THE **HEAD** GAME

THE **HEAD** GAME

HIGH EFFICIENCY ANALYTIC

DECISION-MAKING

AND THE ART OF SOLVING

COMPLEX PROBLEMS QUICKLY

PHILIP MUDD

LIVERIGHT PUBLISHING CORPORATION
A DIVISION OF W. W. NORTON & COMPANY
NEW YORK • LONDON

For information about permission to reproduce selections from this book,
write to Permissions, Liveright Publishing Corporation, a division of
W. W. Norton & Company, Inc., 500 Fifth Avenue, New York, NY 10110

For information about special discounts for bulk purchases, please contact
W. W. Norton Special Sales at specialsales@wwnorton.com or 800-233-4830

Manufacturing by Courier Westford
Book design by Fearn Cutler de Vicq
Production manager: Julia Druskin

ISBN 978-0-87140-788-7

Liveright Publishing Corporation, 500 Fifth Avenue, New York, N.Y. 10110
www.wwnorton.com

W. W. Norton & Company Ltd., Castle House,
75/76 Wells Street, London W1T 3QT

1 2 3 4 5 6 7 8 9 0

This book is for Meredith and Dave.
And for those little ones, Jacob and Nora.
You all bring such joy. Thank you, every day,
for letting me into the family. I love you guys.
What else is there to say?

CONTENTS

Analysts often acquire data and knowledge without carefully considering how that expertise helps a decision maker solve a problem. Many experts fail to bridge this gap, the transition from capturing knowledge for a presentation to anticipating the decision maker's needs. The best analysts think backward, providing decision advantage by molding briefings, papers, e-mails, and other communications so that they answer a decision maker's question with maximum efficiency.

Analysts often believe that questions are self-evident. Experts studying political stability in a foreign country might focus on a simple question: Will the opposition movement succeed? Focusing on better questions (How can we understand those characteristics that might decide whether this opposition movement threatens the government?) leads to better answers. The questions are the hardest part of many analytic problems, but they are the analytic step most frequently ignored by analysts.

The human mind has a hard time juggling mounds of information simultaneously, so all of us revert to weighing just a few pieces of knowledge when we answer everyday questions. To break down hard questions analytically, we need an approach that allows us to escape the limitations of our minds and look at many characteristics of problems simultaneously. We will call these characteristics drivers, to emphasize that these elements of a problem—such as the characteristics you might look for when you buy a house—drive how analysts break down and answer hard questions.

Experts with years of experience apply intuition to every problem they face: With a wealth of experience, what does my personal compass tell me about where this problem is headed? Without metrics to measure how an analytic problem is changing over time, expert or intuitive judgments about complex problems risk using yesterday's events to explain tomorrow's.

Increasing amounts of data can be unmanageable, and the problem of sorting through data overload may only worsen in this digital era. Rather than looking at each bit of information as a discrete data point, we want to look at our drivers and sort the data according to which driver it supports—in other words, sort the data into each of the half-dozen or so driver categories, so analysts have a few piles to deal with rather than a thousand discrete data points.

At some point in this thinking process, we have to step back and make a basic assumption: complex analysis isn't easy, and even a highly trained analyst can make a mistake. How can we assume that an analytic process is flawed and then find ways to check for gaps and errors?

The steps through the analytic process in the book start with thinking about the decision maker first and then breaking down the decision maker's question into manageable parts, before we finally sort data. At the conclusion, we want to put all these pieces of an analytic puzzle back together into one multistep process that we can use to attack a wide variety of analytic problems.

PREFACE

Sometimes life's choices are overwhelming. Start with the data explosion we all live with, from Google searches that produce a million results in a split second to software programs that generate data analyses faster than we can read them. You would think that with all this data at our fingertips life would become more manageable, and decisions might come easier. It hasn't worked out that way in the digital age. As any Google search will tell you, more data can mean more complexity, and more information to sort. Do you want to buy a car? Three hours after you start your search, you've compared dozens if not hundreds of vehicles, but you may be no closer to a decision. In fact, there's a good chance you feel more overwhelmed than ever, drowning in a sea of data.

I walked into my first management job at the Central Intelligence Agency in the late 1990s, when the agency was already living in the world of data overload. I had started nearly fifteen years earlier, as the CIA transformed rapidly from paper to the digital age. Throughout my career, most of the information we sifted through—"we" being me plus the thousands of other analysts and managers—was classified top secret data. My own responsibility was the unit tasked with analyzing Iraq's politics, military capabilities, stability, and economy, in the years before anyone conceived that a war to oust Saddam Husayn might be around the corner. The analyses we prepared were based on data from every corner of the planet, supplied to us by a network of secret human informants, media reports, intercepted communications, satellite photos, background from friendly foreign security services, and an intelligence soup of other material.

The questions we wrestled with were as varied as the data sources that streamed in every hour of every day. What was Saddam's intent toward Kuwait, a country he had invaded in 1990? Would he ever try to retake this neighbor to the south? What did we know about internal stability in Baghdad and elsewhere across the country? Was there any chance Saddam would be under threat himself—that he might face the same type of bloody insurrection that Syria's President Assad later faced, or that brought down President Mubarak in Egypt? Was Iraq's military capability a growing threat to neighbors, or a declining shadow of its former might? What were the possible ramifications of Saddam's relationships with the Russians and Chinese? How was Saddam attempting to erode sanctions? And, of course, did Saddam have weapons of mass destruction (WMD)? If so, how was he hiding them? And where?

After formulating these big questions, we would then turn to sift through piles of information, hunting for the clues and nuggets that might lead us to answers or at least a slightly clearer understanding of what was happening behind Saddam's curtain. In the case of prewar Iraq, this pile of secret intelligence included information on tactical military movements by Iraqi forces, press reports detailing Saddam's speeches, debriefings of informants about Iraq's diplomatic maneuverings, messages from friendly security services, reports from Iraqi defectors and opposition groups outside the country, intercepts of official Iraqi communications, and satellite images of Iraqi military and government facilities. Altogether, this volume of data totaled hundreds of thousands of pages, enough to fill up your local library. How can you make sense of this morass of material? What's important, and what gets dumped?

Data overload isn't, of course, unique to the secret world of intelligence. If you're buying a house, look in the For Sale ads in your local newspaper, or glance at any online realty website. Start leafing through this information, asking the same questions we all might ask ourselves: Which of these houses looks the best? What's in my price range? Which offers the shortest commute? How are the schools in each neighborhood? Are these prices fair? Then walk through fifty of the houses you choose, visiting so many that you forget, by the time you get to the end of your list, what you looked at when you started.

Whether you're dealing with questions of national security or which house to buy, many of the guiding principles that will help you make sense of complexity are the same. The key message of this book is about how to manage tough decisions and piles of data by applying a few consistent guiding principles. The short version is simple: there is a better way to sort through life's questions than simply sitting down with the loads of available information and treating every decision as a unique process without guidelines that help bring order to chaos. Amassing more and more data often isn't the answer. Figuring out how to make sense of hard questions efficiently and effectively is: we want High Efficiency Analytic Decision-making, or HEAD, not a data dump.

Here's how to conceptualize where this book on efficient thinking will take you. When you get in your car before a road trip and figure out the best route to your destination, you don't simply shift into gear, test out a hundred different routes, and then decide which was your favorite. Instead, you get a road map, locate your final destination, and then ask yourself a simple question: What's the shortest, quickest way to get there from your starting point? You might also ask a few subquestions while you're poring over the map. Those go beyond a simple "What's the fastest route?" If you're going on a long trip that takes several hours or more—across the state, let's say, to visit a historic site—you might say to yourself, "I want something scenic, and I have a few spare days. I'd prefer to avoid interstates. They're boring." You might also have a related interest in seeing old historic towns that feature interesting architecture, charming main streets, or quirky antique shops. Remember, you haven't begun to look at any data. You've simply focused on the end result you want.

Without thinking too much about it, you have already changed your original question, from how to reach your destination by the fastest route to how to get there via a route that's more interesting or historic. Throughout the book, we'll use this same approach, one of thinking carefully about the end goal we're trying to reach and then working backward before we ever look at data. As we perfect this technique of starting with the question and working back to the data, we can then begin to apply this methodology to more complex and important problems. You may find that you already default to asking these kinds of questions when you're at home, planning everyday tasks. You can use the same approach at work.

For me at the CIA, the path to this process started to become clearer only after a decade or so of analytic service. It first appeared as a dim idea, when I couldn't get my arms around complex problems and reams of data, and it grew brighter as I realized that some order could be applied to the chaos I was faced with on a daily basis. The path came into even clearer focus when I left government and discovered that the problems and decisions among private-sector business leaders and investment companies had characteristics that reminded me of what I saw in government.

These postgovernment revelations led me to a simple conclusion, one that took more than two decades of hard lessons to learn: that the repeatable methods I had started to understand inside the world of secret intelligence require neither an advanced academic degree nor special information inside a secret vault. The uniqueness of the approach in this book stems not from any individual experience— such as an easy summary of how CIA analysts learn their craft— but from the combination of experiences that I benefited from in the government, which included a whirlwind life of training and more complicated intelligence assignments, both successes and failures.

I grew up in CIA's analytic directorate, at CIA Headquarters in Langley, Virginia, where the internal training program started with classes on critical thinking and analytic methodology. As an entry-level CIA analyst, a twenty-four-year-old with a graduate degree in English literature, I was teamed up with career analysts who had spent decades trying to understand, write about, and speak about the sort of issues that I'd only heard about on TV. I remember clearly the feeling of overwhelming intimidation in the first days of my initial assignment as I watched analysts around me discuss how foreign policy in the Kremlin might evolve or when a country's nascent ballistic missile program might advance to threaten the United States. These experts had years on me, and not all were particularly polite or patient in imparting their wisdom. I just couldn't figure out quickly enough how to think clearly and efficiently. There was no textbook.

During that first assignment, the team I was assigned to gathered in one of those classic, nondescript government offices, with about a dozen of us clustered at desks separated by chest-high cubicle dividers. As you can imagine, there wasn't much privacy. If you wanted to make a personal call without broadcasting across the sea of identical cubicles, you had to head to the pay phone outside the office, toward the cafeteria. When we weren't actively working together, we were seated at our desks in front of what were called "tempested" desktop computers—bulky devices built into heavy metal casings designed to prevent electronic emissions that a hostile intelligence service (think the KGB) might be able to intercept.

The sense of bewilderment was an everyday experience for me then. Early on, when our small team celebrated a birthday at a neighboring desk, instead of walking, I wheeled my chair over to the group gathered around the breakfast bagels and orange juice. I'd forgotten to wear a belt that day; I knew I'd be humiliated if any one of these seasoned pros noticed. And I kept my suit jacket on, all day long, trying to hide the empty belt loops. With that as an inauspicious start, the path afterward went from basic analytic problems to some of the toughest questions the CIA ever faced, and the lessons of how to grapple with that variety of problems still live with me today.

Over time, this combination of classic analytic training and growing up in an intense analytic environment shaped my thinking and forced me to introspection about the craft of looking critically at complex problems. Along the way, I grew, and the analytic approaches in this book stem from witnessing or participating in so many error-plagued problem-solving processes that I've lost track of them all. These were analytic mistakes from a quarter century at the FBI and the CIA, mistakes in how to think clearly, the same kinds of mistakes you might make in your own career. And some of the stories are drawn from tough analytic questions in the private sector, where there are often no clear right or wrong answers. As a result, the lessons here derive as much from failures that none of us want to replicate as it does from successes that we'd all rather remember.

This approach won't come without work. Connecting these lessons into one cohesive methodology was never easy for me, and the lessons surely won't be easy for you to absorb and put into practice correctly. But as you start the first chapter, just keep reminding yourself that there really isn't any such thing as an easy answer, especially to complex problems. If you think you're going to finish and have some sort of breakthrough moment, then think again. This is more like beginning an exercise program when you're out of shape. You can read a good fitness book, or even the best fitness book, but that book doesn't begin to shed fat and mold muscle. The same holds true for your mind.

This parallel between mind and body doesn't end there. Just as the greatest pain that punishes your body comes when you first start down the road to fitness and a healthier life, the worst part of exercising your mind using this analytic process will come at the outset, and you will be tempted to get off the mental treadmill when you start reading this book, because the mental exercise hurts. Persist, though, and I will make you a promise: if you abide by a handful of simple principles and practice them frequently, even daily, your mind will become more agile over time, and this process will become second nature. You may even find that you enjoy it. Just not at first.

So get on the mental treadmill, start slow, and keep going until you get the hang of it. It'll be a little like the most memorable life lesson I learned in college, in one of those teaching moments that don't seem like much when they happen but that you reflect on throughout an entire lifetime. In my freshman year, I was an economics major, and one of my classes was in business law. After class one day, I ran across the professor in the hallway. "The reading assignment you gave us for today was really tough, and I'm having a hard time understanding it," I said to him, looking for sympathy. We were reading a thick volume of legal cases that were intimidating for a college freshman just six months away from high school and unaccustomed to so much complexity, or to tough intellectual challenges. The professor provided no reassurance, though. "The case you're reading is an important lesson, and a good one," he answered. "If it's tough, then read it again." He turned his back and walked away. A hard lesson, but I learned over time that he was right. Sometimes, the important stuff just doesn't come easily.

THE **HEAD** GAME

CHAPTER 1

THE ART OF THINKING BACKWARD

Imagine that you are reading something from a piece of paper or your e-reader. Not hard to imagine, probably, since you're likely doing it right now. Even if you're listening to the audiobook, you're likely visualizing the words on the page as you hear them. Your eyes are moving from left to right, because that's the way the English language is written. Now imagine starting from your right (the end of a sentence, for example) and moving your eyes to your left. Maybe even give it a try. It doesn't feel even close to natural, does it?

Thinking backward—right to left—may not feel natural at first either, but it is central to HEAD. (High Efficiency Analytic Decision-making). This chapter will explain why, and how you can learn and practice this essential skill. You can accumulate huge amounts of knowledge to become an expert, but that doesn't make you an analyst, somebody who practices critical thinking. To make that transition from expert to analyst, you have to get out of your thinking comfort zone.

CREATING DECISION ADVANTAGE

Watching the news today is frustrating. The repetitive cycle, along with the exploding availability of viral videos from smartphones and local cable TV stations, gives television producers plenty of murder and mayhem with which to saturate the airwaves. While some of this coverage might help improve your quality of life, such as weather reports that tell you that you'd better plan for a nasty storm or a report debunking myths about vitamin supplements, most of the breathless, breaking "stories" seem less useful. Why do I need to know about a gruesome murder by a psychotic gunman a thousand miles away? Maybe the story results in a few nightmares, and maybe it forces a viewer to reflect on evil in the world and ponder the tragedy a family somewhere is enduring, but it doesn't help shape decisions about life.

Think of the questionable value of this constant stream of news information in the personal decisions you make every day. How much information do you see or hear during the day, from radio or TV news to books and magazines and conversations around the office? Now ask yourself another question. How much of the news coverage you see feeds natural human interest—in the same category as gossip about the neighbors' marital problems—and how much of it actually helps you educate yourself to make better life decisions? Divide the stories you see on an average day into two categories: news that's interesting but not particularly relevant to your everyday life, and news that helps you think smarter about how to lead your own life. Information should give us some kind of decision advantage, a leg up on how to squeeze a little uncertainty out of the world. Almost none of what you see will meet that standard.

Our goal here is to make complex problems more manageable so you, or someone you're working for, can use that analysis to make better decisions. We want to start this book with an approach to help you reshape your thinking process, beginning with this concept of decision advantage: the analyst helps a decision maker narrow uncertainty by applying knowledge and experience after the analyst understands the decision maker's question. A Realtor, for example, takes a home buyer's problem (How do I understand the housing market in this new city, and where are there areas and homes that satisfy my needs?) and saves the buyer time and trouble by outlining the local housing options based on the buyer's needs. The Realtor, though, isn't the final decision maker; that's the buyer. In the complex area of national security decision-making, the analyst doesn't make the decision of where to deploy the US military against a foreign adversary, but the analyst should provide an advantage to the decision maker by explaining, for example, how the military capabilities of the adversary compare to America's and where the adversary might have strengths and vulnerabilities. In both cases, buying a home and deploying US forces, the analyst has provided an advantage in the decision-making process.

This simple goal—using information to help make better decisions—should be the goal for any analyst studying a problem. Remember, an analyst isn't simply trying to answer his own questions or to summarize data he's built up over a long career spent building expertise. That analyst's expertise isn't particularly relevant if it doesn't help the decision maker think more clearly.

As you think about this contrast between expertise (summarizing data expertly) and analysis (massaging the data into a format that helps a decision maker), start to cement in your mind the following basic distinction: when we're working on how to analyze a problem, we shouldn't start with the data or information that we know and then build a case from there. Instead, we should begin with the question of what we need to know, or our customer or boss needs to know, to solve a problem.

You have seen this problem in life—experts who drone on for an eternity before they get to the information that helps you solve your problem—and I saw it as well, in the national security arena. In one of the most enduring memories of my intelligence career—not because of its significance, but because of the analytic lesson that jumped out during the conversation—my colleagues and I were dealing with a stream of threat reporting at the CIA, information from a human informant (referred to as a "source" at the CIA) within al-Qa'ida that another attack might be coming.

The CIA director from 1997 to 2004, George Tenet, was renowned for bringing CIA officers from across the agency to the White House to brief President George W. Bush. The director had a comfortable enough relationship with the president to introduce him to expert subordinates and then step aside during the conversation that followed. Some of these CIA operators and analysts were buried well within the agency's bureaucracy, not the kinds of senior officials who would typically speak with the president in the Oval Office or White House Situation Room. These briefing opportunities were common: President Bush was an avid consumer of intelligence, and Tenet, along with a full-time analyst whose only job was briefing the president, walked into the Oval Office almost every weekday morning with a binder of classified material prepared especially for the president. This daily access fostered a familiarity that was almost unique in the history of CIA directors and presidents.

Tenet called me one Sunday evening in 2003, when those of us at the CIA's Counterterrorist Center were in the midst of trying to understand yet another in the endless stream of threat reports that we received. During those first years after 9/11, new threat reports were constant, with suicide bombers, al-Qa'ida operatives, and simmering plots popping up all the time, from every corner of the world. We worried most about potential attacks on the US homeland, and our sources ranged from detainees who might talk about unnamed "Westerners" who were training for a mission to intercepted messages that made references to plots we couldn't understand.

When the director called, we were handling one of the few threats that escalated quickly to the top of our list of concerns, rising above the pea soup of lower-grade threats from nutty call-ins and sources who tried to inflate their worth by fabricating stories about the next 9/11 attack. This threat emanated from a reliable source within al-Qa'ida. More immediate, even, this source was ready to tell us about his recent operational contacts who might be involved in training terrorists to strike in Western Europe or North America.

That Sunday, I picked up the secure phone on my desk after a few rings. "Phil," the director abruptly started, "we're going to the Oval Office early tomorrow for the morning PDB session." He was referring to the President's Daily Brief, the highly classified daily intelligence briefing on global issues prepared for the president and his senior advisers. "You've got to brief the president on this threat stream. Meet me tomorrow morning at my office in the Old EOB." The director was using the acronym for the wedding-cake-style Eisenhower Executive Office Building adjacent to the West Wing and the Oval Office, which houses some of the White House staff offices, including the White House national security staff. The director often used his downtown office to prepare for the president's morning briefing; it was a walk of just a minute or two from there to reach the West Wing awning and then over to the waiting room beside the Oval Office.

My first reaction to the director's call was one of unease: *I'm on live with the president tomorrow morning, so I'd better figure out pretty fast what to say and how to say it.* I had started in the service of the CIA as an entry-level junior officer, and it was an honor to reach the point of sitting across from the president in a private setting to discuss the most important national security issues facing our country. That said, coming up with the right story line for the President, especially on a Sunday evening when I couldn't bounce ideas off other analysts, required some quick thinking. The director was a great boss, but his guidance in these situations, I found, was often abrupt: "Phil," he'd say, "just tell him the story."

I don't remember my initial evaluation of the threat when I hung up the phone that day, but I suspect it was some version of "OK, what are the key facts we know about these new reports, and how should I put them together succinctly and comprehensively?" In these early years after the tragedy of September 11, there was still an urgent sense that we would inevitably witness another al-Qa'ida–directed attack. The when, where, how, and who were the questions; but not, ever, the "if." We all simply assumed we'd suffer another catastrophic, 9/11-style event.

This report related to al-Qa'ida's operations at its core, in the lawless lands of Pakistan's tribal belt, the large strip of mountainous terrain that runs along the no-man's-land that borders Afghanistan. This is the same tribal belt that has harbored the remnants of al-Qa'ida since Osama bin Ladin and his followers fled Afghanistan during the invasion of 2001. Al-Qa'ida's most senior operational leaders had settled in that border region after their hasty departure from Afghanistan and their quick realization—after several CIA-backed captures of high-profile terrorist leaders in the urban areas of Pakistan's teeming cities—that they had to find less urban, more impenetrable territory, outside the reach (they thought) of both the Americans and the Pakistani paramilitary and intelligence services.

The region they settled in was, and still is, dominated by fierce tribes who are governed, loosely, through a web of uneasy agreements between local tribal leaders and Pakistan's government. It is a land that time forgot, where the writ of the Pakistani government extends about as far as the reach of the British Empire during its high point in the nineteenth century, when Britain ruled most of the Indian subcontinent. And it is the same territory that served as the main entry point for weapons—and fighters—who were headed into Afghanistan in the 1980s to fight the Soviet Army. This was familiar territory for al-Qa'ida, some of whose members had cut their teeth in the terror organization during the insurgency against the Soviets.

Some of the information we had acquired was highly credible, based on information we had been able to corroborate during the intense period following 9/11. In other words, it had a rare combination of characteristics—timely, credible, and from key al-Qa'ida players. In the often seedy underworld of intelligence, human informants can easily slip into fabrication if they sense that magnifying a threat or reporting on activities they know very little about may earn them a better paycheck.

This stream of threat reporting wasn't embroidered or exotic—we didn't have much detail beyond a basic outline of the disturbing threat—but the quality of the information vaulted this particular plot to the top of the jumble of daily entries in the Threat Matrix. At that time, the matrix was the US Intelligence Community's consolidation of threat reporting from agencies across the US government. Everybody in town read it.

The following morning, Tenet and I talked in his EOB office, one-on-one, about the threat reporting and its source, and we spoke in some detail about the presentation I'd make to the president. Tenet had pursued the al-Qa'ida problem with great vigor before 9/11, and he was passionate about the counterterrorism mission the CIA was managing as we hunted the architects of the 2001 attacks. He knew the counterterrorism work we did in the Counterterrorist Center in tactical-level detail, both before and after 9/11, not just because he immersed himself in it but also because, for years after the attacks, many of the morning briefings for the president were dominated by the issue of terrorism generally and al-Qa'ida specifically. So when we walked into the Oval Office to talk to the president and the small group of staff gathered there—which included the vice president, the national security adviser, the secretary of homeland security, and one or two others—Tenet was already well briefed on our al-Qa'ida operations, though this threat stream was new to all of them, and to us.

Preparing to speak to the president and his advisers amid the distraction of a Marine One presidential helicopter that was landing outside the Oval Office, I thought of the value I could bring to the room, specifically related to this breaking threat we were learning about. In particular, I thought I should add detail about how we acquired the information and why we believed it was credible. Why did this one bubble to the top?

This all sounds pretty straightforward, doesn't it? Summarize what you know of the facts, without wasting the president's time, by using the briefing skills you've practiced and perfected during two decades of working in the world of intelligence and counterterrorism. Get in and out of the briefing quickly; in other words, don't pretend that you'll have more than fifteen minutes for the presentation, plus questions and answers. If the president has more questions, he'll ask. And if he's really interested, he'll delay his next meeting a few minutes to keep the conversation going.[*]

Here's how the briefing started. We sat down in the upholstered sofas beside the president's desk in the Oval Office, with the president in one wing chair at the head of the coffee table and Vice President Cheney in a wing chair next to him. Director Tenet, sitting immediately beside me on the sofa, quickly turned to me to deliver a few minutes on the threat data, with precision and up-to-the-minute detail.

After I briefed the details of the threat, clearly and cleanly, I was satisfied. No "ums," no stumbling. No distracting notes that would have meant I'd break eye contact with the president. Just as quickly as I'd spoken, though, a painful realization swept over me. I knew the briefing was wrong when the president asked his first question. "What do we do about this?"

---

[*] Which he later did that morning. His assistant phoned the Oval Office from the adjacent room; a prominent foreign leader was on the line. "Tell him to wait a few minutes" was the president's answer.

That day, the president's problem wasn't in understanding the details of that particular threat stream. It was determining what to do in response to the threat, such as whether to say something publicly to the American people or how to take defensive action somewhere in the United States. The difference between the two questions—whether to start with details of the threat reporting or with how to add context for the president, so he could figure out how to respond—might sound subtle, but it's not. It is at the center of good analysis.

Repositioning the Oval Office conversation took just a few moments, thankfully. Not that there was more time than that anyway: the president was asking questions, and he wanted on-the-spot answers, immediately. There wasn't time to head back to CIA Headquarters, take a breath, regroup, and consider carefully what to say. The president, of course, had the responsibility of thinking about Americans' safety, and whether the country faced a threat that could disrupt a national holiday. As the conversation proceeded, his question clarified, and quickly. *Should we cancel the event*, he asked?

So I took the question and turned it around quickly enough (I hoped) that no one would notice. Rather than focusing on that one threat in isolation, I reframed it with context drawn from the many other significant threats we had witnessed. I remember the moment clearly: *Yes,* I said, *this one threat is worth keeping on our radar because the reporting is highly credible. But compared to the other post-9/11 threats we've handled, this one is not in the upper 1 or 2 percent, at least not quite yet. It might rise to that level quickly, but we don't yet have the gold standard in threat reporting: information about when and where the attack might take place, or even who the plotters might be—details that would vault the threat to the level of a flashing red warning light. Even if you wanted to do something in response to this vague threat, the lack of specificity would not allow you to design and implement a prudent plan.*

The reoriented briefing went off without a hitch, as far as I can remember. With the added context, the picture during the second half of that Oval Office meeting looked much different than the initial sketch of the threat. The lack of specificity about the threat left us with a picture that was too fuzzy to rank this as what we would call "actionable" intelligence. "Actionable," in intelligence-speak, translates as information that is clear enough (without, usually, perfect detail—even the best intelligence, such as the information that resulted in the raid on bin Laden's compound in Pakistan, is almost always frustratingly fuzzy) to allow a decision that leads to steps to counter the threat. That conversation concluded with a few quick comments on when we might have more detail on the threat, from our current source or some other.

———

Step back, for just a minute, and focus on answering the following question: Why do you think the approach I initially took, which seemed perfectly straightforward in those moments, was misguided? We're clear on one point: the error wasn't a question of presenting information accurately, clearly, or quickly. Reflect for a moment on what approach you might have taken, or what mindset you might have gotten yourself into. Here's a hint: What does the president need, beyond the facts? When does his initial question, after I opened the briefing, tell you about what I didn't answer with the summary that I gave him?

If you're frustrated that the answer doesn't seem to be in your grasp, don't worry; I missed it, too, and I'd already been in the problem-solving business for two decades. Here's the Cliff's Notes answer to the flaws of those few moments. The mistake I made was in starting with the facts and quickly making the classic error all analysts make at one time or another: assuming that just by presenting information or expert analysis, I was making it possible for the person on the other end of the briefing to figure out what to do with it. I assumed, in other words, that a crisp summation of the facts was the same as a good presentation of what the president needed to know to make an informed decision.

My errant approach meant that the president, armed with the reporting about a single threat stream, briefed by me in isolation and without context, was forced to figure out how to weigh the seriousness of the reporting and balance it against his own personal understanding of the counterterrorism universe. Instead I should have discussed how this threat compared with what else we knew and what other threats we faced. Why did he have to do the weighing? Why hadn't I done it for him? I should have put the threat into context for him, so he wouldn't have to determine how it measured up against the high volume of serious threats we faced every day.

I assumed that I should just brief everyone on the facts about the individual threat without thinking enough about the actual purpose of the briefing. Ultimately, I didn't ask the question that now seems obvious: What would help the president of the United States understand this threat so he can make good decisions about how to respond? It was sort of like a weatherman who gives you the weekend weather on Wednesday when you really want to know whether to carry an umbrella tomorrow. His forecast is all well and good, and it may be accurate, but he hasn't given you the decision advantage you needed. He thought about what he knew, not what you needed to know.

Keep the purpose of the briefing in the back of your mind: an analyst is supposed to help a customer or a client make more informed decisions, regardless of whether the subject is buying a car or explaining a national security threat. Just based on this short conversation in the Oval Office, think of how two factually correct presentations could lead in two fundamentally different directions:

1. A straight-up presentation of deeply troubling threat reporting, in a Washington environment in which almost any observer, at that time, anticipated another catastrophic attack on US soil.

2. A presentation of that same threat reporting with context (How severe did this threat look, ranked against all the other threats we'd handled?) that allowed a nonexpert listener who had to make a decision about an upcoming event to better determine how alarmed he should be.

It's not a stretch, not by a long shot, to judge that the first briefing could lead the listener to assume, rightly or wrongly, that this was a threat that should result in a high level of concern, if not alarm. The second briefing, also perfectly accurate, could (and did) result in an entirely different conclusion, one that would leave you not with a sense of calm, certainly, but maybe with the notion that this threat didn't jump to the top of the list on the Threat Matrix when compared to all the others we had resolved since 9/11.

We're now at the heart of the matter: if the purpose of the briefing was to provide the president with decision advantage, the first briefing might have led to a decision to take immediate action; the second led to a decision to wait and see. In retrospect, it's pretty hard to claim that the first briefing provided an advantage. The second half of the briefing, with the added context, got us into the realm of decision advantage, without my telling the president and his advisers what to do.

This question-formulation process sounds deceptively simple, because it appears to be so basic on paper. The ugly secret for proud analysts is that this 90 percent of what they know (the data) might be useful at some other time, but it isn't today. A good analyst has to have the humility to accept that.

THINKING ABOUT BIAS:
THE ANALYST AND THE DECISION MAKER

We should return to the concept of decision advantage, now with the advantage of a real scenario, the presidential briefing, to add context to this idea.* Analysts who are responsible for trying to provide an advantage most likely will have views on what the decision maker should do, just as I had thoughts that day on what actions the president should take. Before we continue, though, we have to lay down one marker, a side note about the importance of separating analysis from decision-making. The analyst is responsible for helping the customer—whether it's the president of the United States or the CEO of a Fortune 500 company—so that the customer can make decisions that are founded on a solid combination of fact, supposition, and expert judgment. The analyst is not, however, the best-positioned person in the room to make the final judgment about what the president or the CEO should do. Often in the analytic world, there is and should be a separation between those trying to understand and analyze an unfolding situation and those who are making the decisions.

Here's an example of why. If a weather analyst tells you she thinks it's going to be a gloriously sunny day tomorrow, she's given you an advantage in your decision about whether to proceed with your annual office picnic. "Yes," you might say, "we don't need to shift to our rainout day, because it looks like the rain will hold off for a bit." The weather analyst hasn't told you what to do for your picnic; she has simply reflected on what she knows. She's combined that with a bit of uncertainty (what she doesn't know about weather patterns, such as whether the winds will shift) and come up with a judgment you can use to determine whether to postpone.

---

* For more on bias, see Appendix A.

In this scenario, the weather analyst might look at new data two hours later and issue a different report. "Winds have shifted suddenly," she might say, "and, based on this new set of information, the forecast for tomorrow has changed. We are now more likely to get rain than not, though there's still a 35 percent chance that we'll see a sunny afternoon."

If that weather analyst becomes directly involved in whether to hold the picnic on schedule, though, she immediately gains an interest in the outcome, even if she doesn't realize it. Why? The analyst becomes a participant in how the weather patterns are being perceived. After all, the office picnic organizers want a sunny day: if the prospects for rain increase, they have to go through the trouble of shifting the date. As a result, when the weather analyst joins the picnic-organizing committee, the chances that she wants to maintain her sunny-day forecast might increase. Now, instead of building the forecast based solely on information such as radar images, seasonal variations, history, local expertise, wind patterns, etc., our weather analyst is, consciously or not, factoring other, non-weather-related variables into the decision.

The lesson is clear: be conscious about whether you are allowing the people who are analyzing the problem to also slip into the role of decision maker. If they do, their ability to remain disinterested in the outcome becomes questionable.

This notion of a divide between analysts and decision makers has direct implications in all sorts of professional arenas. An analyst in an investment firm who has the twin responsibilities of both researching a stock and then participating in conversations about whether to buy or sell the stock faces a challenge you can see anytime a human being stakes his reputation on a judgment. If that analyst wants to offer judgments based on incoming information— what's happening in the stock market, what's happening within the target company, what's happening with the company's competitors and in the marketplace—that analyst can judge new facts, trends, etc., in a process that does not have the analyst participating in the decision. You want to buy? Fine. You want to sell? Also fine. What I offer, the analyst might say, is simply a well-founded understanding of what this company looks like today, and I may well change what I think tomorrow. This mixing of analysis and decision-making happens all the time in everyday life, and it would be naive to pretend that the mix is unacceptable. It simply opens the door to bias.

Like the weather expert, though, our financial expert, as soon as he participates in the buy/sell decision, whether for himself or for another party, faces the human problem of wanting to defend that decision. For example, let's say the analyst makes a strong "buy" recommendation for stock in a major Silicon Valley software company. When new information comes in that suggests that the management team at the tech firm is turning over quickly, the analyst who has participated in a "buy" decision might, knowingly or not, feel pulled toward explaining why that turnover supports his recommendation, or at least doesn't undercut it. "This management turnover isn't necessarily a bad thing," he might feel compelled to say, "because the new blood in the firm will revitalize a brand that was building market share but needed an infusion of fresh ideas. And the new team has a great pedigree."

Here's the problem: while the analysis might be correct, it might be based less on a cold-blooded breakdown of the implications of the firm's turnover, the quality of the new team, and the disruptions that a change might bring than it is on the analyst's human inclination to defend his "buy" advice. All analysts should have the best window possible onto their customers' decision-making—otherwise, they wouldn't know where they could best help the customer—but that's a different job than actually serving as both chef and restaurant critic.

Post-9/11, we had to deal with this problem routinely, and my experiences during those years reinforced for me the traditional CIA view that analysts who participate in decision-making based on their analysis are prone to bias, however unintentional. Try another real-world example to highlight the point. After the attacks in 2001, the CIA was obviously among those agencies that were front and center in preventing follow-on attacks. CIA analysts were also critical in sorting through all the intelligence coming in from al-Qa'ida. The CIA, in other words, had the responsibility of both taking action against al-Qa'ida and explaining to US policymakers, from the president on down, how the United States was faring in the global counterterror campaign. The CIA played a role in grading its own homework.

Keeping this dual role in mind, let's ask a few questions that will help illustrate quickly how an analyst in that position might be susceptible to what we might call "decision maker's bias." We can use two scenarios that center on one basic question: How effectively is the United States waging this counterterror campaign?

The analyst might be involved in judging whether the CIA's strategy and tactics are succeeding in the counterterror campaign. Because it's the CIA that is prosecuting the counterterror war, it's plausible that the analyst might feel just the slightest twinge of discomfort if he assesses that the global counterterror campaign is flawed. In this case, then, the analyst is in the position of critiquing his own organization. Self-critiques are part of everyday life, but once that analyst has to present a position outside the CIA—to Congress, the White House, or the American people—the analyst's view might be colored by an interest in portraying the CIA as successful. This has nothing to do with integrity—it's not necessarily a case of willfully changing analysis to support a particular judgment—and everything to do with human behavior.

This divide between analysis and decision-making is not a distinction you can sustain during every analytic process you oversee, but it's a divide you should be conscious of if you choose to breach it. And it represents a fundamental truth in analysis about the risk of growing attached to the decisions that flow from any analytic process. Many good analysts certainly participate in decisions that are based on their analyses, and we do this every single day, such as when you talk to your Realtor, for example, about how to choose among different neighborhoods or houses. The decision maker's bias is common; just be clear about making this bias a conscious concern when you cross the divide from analysis to decisions, and when you defend decisions that are based on your own analysis.

To close the loop on this point, my own job at the CIA, during that conversation with the president, was not to tell him what he should do. *If you want to take action based on this threat, Mr. President, that's your in-box; I'm just here to ensure that you have the best possible decision-making advantage as you make that decision.* In this case, the president was making a decision about how concerned he should be, at a time when he was speaking regularly to the public about the threats America faced, and as he made decisions about whether to proceed with or cancel various public events that might be under threat. My job was not to warn him that he should be more outspoken about the threat, or that he should proceed with or postpone these public functions; nor was it to advise him that he didn't have to stand down on warning the American people about incoming threats.

PRACTICING PATIENCE:
THE IMPORTANCE OF SLOW THINKING

One of the reasons we need to slow down and focus on asking good questions first, right to left, is that people prefer to answer quickly when they're faced with a question, particularly in their area of expertise. Humans don't like dead air, the embarrassment we all feel when we find ourselves in the midst of a long, awkward silence in the midst of a conversation. Those silences prompt a simple response: regardless of our upbringing, some urge tells us, "Say something. Anything. Just fill the void." So when we face a question, our first instinct is not to remain silent but to answer on the spot. In this sense, we're not much different than the TV professionals who answer questions for a living. During an interview at a moment when the interviewee stops for more than three seconds and seems to struggle for an answer, human instincts kick in, naturally. Even a few seconds of quiet seems uncomfortable.

Now imagine that if every time you are asked a question, you wait thirty seconds and try to step through a clear articulation of what you know and what you don't. If you did this, you might end up a long way from where you would if you answered immediately. I've noticed this during every live TV interview I've ever done. Allowing dead air during a live news interview doesn't work; the producers will never book you again. So you're forced to respond quickly, as soon as the interviewer poses the question on a live camera shot. The inevitable result is that you walk out of the TV studio ten minutes later and realize what you missed in your answer, what you stated poorly, what you forgot, and how an answer with just a little more thinking would have been a lot more useful. The HEAD process we want to emphasize centers on this kind of slow thinking, with a lot of downtime at the beginning of the process to shape key questions.

Try an example. You're walking down the hallway at work. A colleague stops you and asks a question. "I'm really excited about the weekend," she might say. "Have you heard whether it's going to rain on Saturday or Sunday?" The chances that you're going to stop for fifteen seconds, juggle the factors that might help you formulate the answer—whether you've heard the forecast, what the weather is like at this time of year, whether wet West Coast weather usually moves east into your particular region at this time of year—are low.

More than likely you'll answer right away. "Yes," you might respond quickly, "it's been raining all week, and it'll probably rain again tomorrow. I've lost track of the number of weekends we've missed to rain." Or, "No, I think we're in a dry spell for a while longer, and there's no sign of a break in the weather this week." It's just hard for us, as social beings and smart people, to avoid answering questions when we're asked something directly. In these conversations, we're all instant weather forecasters, whether we know something about the weather tomorrow or not.

It might also seem rude to stay silent, or to come up with something like "I just don't know whether it's supposed to rain. I'm not an expert, and I'd have to look at a few variables to come up with a good answer." It might be an honest answer, but how often does anyone answer with something that analytic? Next time somebody asks a question that requires just a bit of analysis—"What do you think about the front-page story in today's paper?" is the kind of question we're talking about—try answering with "Let me think about that and get back to you." In most conversations, this just doesn't sound right.

Awkward pauses, however, aren't the only reason we don't spend time coming up with well-considered analytic answers to the questions we face in everyday life. For starters, analytic processes are frustrating. Picture this: I'm sitting at the CIA's Langley, Virginia, headquarters, assessing a fast-breaking question about al-Qa'ida's terror capabilities in the wake of a car-bomb attack that devastated a hotel in an Asian capital. Information is flooding in, ranging from media reports to secret analyses. Meanwhile, senior officials in Washington are pressing for answers about what just happened, and the director of the Central Intelligence Agency needs a quick briefing paper as he prepares to head down to the White House for a meeting on what kinds of assistance the United States might provide and whether the incident presages an attack on American soil.

Unfortunately, in situations like this you can rarely call for an intermission. Instead, you have to quickly stitch together the intelligence to come up with rapid answers. There's a time and a place for this kind of rapid turnaround, the I-need-an-answer-now sort of thinking, but it's not here in this book. Tough questioning and serious analysis take a conscious commitment to think through the analytic process before you embark on the effort to come up with an answer.

THE MARRIAGE QUESTION:
IS SHE PERFECT? OR IS SHE RIGHT FOR ME?

Riding in a car with a good friend a few years ago, I listened to him speak about how he came to the decision to propose to his girlfriend. I know her well; under any definition of a good partner, she is great. She is smart, even-tempered, beautiful, and good-humored. But, as my friend said that afternoon in the car, she and he differed occasionally, as they got to know each other and as any healthy couple would. "She can be tough," he said. "She stands her ground, and she's not shy about telling me when she thinks I can do better."

He kept explaining as I drove. Allow me to let you listen in on that conversation briefly, because the conclusion helps drive home the point that this book isn't just about theoretical problem-solving from a former CIA analyst. We all use this process, even if we don't verbalize it, or understand it.

"I thought about this for a long time," my friend said. "Not every day is perfect between us. Some days are difficult, because I still have to learn how to become a better partner." Without articulating his thought process clearly, he was on the path to saying that the question that initially troubled him was: Is every day perfect? While it might have been the wrong question ultimately, it was still the one that he had been stuck on for many months.

He did get over this hump of questioning whether they were right together, and he did ask her to marry him. She accepted, and they remain a very happy couple, and just a lovely, joyous family, after years of marriage and the trials of starting a family. First, however, my friend had managed to capture the importance of settling on the right question without using the same words, or articulating the right-to-left methodology. That day in the car, he came to look at all the wealth of good she offered and concluded that the question of whether he was sometimes out of his comfort zone wasn't quite right. The question he eventually grew into sounded something like this:

- For me, this person has a unique combination of personality traits, intelligence, and beauty that fit us together, and I admire her every day. Plus, I could use a little firm guidance now and then. I'm not perfect. Is there a better definition of two people who should be together? Is there a better definition of a life partner? And what two people agree every single day? That's unrealistic, and probably unhealthy.

We could also ask the original question in reverse, to underscore the point that maybe it isn't the right question to start with:

- If I were with someone who never challenged me to grow, would I feel fulfilled? Would I respect my partner? And could I become a better person?

This right-to-left approach isn't the toughest part of the analytic process, but it is one of the most conceptual. So let's close the chapter with just one more variation on how to understand this different way of analytic problem-solving. For this example, try thinking about how you read a novel. Start by opening the book.

Once you leaf through the pages with the copyright information and you arrive at the first real page of the story, your eyes move down and you settle on the first sentence of the first chapter. As you start every sentence of the rest of the book, your eyes will read from left to right, page after page after page. At the end of the book, as you're churning through the final paragraphs, all the story threads come together, and the picture woven through the narrative comes into focus. The boy and the girl marry. The hero or heroine dies, tragically. The protagonist's journey comes to an end, with the main character having learned critical life lessons along the way.

The point is this: as you have read a few hundred pages, you've accumulated all the threads of the plot, with all its ups and downs, as you slowly move from start to finish, reading left to right. You didn't quite know where the story line was taking you along the way, but at the end, you reach a neat conclusion that tidies up disparate plotlines that might have seemed disconnected midway through the book.

Stop, though. That's not the only way to read a novel, or to even think of a plot. You don't have to start at the first page and grind through a few hundred pages before you fully understand where the story will take you. What if you pick up that same novel, skip the initial 95 percent, and instead read the final chapter first? You could then turn around and read the entire book, start to finish, beginning with the first chapter. (We all, no doubt, have done this a few times, or we've at least seen a movie adaptation of a book we've already read, so that we know the end of the story before the opening scene.) As you know, here's what would happen if you started at the back of the book: instead of wondering how the threads might eventually come together, you would clearly see, as each page turns, how each fragment of dialogue and each scene contributes to the story and the plot. If it's a mystery novel, you'd spot the secret clues as they're sprinkled among the pages.

Now let's take this approach of right to left, backward rather than forward, one step further. Rather than being the reader of the novel, let's make you the author. You're sitting at your desk, with a new yellow legal pad and a pile of freshly sharpened No. 2 pencils, and you're ready to write. As you begin the drafting process, think about two scenarios. You can choose either path, but first see which one you think might be simpler and more efficient.

In the first scenario, you start writing as you would start reading, beginning with page one and then proceeding from left to right. You haven't mapped the plot or sketched the characters; you don't know anything about the story. As you write, page by page, without knowing exactly where you're headed with your narrative, you introduce new characters, along with new scenes, new dialogue, and the beginnings of the plotline. You haven't mapped out how the book concludes, which characters live and die, what they say along the way, what subplots you want to develop, or how the threads ultimately will converge in the final scenes—you're making it up as you go. Some authors can do this brilliantly. Think of Jack Kerouac's novel *On the Road* as an example, a book written in what must have been a manic three-week period.

Others can't. A lot of us, especially those who aren't professional novelists, might struggle with writing a book without first sketching out the plot. In this second novel-writing scenario, you either write or conceptualize the final chapters first, so you know exactly which characters live and die, which disasters strike during the story, and who gets married, who's happy, and who ends up distraught. You think about where you will need dialogue along the way to reinforce character development and to build the plot. You decide where you want to develop characters and how the various parts of the overall story will flow. You chart out the personalities of your main characters, plot a few central story lines, and think about key points during the story when the characters will define themselves.

No matter what kind of author you are, writing from the first chapter without knowing the final destination almost guarantees that you'll have to go back through the novel a second time to weed out large patches of character development that go nowhere. You might have to delete pages of dialogue that take the plot or the characters away from your theme, or plot strands that take you to dead ends. This is the same scenario that might evolve if we start on a road trip toward California without a sense of where exactly in California we're going and what route we're going to take to get there. This kind of random road trip might be fun as a college lark, but it would no doubt prove to be less enjoyable if we want an efficient trip because we've got screaming children in the backseat.

VISUALIZING THE CONCEPT: THE RIGHT-TO-LEFT MODEL AND THE INVERTED PYRAMID

We can take this concept of how the analyst should start with the decision maker's question and make it visual, as a way to help remember the concept. We've already captured the idea in the phrase "decision advantage"; now we will visualize it as right-to-left thinking, where we will start on the right side of the problem (what the decision maker's problem is) and end up on the left side (what we experts and analysts know). For most of us, right to left is backward: we are trained to start at the left side of a sentence and read forward and to the right, across the page. That's exactly the point. For this analytic process, we want to think in reverse.

Let's apply this backward-thinking process to a case in everyday life. Imagine moving to Memphis, Tennessee, which is exactly what I did in the spring of 2013. The Bluff City, as it's known here. (The city sits on bluffs along the Mississippi River.) If you're moving to a place you don't know well, or at all, your first instinct might be to ask a Realtor or friend an armload of questions as you search various realty websites. You're trying to get a feel for the city, in other words, by poring over masses of data and letting the details slowly sink in. As you scan scores of listings, you might ask questions such as: What's the market like? How do prices compare to where I've come from? Where do other people around the office live? Which neighborhoods are a reasonable commuting distance from the office? Where are the best schools? This is thinking forward, taking data and spending large amounts of time sorting it. You're thinking in the wrong direction, left to right.

Rather than immediately searching the real estate ads, try this question: What kind of life experience are you looking for as you move to a new town and start a new life? It may take awhile to sort out your mind so that you can summarize the question even more cleanly, so that it's both succinct and comprehensive, and maybe this isn't precisely the question you want. But even if you spend another hour or two at the front end of your search, ironing out what your real question is, you will save a lot of time and trouble at the back end of your decision-making process. You've started thinking backward, not even touching the data until you know the question, the destination.

Different people will have different definitions of what they mean by city living, or they might be looking for an entirely different lifestyle when they think of a move from the Northeast to the Mid-South. If this is your move, are you thinking back to Tara, the huge plantation that features in *Gone with the Wind*? Or are you dreaming of a condo in a thriving downtown district? Or do your thoughts drift to Spanish moss swaying in the branches of live oaks? Sipping bourbon? Sampling barbecue? Hold on; we're getting ahead of ourselves here. Let's start with the bare basics that might define your choice, and that did define my choice.

Now that we've invested the initial time and energy to whittle down something as fuzzy as where to live to a simple core question—Where can we find the genteel southern style of living we've decided we want?—we can look at areas of town, neighborhoods, or geographic quadrants near our office, schools, or whatever is of interest to us. You want to try downtown Memphis, you say? OK, it's a rejuvenating, lively, action-oriented center, with cafés, restaurants, plenty to do, and some serious history centered partly on the bustling, music-oriented Beale Street.

This downtown section of Memphis is vibrant on both week-nights and weekends, and condos right in the heart of the action are affordable. The architecture is fun, too. Many of the most interesting options are beautiful exposed-brick lofts in restored buildings, with the kinds of historic interiors and vestiges of life decades ago that add character to modern urban living. All these features could equal a great place to live, no doubt. But if you want to sip iced sun tea on a big porch off the front of a high-ceilinged 1920s house—not a bad definition of a southern life, and coincidentally the definition I had come up with for the life I was trying to find—downtown Memphis might not be right for you. I haven't looked at a single real estate ad, but I know this lifestyle doesn't begin to answer my initial question. Why bother looking at the ads? I'm not moving here.

If you get into this rhythm of reshaping questions consciously when you start any process, you should find that some of this questioning comes naturally with practice and patience. We don't always mold good questions consciously, though, and you're going to have to work to avoid slipping into data before you settle on the question. Further, this approach doesn't come quickly with just a few practice sessions. Think of pushing yourself to try this for months and years, the kind of time a professional athlete invests to get into game form. Making this switch in your analytic mindset is long and hard. Be patient with yourself, and don't lose faith if you feel like you're occasionally pounding your head against a wall. That frustration doesn't suggest you're somehow a poor student, or that you can't learn this.

It just means you're trying. It's the same pain your legs feel when you start running: you're training, and you're not in shape yet.

Now that we've gone through the backward-thinking concept, we can try a diagram. Think of a pyramid, with a thought process starting at the broad bottom with a mass of data and then working toward the pointy top, where an analyst who's worked through the data might provide a one-sentence answer. The bottom represents a jumble of undigested information; the top represents the analyst's distillation of this information into judgments for a decision maker.

This type of problem-solving reflects exactly the process that we want to avoid. Here's how to avoid it, using the pyramid diagram. Begin your analytic process by turning the pyramid over on its tip, literally flipping the pyramid so that the broad base is on the top, with the pointy tip at the bottom. This isn't a sustainable design from an architectural perspective, but it'll help you order your mind, not to mention remember the principles of this book more readily. At the top, you have your big question, our starting point. It's the broadest, most basic part of the analytic process, so we represent it at the top. Only at the end, after having turned the process on its head, do you begin to sort through the bits of data that help you answer the question.

It bears repeating. Invert the pyramid. Start with the base, the big question. Then work your way down to the tip, the bits and pieces of data.

THE TROUT AND THE ANALYST:
RESISTING THE CURRENT

These visualizations will allow you to think of efficient analysis as a process, working from one part of a visual representation across to the left, or down to the tip, but it will take conscious effort every time. As we transition to the heart of the analytic process in this book, try to remember an image that has stuck with me for years, as I struggled to understand why analysts resist hard thinking. It's the trout analogy. For eons, trout have had to adapt to life facing upstream, typically in fast-moving water and in a constant battle to maintain position. As even the most amateur trout fisherman can tell you, trout conserve energy by finding pockets of water that shield them from the current. In the midst of a boiling stream, you will find trout sheltering in less turbulent water behind boulders, in cuts underneath stream banks, or in eddies that swirl under fallen trees. These trout are making minute-by-minute calculations about energy conservation as they fight the current, just as we conserve energy by taking analytic routes that provide quick answers without fully engaging our brains. In the trout world, the fish doesn't want to expend the energy to fight the current, just as we try to find ways around spending the energy to think.

This is the same concept we need to employ in handling complex analytic problems. Too often, we think we're coming up with high-end solutions to analytic questions solely because we're the experts. We spend no time on fashioning the right question, and we revert immediately to forming a quick "expert" opinion that reflects more knee-jerk intuition and a quick data dump than slow analysis. What are Vladimir Putin's prospects? Where is the stock market headed? Is it going to rain this weekend? Experts in these areas often will give you the answer in five minutes. That's convenient. But it's too fast to reflect serious thinking.

If we choose the right moments to move out of the ease of quick answers to the challenge of fighting the current, the analytic return is high. These conscious decisions to engage aren't meant for every problem: there's enough of an energy cost to engaging our brains on a high level that we don't begin this process if a question is not among our higher priorities. Conversely, though, when we have to handle questions we think are particularly important, we have to make a conscious decision before answering. Going out into the current has great potential benefits, but only if we're willing to dedicate time up front to an arduous mental exercise. The first step in heading out into the current is one of the most frustrating: spending time ensuring that you understand what you're asking. So before you immerse yourself in the data, and combine it with your knowledge and experience, step back and test your brain: Do you understand what question you're answering in the first place?

———

It takes a long time to learn that experts master data, but they only transition to becoming analysts when they realize that an impressive recall of data has little to do with analysis and understanding complex problems. Increasing the efficiency of how we think—of how we provide an analytic advantage—requires more time than we'd care to spend on questions that might seem straightforward initially. This distinction between expertise and analysis might sound superficial, or at least obvious, at the outset. Before you come to this conclusion, though, reflect on this question: If you went to college, how many classes did you take in your major area? A dozen? I was an English literature major; through five and a half years of undergraduate and graduate school, I'm guessing that I took twenty or more literature classes. All of them emphasized information, or data, about books and authors.

Now answer another question: How many classes did you take about how to think critically? Maybe none. In my entire academic career, I only remember one, and I only signed up for it by accident, because it fit my schedule. Fundamentals of Logic was the class.

We assume that we'll learn critical thinking by osmosis, or just naturally—that somehow taking twenty literature classes will leave a student with a well-trained mind and an ability to analyze. It doesn't. That's what this chapter and the following pages are about, making up for all the lost time in college classes that trained all of us to be experts but not efficient analysts.

CHAPTER TWO

WHAT'S THE QUESTION?

Crafting the right question should always be the first step in this analytic process of moving from right to left, once we realize the need to have the customer's or audience's interests in mind and not our own. I use the word "craft," or "create," because we often assume that questions create themselves. Good questions, though, are hard to come up with, and we typically over-invest our time in analyzing problems by jumping right to the data and the conclusions, while underinvesting in thinking about exactly what it is we want to know. We started by reinforcing the point that the decision maker has to be the start of how analysts think about hard problems. We're now staring at a blank page that represents how we start attacking a problem: How do we think about what that question is?

Think of the first chapter, and the White House briefing. If you received a call asking you to offer a briefing on a current threat, how might you frame the question? Here's a guess:

Who is the source of the new threat reporting, and what does he say about the current threat?

This seems easy, but as we've seen, it's a trap. This simple question doesn't lead to a wrong answer, just to an answer that doesn't help provide decision advantage to the person at the head of the table, the decision maker. If you had spent time working on the question, you might have come up with this instead:

- How serious a threat is this, compared to the other threats we've worked through?

Try another, more practical question we ask all the time and one we've discussed before. What's the weather going to be like tomorrow? Think of how different the answers might be if you framed that question in one of the following ways:

1. Is it going to rain tomorrow?
2. What's the weather going to be like tomorrow?
3. I'm having a picnic tomorrow. Will we have some sun in the afternoon?

Each one of those questions might get you a different answer, and each answer might be accurate. But if your core question is the third—you want to know whether you have to postpone the picnic—the first two questions might get you factually correct answers that mislead you. Try these:

1. Yes, it's going to rain tomorrow. (It'll rain in the morning, not the afternoon, but you didn't ask!)
2. Tomorrow's weather will be a mix of rain and sunshine. (The sunshine's in the afternoon, when you've scheduled your picnic, but you didn't ask!)
3. Yes, it'll rain in the morning, but it should clear by noontime. (Enjoy the picnic!)

THE TRAGEDY OF SOMALIA:
WHAT SHOULD THE QUESTION BE?

This problem of kneading a problem again and again to arrive at the right question will come up throughout any analyst's career. It might take an hour or two to start, and the right question might only crystallize over days or weeks, or even longer. Don't despair. It's never fast, and it's never easy. For me, one of the most glaring examples of the trap of avoiding this step—of jumping too quickly to the data and skipping the question—happened late, two decades into an intelligence career.

After 9/11, a collection of senior executives met every day, at both the CIA and the FBI, to discuss the terror threats and plots that streamed in endlessly during that unique period in time. The CIA meetings happened each evening at 5 p.m. in the CIA director's conference room. At the FBI, Director Robert Mueller convened us in the morning, shortly after 7 a.m., to talk about terror investigations in the United States. It was at these latter meetings that I learned one of my toughest lessons in asking good questions.

During the early 1990s, Somalia took a turn for the worse. Refugees fled as the country descended into years of chaos and the United States turned to other problems, in the wake of an ill-fated military aid mission that led to the shooting down of two American helicopters in the capital of Mogadishu. Eighteen US servicemen died in the incident, which was captured in the book *Black Hawk Down* and culminated with gruesome TV images of Somali militants dragging the bodies of American soldiers through the streets of the city.

Years later, in the mid-2000s, war-ravaged Somalia recaptured front-page news coverage as radical Islamists banded together to take Mogadishu and impose a harsh version of Islamic rule. African forces from outside Somalia, concerned about the blowback effect across borders into their own countries and spurred by stories of atrocities committed by the militias, decided to intervene against the newly installed Somali radicals in 2006. These new Somali Islamists, called al-Shabaab (the Youth), fought back, gaining support among the group of expatriate Somalis across Western Europe and the United States who opposed the foreign invasion of their homeland. Meanwhile, on the list of those countries that supported the African intervention was the globe's superpower, the United States.

Many Somalis, after their country had slipped into civil war in 1992, had fled to the United States and settled in cities across America. San Diego, Columbus, and Seattle hosted significant populations, along with Minneapolis, which remains home to by far the largest expatriate cluster. These communities of recent refugees— or children of refugees—kept in close touch with contacts back in Somalia, and the Internet age fostered a flow of information from news services, relatives, and friends that would not have been possible even as recently as the 1990s. As the Islamists gained control over greater swaths of territory in the 2000s, this new media facilitated unprecedented information exchange and personal contact. In this flow, expatriate Somalis in America heard of the arrival of African forces from friends and family, and they knew US policy backed the African intervention.

Some of these refugees, in the United States and elsewhere, saw al-Shabaab's tough justice as a way for chaotic Somalia to regain some semblance of order. As this loose Somali militia gained power, those few sympathetic refugees provided financial support through fund-raisers operating in Somali refugee centers scattered across America. During this same period, the FBI opened investigations into these fund-raising channels; the US government had formally named al-Shabaab as a terrorist group, and fund-raising for the organization constituted a violation of federal law. These were serious charges, in other words, and investigating this kind of financial support for terror groups was, and is, a high priority for the FBI. The fund-raising cases cropped up in multiple locations across the United States, and they were a regular feature in the FBI director's morning threat briefings. They all had one characteristic: they showed that there were a number of expatriate Somalis in the United States who were knowingly raising funds for al-Shabaab and funneling the money to the group. I remember because I was there, at the table, listening to and participating in the director's briefings on significant cases.

That's the historical backdrop to some of the decisions I witnessed as these Somali cases moved along at the FBI in the mid-2000s. You might be able to pose a few basic analytic questions here, all of which are real questions you'd have to answer if you were facing this problem. Start with these:

- How extensive are the fund-raising networks for al-Shabaab in the United States?
- Are there fund-raising networks other than those we're already investigating? Do we see new or emerging linkages to these individuals we're investigating that we need to investigate further?
- What else is happening in these cases, beyond fund-raising? What are they up to?
- Once we think we understand the extent of these networks, do we have enough evidence to prosecute the individuals involved? Can we destroy these networks by putting the key players behind bars?

It is often the case in complex analytic decision-making that one of the challenges we face is that we're not choosing between right and wrong questions, and this fund-raising case is no different. It's a classic HEAD Game example. Not only is there nothing wrong with these questions, but they're also clearly questions we have to resolve, regardless of whether there are other issues we must turn to first. If the cases in fact involve fund-raising for a proscribed terror group, the fund-raisers should spend some quality time in a federal prison. That's not, though, nearly the extent of what we need to know. It's not even close, as it turned out.

The information the FBI collects in cases like this originates with a local field office somewhere in America that conducts on-the-ground investigations, goes through the counterterrorist component at FBI Headquarters, and then, if the case is significant enough, is handed up to the FBI director himself. If we're thinking about decision advantage, then, the decision maker in this case is the FBI director, who sits on the right side of this right-to-left analytic exercise. His responsibility is to protect the United States and its citizens using policies and practices that adhere to US law. While fund-raising for terror groups is a criminal offense, raising funds for overseas groups isn't the highest concern of an FBI director in the post-9/11 era; preventing attacks on American soil is. If we stop a fund-raiser but a lethal plot later succeeds because we missed a few participants in a conspiracy, we've failed.

We didn't realize during that time, until it was too late, that the al-Shabaab extremist infection in American cities spread well beyond fund-raising. Somali parents in American cities were unaware that their sons had been recruited to fight in Somalia, until these young men turned up in Somalia and their families started asking what had happened to their children. Somali communities were outraged, and the fund-raisers who had gathered the funds to support al-Shabaab's violence in Somalia were prosecuted. What we missed was the recruiters of young fighters who would travel to Somalia to join the jihad. These recruiters used different networks than the fund-raisers, and they talked to different people. If we thought we had a good picture of extremism among Somali youth in America by looking at the fund-raising cases alone, we thought wrong. We had a very narrow window on Somali extremist activity in America. In other words, we didn't ask the right questions.

The end of this story is telling. In 2008, Shirwa Ahmed drove an explosives-packed vehicle into a building in Somalia. Ahmed was a naturalized American citizen; he went to high school in Minneapolis. Shirwa Ahmed was America's first suicide bomber.

Before you judge that we could have stopped this tragedy with just a few well-considered questions, let's take one step further, and consider the complications of trying to search for the answer to this opaque question of how far extremism had penetrated America's Somali-origin population. As it turned out, the fund-raising networks were different than the networks of people recruiting youth to fight in Somalia, so the intelligence collection we had on fund-raising didn't give us an understanding, or even a hint, of the youths' recruitment. We might have put in place different collection programs to look for this activity; in fact, we should have, as long as we respected the fact that this is America, and the FBI and state and local police cannot simply collect intelligence against local communities, without a good reason to do so. Finally, if we had started down this road, we would have had a tough decision: With known, ongoing cases of terror fund-raising, how many resources do you transfer off these solid cases to work the fuzzy question of whether there are better cases out there relating to the recruitment of Somali youth in American cities?

We'll never know the answer to these questions, but after all those years of analysis, the narrow focus I remember did not help answer the real decision-advantage question: Are we helping the director understand whether there's more going on here? Would the world have turned out any different? Would we have seen the recruitment networks in America sooner? Might we have caught just one teenager from a poor neighborhood in Minneapolis before he got on a plane to East Africa, destroying not just his own life but his family's new life in America?

———

As we examine this Somalia case, we are at risk of the common analytic problem of hindsight bias: looking at how the events developed and judging, because the pieces seem to line up so neatly in retrospect, that we should have been able to see this coming. Of course, we could not have known what would happen among Somali refugees in America beforehand. We could, though, have asked better questions by engaging in a little more right-to-left thinking, and focusing more aggressively not on what we knew about fund-raising but on what we didn't know about which other aspects of extremism might be spreading among Somali-American youth.

We can also transfer this concept of how to think about good questions from the outset to a tougher, multifaceted case, one that both turned out better and offers further insight into crafting complex analytic questions. You're familiar with this case already, even if you don't know it. In 2005, plotters developed an ingenious way to put together a liquid explosive on an airplane, and it led to the prohibition of carrying liquids on planes. Let's step through the plot, applying the right-to-left question process to a real-world problem.

As we watched the case unfold at the FBI, the members of a large terror cell in the United Kingdom were entering the final stages of a plan to take down numerous planes in midair over North American cities. They intended to drill holes in the bottom of unopened plastic drink bottles, refill them with explosive material, and then reseal them so that they would appear new to an airport security officer. This was easily the most ambitious al-Qa'ida plot those of us at the CIA and the FBI had seen in the post-9/11 years, in terms of its sophistication, the size of the cell, and the support (such as training) al-Qa'ida members in Pakistan had provided to the UK plotters. The plot had been brewing for some time, with UK investigators putting together the seemingly disparate pieces while US law enforcement and intelligence operators tried to determine whether there were co-conspirators in America. Our key points, then, are as follows:

- The plotters were pursuing an innovative technique of refilling energy drink bottles that might appear unopened to an airport security officer.
- The plot was expansive, in terms of both the scope of the targeting (many airplanes) and the number of plotters.
- The plot reached into Pakistan to al-Qa'ida operational planners, raising the sophistication of the plotters' security practices, explosives expertise, and target selection.
- The British security services mounted a massive security effort to track and stop the plotters.

These points summarize what we know, but our first question has to start with how we provide decision advantage to the key officials in Washington who are responsible for responding to the plot. Not until we understand their responsibilities can we start to understand how to take what we're learning, as analysts, and package it in a way that helps the decision maker understand and respond. Not all these decision makers need to know everything about the twists and turns of the explosives plot. In this case, a small sample of the officials who would be responding in Washington might include the secretary of state, the head of the Transportation Security Administration (TSA), the FBI director, and the CIA director.

Following is a quick attempt at sketching out the responsibilities of these key customers and what questions we might start with that will help provide decision advantage to them. First, their responsibilities:

- Secretary of state: Work with foreign countries to further US national security and US interests abroad.
- TSA administrator: Secure passengers and aircraft on domestic flights and on international flights entering and leaving the United States.
- FBI director: Follow federal laws, regulations, and procedures to oversee investigations of violations of US federal law.
- CIA director: Locate, track, and dismantle terror networks, working unilaterally or with US partners and partner security services overseas, to keep Americans safe.

With each customer, we can start with a basic question that helps us shift into the right frame of mind, away from a simple recitation of what's happening as the plot unfolds. What is each individual decision maker most concerned about, based on the responsibilities of his or her position? How does the decision maker's area of responsibility relate to the plot and plotters, and how can we analysts use our knowledge to provide a decision-making advantage? How can we limit uncertainty for the decision maker?

That's a start. Now we can continue refining. Here's a next step: Is the threat changing in a way that means US officials have to act immediately, forgoing the opportunity to collect more information that might help us answer open questions about gaps in the investigation, such as whether there are additional conspirators? Ideally, we can spend enough time on the investigation to ensure that when the conspirators are arrested, we're confident we got all of them, not just a fragment of a larger conspiracy. If we miss a few fringe conspirators, there's a decent chance they'll cook up some other conspiracy down the road. We're looking to dismantle the entire operation, in other words, rather than disrupt just the core elements.

Beyond this broad concern about mapping the conspiracy, though, we have to get back to answering the individual needs of the four customers listed above. Unless we try to understand their specific concerns, we risk giving them information that doesn't help them address their unique problems. What follows is an exercise in how to think about providing this kind of decision advantage to varied customers who are dealing with different dimensions of the same problem.

The secretary of state. If we previously told the secretary of state that the plot's origins clearly link back to al-Qa'ida trainers in Pakistan, are we more or less confident in this judgment today? What are the Pakistanis doing about the problem?

There is a related question here that we have to pair with this al-Qa'ida assessment. The secretary is the point person in the US government's relationship with Pakistan, and she's going to want to know about the origins of this plot there because she will undoubtedly be speaking to Pakistani officials about their role in breaking up plots like this. One question we might pose to her, then, is how we assess current Pakistani efforts in al-Qa'ida strongholds, and whether those efforts are more or less intense than they were last year.

Here's why this is critical: if the plot originates with al-Qa'ida trainers, operational planners, and ideological leaders in Pakistan, we can guess that the secretary is going to have to initiate some difficult conversations with Pakistani officials in Islamabad, pressing them for more action against al-Qa'ida to limit the prospect that the group can brew further plots that threaten London and New York. One of the questions she'll have to ask is whether Pakistan's security services can conduct more aggressive operations against al-Qa'ida, and whether Pakistan's political leadership can do more to press forward against al-Qa'ida.

The head of the Transportation Security Administration. His responsibility is to protect air travelers on domestic flights and those going into and out of the United States, and he has to add to that burden an understanding of how plotters are changing tactics in novel attempts to down an aircraft. Finally, he might want to keep abreast of US government efforts to put known and suspected terrorists on travel watch lists, and to monitor how closely foreign airlines flying into the United States check their passenger manifests against these watch lists.

Rather than running through every one of these responsibilities to try to determine how we would work backward into our analytic questions, let's just pick one key aspect of the TSA administrator's job and play it out: the administrator has to prevent airplanes from falling out of the sky as a result of terrorist strikes.

We know we don't want to present the TSA administrator with a simple recitation of the facts surrounding the plot. Instead, we might start by thinking about his specific responsibility to protect air travelers and ask, as we did with the secretary of state, a few key questions relevant to his specific interests in the plot: If the terrorists had progressed without detection by UK security services, what is the likelihood that baggage sensors would have detected the explosive materials at UK airports, or US airports? Have US analysts replicated the materials in US government labs and tested how feasible they are, and how easily they might bring down an airplane? If US intelligence analysts don't think current airport security techniques would have detected the devices, what kinds of policies do we need to put in place to prevent such a plot from succeeding? How much will new defensive measures cost, and how slow and intrusive will new airport checks prove to be?

The FBI director. If some piece of the plot emerges in the United States, and a few random plotters conduct some sort of terror strike—even if they're at the far periphery of the core conspiracy—

the FBI will have failed in its mission. The standard is high: one mistake in this investigation and you lose. Innocents die. To start with, then, the FBI director's question might be something like: How do we ensure that we find any sign of whether this plot has tentacles that touch the United States? Because the core plot is outside the FBI's jurisdiction—the core investigation is in the hands of British authorities—how can I keep abreast of the UK investigation, and stay in regular touch with my UK counterpart, to work through the inevitable rough patches in any complex, transnational investigation like this one? Meanwhile, the director might want to step back periodically and ask questions about whether there are lessons learned in this plot that the FBI could apply to other investigations. What are the key characteristics of these plotters, he might ask—such as their communications, travel, or purchases of precursor materials for improvised explosive devices—and can we put in place policies or procedures that would allow us to spot this kind of conspiracy in the United States?

Some analysts or operators working on a case like this might walk into a morning update with the director and begin a presentation by summarizing what's happening with the UK's investigation. I'd probably suggest a different approach: start with whether anything in the United Kingdom suggests that there are plot tentacles reaching into the United States, and think through whether the director should be making decisions about what steps the FBI should take to look harder. You can get to the question of what's happening across the Atlantic, but that can come later. If you brief the UK plot alone without adding in even tangential US angles, you're forcing the director to filter out what you've said so that he can capture what he needs to know. He will never have the detailed grasp of the investigation that the FBI case manager has, so he might not always know the right question to ask.

The CIA director. This liquid-explosives plot in the UK turned out to be perhaps the most sophisticated attack planning by al-Qa'ida-trained terrorists since the September 11 attacks. One key reason was the training some of the conspirators received from al-Qa'ida operators in Pakistan. If those trainers had access to these kinds of trainees in the UK, who's to say al-Qa'ida wouldn't have access to similar sets of potential terrorists in North America, or in Europe, just a plane flight away from the United States? How can we assure ourselves that this hasn't happened?

While the FBI director asks questions about how the plot might reach the United States from the UK, the CIA director might set his sights in the opposite direction, toward Pakistan. What are we learning about the al-Qa'ida members who worked with the UK plotters? Have they appeared in earlier intelligence reporting, especially reports that suggest they're targeting the United States as well? Can US intelligence collect location information so that the United States or Pakistan can mount operations to capture or kill them? Meanwhile, the CIA director, to avoid crossing wires, might be coordinating with the FBI director and the heads of the various UK security services. Does the United States have access to the data from the British investigation, so the FBI can investigate US links and the CIA can exploit anything that helps sketch out the Pakistani connection?

———

This step of focusing on what the customer needs to know rather than on your own knowledge is one of the hardest lessons for any expert to master in the transition to becoming an analyst. Most analysts I worked with never managed to graduate to this level. A Realtor doesn't look at a new customer and offer a summary of everything she knows about the local housing market. A good Realtor starts with questions focused on you, to understand who you are and what you're looking for. A good analyst, walking into the office of the FBI director, shouldn't offer details of a case without going through the same process: What's the director trying to do? What questions do I need to ask to help?

Does this sound simple? It's not. It's the first mile on a treadmill, after you've taken a year off exercising. If you spend time struggling with this stage, it'll hurt. With practice, though, it'll get easier.

AVOIDING THE CERTAINTY TRAP:
THE DECEPTIVENESS OF YES/NO QUESTIONS

All experts, or even pretend experts, gravitate toward certainty when trying to answer questions. Look at the unrest and revolutions that have simmered and exploded in recent decades, from Latin America and the Sandinistas through Algeria's counterinsurgency in the 1990s and the upheaval in the 2010s in the Arab world. Regardless of which of those problems you are analyzing, the questions are the same: Are the insurgents going to succeed? Does the government have the will and firepower to maintain control? Is some revolutionary movement in the Middle East or Latin America going to succeed?

Now let's imagine that you are the expert. What's the answer? Don't hedge. Is it yes or no? Here's another one, for the economists around the world: Is the economy heading into a bull or bear market? Come up with an answer, quickly. For the home buyers of the world, you have the same drive to answer a black-and-white question: Do you like this house? Yes or no?

Our ability to answer with certitude reflects confidence; it projects the image of expert invincibility. We are the experts on insurgencies, or American politics, or home buying. Yes, we say, I know the answer to questions in my area of expertise. Anything else would reflect weakness, and weakness immediately suggests vulnerability. We even joke about this all the time when we discuss the battle of the sexes. What male out there hasn't gotten hopelessly lost in a car because he felt the necessity of claiming that he really knew the right directions when in fact he had little idea? We will refer to the pressure that pushes us toward yes-or-no conclusions as the "certainty bias."

This tendency toward certainty is understandable, but it is treacherous in the business of complex analysis. Not only does certainty sometimes eliminate complexity, but it also drives us to pretend that we know what is inherently unknowable. We can take a knowledgeable position, even an expert position, on an issue such as the future of a revolution or political upheaval, but to suggest that we know with certainty how chaos will evolve over the course of time is analytically unsound. We know some of what to look for, certainly. But we really don't know who will end up on top.

Let's try out this theory of analysis versus yes/no answers on the process a publisher might step through to determine whether to buy and publish a book. On the surface, nonexperts might think that the question surrounding whether to publish a book is simple: Will the book sell? How certain are you? Yes or no?

If we faced a question that narrow, though, we might consider only one answer: "That's not a good question. I don't know the answer, and the truth is, because we can't predict the future, none of us really knows. If people pretend they do know, their certainty should immediately lead you to view their analysis with skepticism." Since we've already acknowledged ignorance about the publishing profession, let's take a step further. If you approach this from an analyst's point of view and define your goal as narrowing uncertainty, one step might be weeding out books that don't show the characteristics that you might typically see in bestsellers. We might then turn for a moment to defining those characteristics we nonexperts think should be important in assessing what we think of a particular book or book proposal. This list of characteristics isn't meant to be perfect, partly because we're not publishing experts. It is designed, though, to underscore the point that with some painful, but effective, analytic thinking, wrapped in the simple methodology we've stepped through so far, even a nonexpert can start necking down from a vague, insoluble mess ("Is the book going to sell?") to a manageable problem that has characteristics anybody can weigh. Here are a few questions we might start with, avoiding the yes/no trap along the way:

- What kind of books sell in this genre? What are the characteristics of those books that sell?
- What kinds of books fail in this genre? What are the characteristics of those books that fail?
- How many of the good characteristics does this book have? How many of the bad characteristics? If we assume that almost no book is perfect, how can we judge whether the good characteristics outweigh the bad?
- Are there ways to work on the weak points, even if we can't fix them entirely?

PRACTICING HEAD GAMES: THE "CALL MOM" EXERCISE AND THE THINKING GAME

You'll need discipline to answer complex analytic questions without rambling, or slipping into jargon, or getting sloppy with loose sentences or imprecise words. Too often, you'll want to rush through these initial stages of analysis, so you can start playing around with the kinds of interesting data that all analysts like to assess. To help you avoid this rush to data, you can try a few basic exercises to test whether you've sharpened your thinking enough to head to the next step in the process. These exercises might sound simplistic, but try them anyway. They work. And they're not nearly as easy as they seem if you read them but don't practice them.

The "Call Mom" exercise. For the first of the two exercises, we need a few rules to live by. The most basic of them is this: if you're wondering whether you've posed a good question, or you're practicing the answer to that question to see if it's both concise and comprehensive, then try using only one sentence to summarize your question. This one-sentence limit, artificial as it seems, will force you to be clearer and more concise than you're comfortable with. Using too many sentences or words to ask your key question or explain your answer is almost always a signal that your thinking is still too muddled. If you can't summarize clearly to yourself, how can you explain clearly to someone else? The addition of even a few extra words to your questions is a simple indicator that you have not sorted through all your thoughts aggressively enough to eliminate extraneous words or thoughts that sidetrack clear-minded thinking. There's no cheating here, either: you get no run-on sentences.

To implement the one-sentence principle, your question or answer summary can contain a maximum of three written lines, and you are limited to one dependent clause in that sentence. When you have whittled away enough excess language to hit this target, shift into the part of this exercise that you might initially find odd. Pretend that you're picking up the telephone to call your mother (thus the reason I've named this the "Call Mom" exercise). Speak aloud the one-sentence question you've settled on. Don't read it, or mumble it quietly; speak it out loud. If you can look yourself in the mirror, speak the sentence, and confidently affirm that your mother would quickly comprehend the sentence, you're in good shape. You're thinking clearly, and your audience should be able to understand you.

Speaking your core summary sentences this way will shake out a few problems beyond hazy thinking. At the most basic level, we all speak more naturally than we write, and your ear will immediately hear and weed out awkward phrases or structure in your ideas and your writing. If what you have written sounds odd to your ear when you read it, don't hesitate: force yourself to change the sentence. If your ear hears something even slightly offensive, don't pretend that what you've written is acceptable because readers won't notice it, or because other listeners will have a different reaction than you did. When we write, we tend to think we need to be more formal, to express ourselves more clearly and to impress the reader. Instead, this formality puts off readers, who immediately recognize language that is staged. Drop this language. Stick with more everyday words, phrases, sentences, and explanations. Listeners will absorb them more quickly.

More than likely, you'll never actually call your mother to practice, and this exercise has less to do with your mother than with your mind. She's a surrogate that will help you step through this quick diagnostic test that helps determine whether your thought processes are distilled enough when you start with your question and finish with your conclusion, or answer.

In addition to the brevity this rule enforces, we should apply a second litmus test to our one-sentence questions and answers: the litmus test of inclusivity. If anything, this standard is going to be harder to meet than the one-sentence brevity rule we set as our first standard. Think through all the kinds of material you will need to provide a decision maker who's receiving the answer to your question. In the case of assessing a terror group, you may need to factor in the group's leadership, finances, training program, expertise, pool of fighters, etc. That's a lot of material to cover. When you pose your one-sentence question to your mother, you have to look at all the data you'll need to include in your analysis and ensure that your one sentence gives you the latitude to cover the subject.

Here's an example: You've been asked to assess whether a terrorist group's capability to attack New York is rising or falling. You run through an exercise to list what you'll need to think about to answer this question. Do they have strong leaders and operators? Do they have trainees who can get to the United States? Can these trainees find weapons or explosives for an attack, or build an explosive device? Good questions, all of them. You think you've come up with a strong, clear question to start your analysis. Here it is:

- How do I understand whether this group's leadership in Pakistan has sustained or grown the infrastructure to support an attack?

This is pretty close, but it's not perfect. If the group has a strong infrastructure in Pakistan, the group's leaders certainly can conceptualize and train for an attack, and then the group can send out trained operatives. But key to the problem is whether these operatives can operate in the tight security environment of the United States, whether they'll make a mistake because they don't blend into the United States, and whether they will know how to acquire materials in the United States. The infrastructure in Pakistan that you asked about in your question is key, but it doesn't pass the "inclusiveness" test; it doesn't include everything you need to answer to assess the threat, because you haven't asked about whether the group can operate in America.

Let's rephrase the question, just a bit, to see if we can capture both the brevity and the inclusiveness, or comprehensiveness, that we need:

- How do I understand whether this group's leadership in Pakistan has sustained or grown the infrastructure to support an attack and whether its operatives can operate effectively in America?

The point of adjusting the question has to do with clarity and efficiency of thinking and analysis. As we step through a complex analytic exercise, we have to make sure we don't lose our way in a sea of confusing data. One way to maintain focus is to return periodically to our initial question and ask how the data we're reviewing relates to the initial question. If you've spent time practicing the "Call Mom" exercise at the front end of your analysis, when you lose your way you might find quickly that returning to your initial question will help you avoid spending a lot of time with data that doesn't seem related to it. And you might add efficiency to your thinking by conserving energy you might have spent thinking about problems that don't relate to your initial question. Do you want to know about the group's capabilities in Pakistan? Or do you want to know how these capabilities match up with the group's ability to operate in the United States? These are both very good questions. But they're also both very different questions.

The thinking game. Another method that will train your mind is even easier to practice than the "Call Mom" exercise, but it's often more frustrating. It's what I'd like to call the thinking game, an exercise you can use on a daily basis while you're driving or on the treadmill or waiting in a supermarket line. Here's a snapshot of the method: take a problem you care about, in whatever sphere of life you know something about. Almost anything counts—you can pick sports, fashion, politics, international security, or food—just as long as you're passionate about it. Once you select something, pick a current debate or subject of conversation in that area. Following is a notional list of the kinds of things you might settle on, from the significant to the small:

— Whether some dictator is going to survive a revolution.
— Whether free agency has been good or bad for baseball.
— Whether Paris haute couture shows have a significant impact on what you will buy in stores this fall.

— Whether the current food fad (from quinoa to kale to sustainable salmon) is a short-term phenomenon or a longer-term shift in global dietary habits.

Let's start with the easy part. You can have an emotional response to the issue—"I'm really angry with the Republicans for gridlock," or "The Democrats' reckless spending habits drive me nuts"—as long as you understand that these responses are not analytic; they're just a quick characterization of why your blood boils. So take a deep breath and pick the side of the issue with which you agree. Let's turn back to assessing an insurgency, whether it's in Latin America, Asia, or the post–Arab Spring Middle East. You might assess that some dictator somewhere will be ousted within twenty-four months; you don't think he can withstand the pressure of surging opposition militias, despite their factionalism. OK, that's our starting point. It's the easy part because, at the outset at least, you get to defend the position you believe in.

Now we're going to force you to push yourself to ask more questions than you'll be able to answer; this is where you'll find yourself growing more frustrated. The thinking game goes something like this: you have to offer a rational, clear answer to every question you ask yourself about the position you're defending. You can't inject emotion, and you can't use loaded judgment words that mean different things to different people (words such as "bad," "good," "appropriate," "inappropriate," "right," "wrong," etc.). On the question of a dictator holding on to power, then, you might start as follows:

Question 1:

Why do you think the dictator will hold on to power?

Notional Answer: The dictator retains control of key levers of power, including a well-armed and loyal military and the financial resources to support the military. He also has deep support among some segments of the population.

Question 2:
Why do you think these are the key characteristics that will define the country's future?

Notional Answer: The country's rebels haven't shown the battlefield capability to take and hold more than a few major cities, and they don't have the political cohesion to mount a diplomatic campaign that might result in greater international pressure on the dictator.

You might be able to handle two questions, but by the time you get to question 3 in this game, you're probably having a difficult time capturing what you think in words. In this case, for example, you might try to ask why you think the current battlefield capability and internal cohesion of the rebels won't change. If you're like most of us, once you get beyond two or three questions that drill down into hard issues, you start to grow frustrated. "I know what I think," you might say, "but shaping a clear, simple answer in my mind isn't so easy." This kind of question practice is a simple method that allows us to get to the bottom of why we think the way we do.

Here's an easier example of how this works. Find something that involves taste, such as a dessert you order whenever you can. Chocolate layer cake, let's say. Here's the first question in the thinking game: Why do you like chocolate cake? Because it tastes good. Why does it taste good? Hmm. Already, after just one question, an issue about which you might have strong views has you stumped. Despite your strong views, you can't quite articulate why it is that you think what you think. Attempting to assess taste provides good examples for this exercise; try getting beyond answering two questions to explain why you like some particular fashion, color, food, or hairstyle. In this case, you might be able to get through question 2: It tastes good because it's rich. OK, now try again. Question 3: What do you mean by "rich"? Just about all of us would be frustrated by this point, but the HEAD Game we're practicing is forcing us to articulate why we think the way we do with a precision that we're unaccustomed to. This is great practice. Stick with it.

We're not through, though, because our goal isn't simply to press you to practice translating feelings or thoughts into clear analytic statements. Our goal is broader, to force your mind to practice mental gymnastics that should help you learn to break down any problem you see more quickly. So here's the next step: take the position you've just articulated. "I think this dictator is finished." Or "I think the new fall colors for casual wear are ugly." Brace yourself: your next task requires you to reverse your position. Work through the same process of asking questions that are increasingly narrow, but this time try to articulate clearly what someone else would say if he or she took a position in opposition of the original position you took.

The first step isn't hard. You're going to end up with a statement such as "I think the new fall colors for casual wear will capture our demographic market," even if you find them repulsive. But remember, the goal here isn't just to help you articulate what you think about a particular problem or question. The goal here is to train your mind to look at a problem and break it down. Saying "I just don't like this color" or "I just don't like this idea" is not the way you are going to explain yourself in a business meeting or defend yourself when you're under attack by a colleague. Stepping clearly through your thought process might help, though, and practicing by taking both sides of an issue will help you do that. If anything, articulating how you would explain the side with which you disagree might be the more valuable element of this exercise. If we're looking for mental agility, it's hard enough to explain what you think. You want more practice? Explain what you *don't* think, and pretend that you believe in this position enough to persuade someone by the analytic clarity of your presentation.

———

You will face the temptation to skip this step of framing the question properly and head right to the heart of the analytic process, but you can't do that. Where you end up in any analytic process is decided from day one, when you settle on the question. Two examples from American business successes should help clarify this.

Howard Schultz. Starbucks sells coffee, right? Wait. Did Schultz (who built Starbucks) decide how to make better coffee? Was that his question? Or did he start in a different direction: How do I build a Third Place—a place for people to gather that's not work and not home? Lots of cafés sell coffee. Starbucks built a business around the concept that the café is a place to go, not another place that sells coffee.

Steve Jobs. Apple sells technology, right? Wait. Did Jobs decide how to build a better technology company? Or did he decide how to build a consumer company focused on style and marketing? Lots of companies build smartphones, and Apple isn't always the first to the market with new technology. Smaller technology companies sometimes are. Apple starts with the proposition that they make hip consumer products that include cutting-edge electronics.

CHAPTER THREE

THE DRIVERS

We are now going to transition from how to think about questions and decisions to how we can pick apart a question and break it down into constituent components. Note the significance of this: without this process, you'll often (and wrongly) start with data, quickly picking bits of information from a mass of data. If you take this approach and you're a stock picker, for example, you might have read an article yesterday about the industry you're thinking of investing in, and that article becomes your first data point. This intuitive data sorting isn't truly analytic; it's the simplest way the human mind can provide quick answers without struggling to expend the time and energy to think harder. We'll get to the data later, only nearing the end of the book. It's the least significant piece of this analytic process. Right now, we are going to discuss setting the question and then breaking it down, as it is far more important.

Think of this step in the analytic process as similar to sorting laundry in your basement. You have your pile of clothes, unsorted, and now you're wondering how you can quickly get them folded and into the dresser upstairs. You can either work through them one at a time, folding one T-shirt and placing it on one side of the room, then folding a second and placing it somewhere else, until you have thirty-seven individually folded items of clothing spread around your kitchen, your living room, and your study. This accomplishes the laundry mission, but it's not the most efficient way to complete your laundry. Quickly, though, anyone who's done laundry since living in a college dorm will decide that the faster route would be to sort the pile, requiring a division into T-shirts, underwear, towels, etc. Before you get to the real work, in other words—the folding—you have a way to divide your laundry-folding problem into constituent components.

Without thinking, you've come up with the concept of sorting bins. In this simplified example, the clothes represent the piles of data we deal with every day. Do we want to start playing with the data before we figure out which pile each bit might fit into? With the complex problems we're dealing with here, that approach would be extremely inefficient. But now, as we start, we don't have a way to come up with the automatic "go-to" bins we can turn to. It's easy to come up with the bins when you're sorting laundry. It's harder with more complex problems. So in this chapter, we will work through a process of how to build our sorting bins, the step between asking the question and swimming in the data.

To shift to a more complex real-life example of how to break down questions, let's turn to another national security problem, one of those counterterrorism questions I remember revisiting periodically at the CIA. Not the simple yes/no question—"Are we winning against al-Qa'ida?"—but instead something harder. Try this: "How well are we doing in degrading whatever terror organization we're fighting today? Where are we weak?" This question requires that we shift into the stream's current and burn a few mental calories. As a start, we might think of the characteristics we'd have to assess to answer the question. After a day or so working on this, maybe as part of a team of analysts working through the problem, we might decide on a list of key drivers that looks something like this:

- Safe haven for terrorists (in other words, the time and space to plan, train for, and execute terror plots)
- Money
- Recruits
- Leadership
- Communications
- Ideological resonance across borders (popular support)
- Access to weapons/explosives
- Training
- Facilitation (infrastructure for travel, documents, etc.)

This driver-based approach not only gives you an advantage by breaking down questions into manageable units, but it also allows you a way to manage your data. We're not at the stage yet of looking at data, but keep this thought in the back of your mind: when information flows in, rather than adding it to one unmanageable pile, sorting through it periodically, and offering a recitation of what appears to be relevant from the most recent stuff you've seen, you can instead file each bit into one of these baskets as it comes in. If you have five hundred pieces of new information flowing in during a given week, you'd face a daunting task to make sense of it unless you resorted to cherry-picking a handful of pieces because you can't manage to juggle anything more.

Instead, you might count thirty pieces of information for the first driver basket, such as al-Qa'ida's financial position. You're already in a more manageable place analytically. You're clear on where you're headed—that's your initial question. You know the elements that you'll need to weigh to break down that complex question—those are your driver baskets. And you have the starting point for how to make sense of your pile of data—that's the process of sorting the data into your driver baskets and keeping a separate pile of data that doesn't seem to fit.

Regardless of what kind of problem we're handling, we will use the same terminology every time we finish adapting our question and turn to selecting our bins. Through the rest of the book, we will refer to this "basket" concept of breaking down questions as "driver" analysis, with the word "driver" representing those key areas (the baskets, or bins) that will drive our judgments about how to assess our key question. What drivers do we need to understand when we assess a foreign country's military capabilities and intentions? What drivers do we need to assess whether we think a company is a good long-term investment?

In short, the driver concept works as follows: for any question we face, a certain number of elements—in general, let's set the number at roughly six to ten—are fundamental to breaking down our question into its constituent components. These building blocks propel us toward reaching a conclusion without having to look at each bit of data as a discrete element.

To make this clearer, let's do a quick check on how to use this concept of driver analysis by breaking down two questions. We'll start with how we might think of a car purchase and then return to a tougher question, how we assess our concerns about terrorism. As for the car, we'll start there because it may resonate with you: you've probably already applied this driver-based process in your life, without using the terms and conscious thought processes that we're employing here. You may have started a new family, for example, and you decided that your tiny compact car is not the right vehicle if you want more safety and room for a baby seat in the back. You've come up with a fair question: What family-friendly car meets my needs? Under any circumstances, you'd probably settle on at least a few of the drivers that follow:

- Cost
- Reliability

- Car-seat adaptability
- Safety
- Size
- Fuel efficiency

This summary is not meant to be exhaustive. For the moment, though, let's stick with it to practice. You can probably guess that with this list of these six basic characteristics, or decision drivers, you can get pretty close to compiling a solid mix of the types of cars that might help you answer your question. Significantly, we did not start with either a brand or any particular data point. We started instead with basic car-purchasing elements that are important to all of us. We did not compare cars on popular websites, and we didn't pick up the free auto sales listings that you find at groceries and drugstores. We started by breaking down our question into bins, or drivers. And we started with a process of listing our key drivers that would probably take a prospective car buyer about three minutes (if that), start to finish.

Think of what would have happened had you started at the other end of the problem, starting not with the few key variables but with the data. Here's the likely scenario: you might pick up that free newspaper in which you'll find ads for a thousand used cars in your area. You then waste two hours, looking at every single ad, just trying to figure out which options jump out at you. This data-first approach might be fun for you, if you're an auto enthusiast or a glutton for wasting your Saturday afternoon leafing through free newspapers. If you've got better things to do on a weekend, though, this approach could waste a lot of time that could be better spent with family or friends.

Try another common car-buying scenario that starts with data rather than drivers. Ask yourself a few opening questions: What are the options from Honda, or Ford, or Subaru, or Toyota, or GM? What do I think of these? What about Honda versus Ford? Or Ford versus GM? You could spend all day breaking down your purchasing process just by posing an inefficient series of a hundred questions that makes it feel like you're sorting strands of spaghetti.

Now go back to that initial list of six basic drivers and focus on one of them. Let's pick the size of the vehicle as a starter. We're focusing on family-friendly cars, which means those that can hold a few people and provide easy access for child seats. We're also, obviously, eliminating everything from a Mazda Miata to a Honda Fit. Weed them out, because they're nowhere near matching the family-friendly driver we settled on. We tell ourselves that what we're looking for is a car that seats five comfortably, because we need a family-friendly vehicle that's at least as big as a sedan— maybe up to the size of a van or an SUV—to fit us, our stuff, our coming family addition, and a few groceries in the trunk. This is four doors and a minimum of some amount of cubic footage that you should be able to figure out from just glancing at standard sedan interior dimensions.

You can do the same thing with the other drivers, not picking any particular car but simply defining what your parameters are. "I want at least thirty miles per gallon," you might say. "Anything short of that would feel wasteful. And I want something in the top five in its class for reliability. I've got a new little one coming into an expanding family, with soccer season just around the corner." You certainly don't want to be surprised if your new car collapses like a tin can in the event of a catastrophic accident.

You are no doubt sensing where we're going here. We've defined our question (How do we come up with a good list of family-friendly cars?) and broken it down into drivers, the baskets any potential buyer might consider in a new or used car purchase. We're already heading into a decision-making process that will save us time when we finally get to the stage of logging on to the websites that allow you to compare an endless selection of cars. By the time we get all the way to that selection process, when we're sorting through the data about Hondas, Fords, Subarus, and every other car make, we should be well on our way to whittling down our list of the final contenders.

When you get to decision time, you may have a few auto options that bunch closely together, because they all match your driver criteria so closely. How can you decide, you might ask, if they all seem so close to checking the boxes you have identified as important? Rather than frustrating you, though, that difficult choice at the end of your decision-making process should leave you with a feeling of faith in the car-buying analysis you've done. You can struggle with your final options, but you might instead acknowledge that whichever option you choose, you've already fulfilled the requirements you set as important. Why lose sleep? If they all are so close to meeting the top six or eight criteria you've set, are any of them really a bad choice? At this point, as you choose among them, you're splitting hairs. More than likely, you'll be perfectly happy with whichever car you pick.

If you really feel compelled to keep whittling away at the list, you can go on to create a second set of subordinate drivers that could quickly weed out a few options. For example, if you live in a city, you might add ease of parallel parking to your list of drivers, and maybe you'll find that you can eliminate one or two of the models that are left on your list. Just be aware that, by this point, you're making a choice based on criteria that aren't that important to you—if the driver wasn't on your initial top ten list, it just can't be that much of a priority. So when you're adding this criterion, you're not using it to dump cars that don't meet your needs and interests. You're just looking to decide between perfectly good options.

When you start this process, push yourself hard: Did you define your question clearly enough? "I need a good new car" isn't good enough. If you need a good new car, go buy a Bentley. Is it too expensive? Too much of a gas-guzzler? Well, that's because you didn't spend enough time defining a clear question. You don't need a good new car; you need a good new car that matches your simply stated goal of reliability, efficiency, size, and safety. Force yourself to be clear about the question and you'll save time on the back end of this process.

When you're through with developing that initial question, try harder than you'd like to refine the first list of drivers. If you've gone through from start to finish and you still have too many options, focus on distinguishing between the ones that are truly significant for your final choice and the ones that aren't. No matter how interesting they may be, if drivers aren't essential to your decision-making, they need to come off your list. (Of course, some of these may turn out to be useful as subordinate drivers later on.)

REDUCING COMPLEXITY:
THE ADVANTAGE OF DRIVER-BASED ANALYSIS

The car example is a good starting point for discussing drivers because auto purchases involve a limited set of variables that are familiar to most of us. For almost all decisions like this, we should be able to make a sound decision by juggling no more than six to ten drivers, which is about the same number we can use for most complex problems, including national security ones. And ten variables is on the high side; more than ten and you are, by definition, starting to consider drivers that don't have a fundamental impact on your answer. If they did, they wouldn't drop below the top ten.

We can practice this basket approach using the kind of complex case I used to spend my time with in the world of counterterrorism. Let's take a question that's standard for any counterterrorism professional—White House policymaker or CIA intelligence analyst—who's trying to assess whether the US and international campaign against terrorism is gaining ground or slipping. If we're playing the role of the intelligence analyst, trying to think for the policymaker, we might return to a question we've asked before, something like this:

- How much progress are we making against the al-Qa'ida group that conducted the 9/11 attacks, and where are our weak points?

Before we get started, we should pretend that this book on analytic methodology doesn't exist. Without the simple, repeatable process we are laying out across these pages, here are the kinds of problems you might face when you put pen to paper:

1. The analyst's initial answer might result from fast, intuitive thinking. An experienced analyst, or group of analysts, will walk into the conference room with some version of a narrative that is anchored in their expertise and personal experiences. Their experiences are critical, but only when they're packaged in a process that's analytically credible. Unless they've broken the problem down into constituent parts and weighed the data with a cold eye to clarifying what they know and what they don't, their answers too often reflect an overemphasis on one person's personal perspective and an underemphasis on those variables that might conflict with the analyst's views.

2. The analyst may pay limited attention to gaps. If we don't line up the elements we think are critical to understanding a problem, including those elements about which we know little or nothing, we risk focusing on what we know without

facing the reality that there are huge blank spaces, or gaps, in our knowledge base.

3. If you're the manager of analysts working on this problem, with less hands-on knowledge of the data than the experts, you won't be able to question them in enough detail to test them. It should be the analyst's responsibility, with training and coaching, to offer analyses that include *all* relevant drivers, including those that are the weak links. Analysts can't pick and choose those drivers about which they have confidence. How would you like to be the patient of a doctor who sold you on a surgical procedure without openly acknowledging the risks? Further, how much confidence would you have that you could identify those risks, if you're not an expert surgeon, just by asking a series of good questions?

4. Analysts won't be able to update their analyses effectively and efficiently. Each time you discuss a complex analytic problem, ask these basic questions: Which driver baskets now include new information, which include only limited or dated information, and which are bare? Are there places where you haven't seen new information for a while? What do you make of those gaps over time? A less structured, more intuitive analytic approach would result in a fuzzier, less efficient conversation. "What's new?" you might ask. If analysts answer by focusing only on the most recent piece of information they've seen, you're already in trouble. If you're managing this process, you can force accountability by requiring analysts to address information changes in every driver basket each time they discuss an analytic problem.

We're not here to pretend that the final choice will appear like magic after you've run through your drivers; it won't be as simple as inserting numbers into an equation and coming up with a hard,

unambiguous solution. Instead, once you inject the human element at the end of your analytic process—whether you're buying
a car or assessing the persistence of the al-Qa'ida threat—you can
be sure that you've forced yourself to become more efficient, more
organized, and more pointed. Rather than arguing the difference
between "al-Qa'ida is still a major threat" and "al-Qa'ida is a spent
force," you're down to a much clearer conversation based on which
individual al-Qa'ida drivers are in dispute.

For this to happen, you can't let yourself off the hook on this
question of how many drivers you juggle. Even for your most complicated problems, you can only have a limited number of drivers
before you overcomplicate the analysis. After you've selected ten,
are you sure the eleventh driver you've added is relevant? When
the president is working on a complex foreign policy issue, such as
nuclear negotiations with Russia, does he consider more than ten
variables? I doubt it.

A final driver principle we need to consider is more complex, but
it's just as important as the simple concept of limiting your numbers.
If you're involved in evaluating a problem that includes analysts
who disagree, this rule will help you narrow their disagreements.
Here's the rule: to keep your analytic process pure—to eliminate
bias—analysts who disagree should select one single set of drivers
they agree on. In our car-buying scenario, for example, they might
disagree on which vehicle they'd recommend. They should not disagree about whether the set of six drivers we selected represent the
criteria we should consider. This is a difficult concept to grasp in
theory, but in practice, it's a lot simpler than it sounds. Don't worry
if it takes you a few tries to get it. Do worry, though, if you try to
pretend that this principle is irrelevant. You can't adjudicate analytic disagreements unless each side is assessing the same criteria.

The fact that these drivers should be agreeable to all sides of an
analytic discussion, whether we're talking about stocks or national

security, is why you might use the word "agnostic" to describe the selection of drivers. This word captures our goal: analysts across the spectrum would accept that price is a factor in car-buying decisions. This driver, then, isn't linked to any argument; it's an agnostic measure that all analysts have to use to assess which car is the right buy. If you complete your analysis and the drivers lead to a result that favors your point of view, that's fine if it is accidental. Agnostic drivers are the backbone of how we want to analyze any problem we look at, and there's no way we can build a valid analytic conversation if we manipulate the drivers from the outset to favor one side or the other.

Let's go from theory to practice. We can try this driver approach on a problem that's much harder than our car purchase. Once again, it's an al-Qa'ida problem, one that I've personally struggled with since 9/11: the emotional question of how much Americans should worry about terrorism. Using the principles of both limiting our driver variables and filtering our drivers to ensure that they are agnostic, we might start the process by assessing key drivers in two basic areas: (1) how terrorism affects the world, the nation, my community, and my family and me; (2) how terrorism fits into the broader context of violence in America and other social ills in the country. When you review the following list of prospective drivers, note in particular that regardless of whether you think terrorism is a problem, it would be hard to argue against using these measuring sticks to come up with a reasoned answer:

- Personal experience. (1) Have I ever experienced terrorism personally? (2) Have I ever experienced other types of violence?
- Local frequency. (1) What is the incidence of terrorism in my community, state, or region? (2) What is the incidence of violence in my community, state, or region?

- National frequency. (1) What is the incidence of terror attacks nationally? (2) What is the incidence of violence nationally?
- Trends. What are the trend lines? (1) Are terror incidents increasing or decreasing over time? (2) Are other acts of violence increasing or decreasing over time?
- Randomness. (1) How random are terror incidents? How likely is it that I might be affected? (2) What is the incidence of random natural events that lead to death or injury?

As we've discussed, there is nothing wrong with deciding, at the end of this process, that you want to worry more (or less) than this analytic process suggests you should.

The conclusion of an analytic process depends heavily on this human component, whether it's an expert's view based on decades studying a problem or whether it's your decision to buy your first new car based on its "feel." But to start the process, you can use this less emotional methodology to help you step back and understand the analysis that might be the foundation of your argument. Is your rationale for your analytic judgment reasoned, or is it based on emotion?

If you're looking at information in the baskets listed above as terrorism-related drivers, you might decide that the threat of terrorism in everyday life, compared to other violent threats facing Americans—such as gangs or drug-trafficking organizations—remains high. But since driver-based analysis doesn't support this proposition, your decision is an emotional one. Now you must ask yourself if you have a clear understanding of where and why emotions have driven you away from a more agnostic analytic process. Are you comfortable with that? Are you relying on intuition or a process that is less personalized?

If you're not careful about looking at all the characteristics of the problem, you'll fall prey to one of the most common analytic faults, the "Last In, First Out" principle: the last item of inventory that enters the warehouse is the first item that will go out of the warehouse. For humans whose minds don't like the trouble of burning the energy to sort through vast amounts of information, the Last In, First Out (known as LIFO) principle means that when you are confronted with a complex problem, you will take the first piece of information that you can think of—which often happens to be the last thing you learned about that issue—and use that single bit of information as the piece of data around which you make your argument.

Remember back to the bombing at the Boston Marathon in 2013, when two brothers built explosive devices using common pressure cookers and placed them near the finish line of the race. The case dominated cable news for weeks, and the tragedy of the injuries and loss of life—coupled with the randomness of the target, a marathon race—rightly resulted in grief across the nation and emotional questions about how such an event could happen. In the Boston bombing case, then, you would look at the tragedy and then create an entire argument or analytic judgment based on the episode, which you turn to because your mind, which has just stored the Boston memory, pulls it out first when you think of terrorism. This is another characteristic of living like a trout: you have to burn energy to put a recent incident into a broader context, and the easiest out is instead to use that one incident in isolation to make your argument.

The single incident that is the tragedy of Boston, though, cannot represent a full analytic argument, simply because single incidents do not, by definition, provide enough of a statistical base to draw conclusions. If you're a baseball player and you fail to reach first base for two straight games, a baseball analyst would be mistaken to draw the conclusion that you are a poor hitter. More precisely, that analyst could clearly say that you have had a poor two-game stretch. Without putting your two-day skid into the broader context of your performance across your career—without, in other words, using a statistical base with enough data points to result in a meaningful conclusion—you are at risk of LIFO analysis. What just happened, in terrorism or in baseball, does not allow for in-depth analysis.

Adding context to the tragedy of Boston, then, would require looking at the totality of incidents over time so that you have a reasonable statistical base from which to draw conclusions. The problem with terrorism, of course, is that there are so few incidents domestically that a professional statistician might tell you that the base is too small for meaningful analysis. In baseball, if you go to bat three hundred times, a statistician would tell you that you have enough of a base to make solid judgments about how good a hitter you are that year. We don't have that kind of statistical base in terrorism.

We need to be especially wary of LIFO when we are employing the analytic process immediately following a traumatic or highly emotional event. If you properly employ the right-to-left method in the heat of the moment—after, for example, a horrific terror attack—you will be perceived as downgrading the significance of a tragedy. This is exactly the point, though: in the emotional period following a major event, whether it's a terror tragedy or a significant error in your business processes, you have to balance the need to address the tragedy or the business error with an understanding of how it fits in context. If you want to respond emotionally to Boston, as we all do, this is perfectly understandable. Failing to grieve at the loss of life is inhuman. To take that emotion, though, and transfer it to an analytic judgment that Boston represents the persistence of a major terror threat to the United States is analytically unsound. Watch out for Last In, First Out. It'll crop up for you every single day—unless you know it's there and guard against it.

ANALYTIC ARGUMENTS:
REDUCING COMPLEXITY WITH DRIVERS

There's more to the driver-based process than giving analysts a way to manage the complexity of tough problems. This process should also give you a method for arbitrating analytic disputes among experts who might otherwise walk into a room and explain, using decades of experience, why their analytic intuition is right. You have a couple of options if you're in the middle of that dispute. You can listen to both sides for hours and try to sort through the judgments they're presenting by yourself, trying to use your own expert experiences to determine which of their competing views makes analytic sense. Or you can start breaking down their arguments using the driver-based approach, sorting what they say into baskets and separating out those baskets of agreement (maybe the beginnings of a compromise) and those of true disagreement (maybe the beginnings of the next round of analysis, to close analytic gaps).

Here's a sample from the national security world. If two counterterrorism experts are arguing about the seriousness of a terror plot, you might raise the level of the debate by using the driver method to tease out where they really disagree—and where you can identify common ground. Despite these two analysts' disagreements, they might start their conversation by settling on the drivers they think are important to assess the terror plot, just as two feuding editors might settle on the characteristics that define books that have succeeded under their publishing company's imprint.

Your first question, then, would be simple: Is the driver list they are using biased in favor of either one of them? After some thoughtful review, perhaps they make a few adjustments to the driver list, and then you might, as a mediator, ask the two to run down the driver list one more time and check off those areas about which they are in agreement. Maybe they both have common views about the access and track record of the informant. Maybe they both have common views of the underlying data: both agree that it's reliable, but they also agree that it lacks specificity.

So we might learn that the disagreement between the two analytic camps boils down to differing interpretations of the lack of corroborating information from any other source. You could end your moderated conversation here, by allowing the two parties to disagree: that is, by asking the analysts to draft their analysis starting with the drivers about which they agree and then highlighting the one driver—corroboration—that they weigh differently. Think, now, of where this conversation might otherwise have started. If each analyst—let's call them Mary and John—had written an independent assessment, or participated in a debate about the threat, their intuitive assessments might have looked something like this:

MARY: I've been doing this a long time, and I think this is a serious plot.
JOHN: I've also been doing this for more than a decade, but I'm less confident that this is a serious plot.

I heard this kind of analytic dispute all the time at the CIA. If you're managing analysts like this, what are you supposed to do with this kind of she-said, he-said dispute, especially if you're not an expert on the information they're debating? And, to add a human dimension, what if the two are hard-headed, more interested in besting the other and proving their analytic prowess than in coming up with a coherent narrative? You then spend the next two hours sorting through why they think what they do and trying to reconcile the two accounts into a comprehensible narrative. Meanwhile, because we're all human, after these two analysts have started down an analytic path, the likelihood that they'll move off their positions declines. They go on defense; you're stuck in an analytic argument that loses its focus on analysis and shifts into the difficulty of getting an already cornered analyst to accept that perhaps there's a different way to attack the problem, and a different way to narrow down differences.

Try instead the alternative resolution we might arrive at if we simply use the driver process to break down the question of how we prioritize this plot. Here's a sample:

> Analysts agree on the credibility of the threat, and they're studying a terror group that clearly has shown the intent to stage such strikes. Some analysts, though, weigh the lack of corroboration more heavily than others. All analysts agree that if we receive even limited corroboration, this plot will rise to the top of the current roster of threats they are following.

We might add another piece here to help a nonexpert sort through this. We could review other major plots that did pan out as real threats and then assess how many of them included corroborating information as they developed. Simply put, if we want to provide decision advantage to someone who has to figure out whether to do something about this plot, we might think about how we can add context. If an elephant lumbers into your yard, almost anyone will think this is exceptional. If you add context—"elephants walk through the yard every afternoon"—the uniqueness anyone would assign to that elephant probably would drop radically.

In the terrorism case above, this contextual paragraph could help answer the inevitable question of whether or not we'll get corroborating information on a potential attack. If so, when and how does this information exchange typically happen? And if the added paragraph indicates that in nine of ten previous high-priority threats you never received corroborating information, the game changes immediately.

This isn't the place to hash out every single angle of how an army of experts would pick apart this plot. The basic theme should already be clarifying: without breaking down problems into constituent parts, or drivers, you're more likely to end up with squishy, imprecise analysis that pits expert against expert and asks the moderator to spend a lot of time herding cats. By breaking the problem down, you might be able to offer greater clarity for your decision maker, along with pressing your experts to get beyond their defensive positions and articulate at a more micro level where their disagreements lie. Further, as the plot develops, you will have clear benchmarks that can guide future discussions, an analytic step we'll consider in the next chapter.

THE PABLO PROBLEM:
GETTING YOUR DRIVERS RIGHT

If you want to understand, in clear terms, the importance of spending some time settling on the correct drivers, go no further than a mistake I made assessing a fun question, just for practice. In this case, the analytic process followed the outline in this book, but the failure to break down the question into the correct driver baskets fundamentally skewed the analysis, and I ended up with the wrong answer. Here's the problem: I was working with Pablo, my university teaching assistant at the time and one of the sharpest students I met while teaching. He had been assigned as my TA after I left government, when I taught a graduate-level class on domestic intelligence—how government agencies gather and analyze intelligence inside the United States. Pablo was Uruguayan, as was his longtime girlfriend. A long university break was approaching, and he hadn't been home to see his family in Uruguay in some time. Pablo and I spent a lot of time together, so I knew a fair amount about him. In the months before the break, he became the source of an analytic problem I practiced with.

I started with a basic question: How likely is it that Pablo will travel to Uruguay over the holidays? You'll note, before I start, that the driver list shows why you need experts, not just professional analysts, owning this process. If you didn't have substantive expertise about Pablo's particular situation—in other words, without being a Pablo expert—you might not have compiled a sound list of drivers, and you certainly couldn't have evaluated the list.

As you glance down the list I made up, pick it apart:

- Money. Does Pablo have enough to travel? Does his girlfriend have enough?
- Geography. Can the two visit both families during the trip, which might increase the chance that they go?
- Time. Do they have enough time to travel to Latin America and back and still enjoy a decent break?
- Relationship. Are they comfortable enough that they would enjoy spending this amount of quality time together?
- Time gap. Have they been home recently?
- Alternatives. Is there some competing priority that they would enjoy more?
- School. Do they have any university projects that would require them to stay in town?
- In-laws. Does each of them enjoy spending time with the other's parents?

For each of these, we should have a simple way to assess whether we have enough information to understand the driver fully. If you're buying a new car, for example, you can quickly assess, with certainty, the cost driver that feeds into your decision of whether a car meets your needs and interests. You can give the cost variable a green light: you have solid, indisputable information about how much the car will cost, so you can assess the cost variable with a great deal of certainty.

Another of your drivers, though, is likely to be the reliability of the vehicle. If the car manufacturer just started to produce the model, how can you assess reliability with the same certainty with which you assessed cost? You can't, of course. The car's reliability doesn't have a track record. So instead of a confident green light for this driver, we should assign a red light—a stop sign. (We'll get back to red, green, and yellow lights in chapter 5.)

In almost every driver category in the Pablo case, the light came up green, suggesting to me that Pablo and his girlfriend would be reunited with their families over the holiday. Still there were a few yellows, mostly because they're the drivers based on "intent," not the "capabilities" pile. With our Pablo list, for example, money falls into the capabilities pile; if Pablo doesn't have a cent in his checking account, he can't travel. His feelings toward his future in-laws, though, fall into the intent pile: What does he want to do? Even if Pablo's words told me that he loved his in-laws, it would have been near impossible for me to understand whether he really meant this (probably) or whether he was just being polite (possibly). I could be confident (green) that Pablo had enough time for the trip; I couldn't be equally confident that, deep down, he would be excited about going.

Well, sadly, Pablo didn't make it to Uruguay during that university break. When he told me why, it underscored the importance of paying attention to the quality of the driver list before going on to add the data to each driver basket. Pablo's reason for not going had nothing to do with any of the drivers I'd listed, or my misreading any of them. He didn't go because his student visa status was murky—so his decision was based on a driver I didn't consider. Every single driver I'd listed was relevant, and my grading of those drivers was on the mark. It didn't matter. Missing this one driver changed the entire analytic picture.

Drivers are the speed bumps that prevent analysts from making the mistake of moving directly from the question to the data. You see this mistake every day. When you flip on the TV and watch even a seasoned commentator answer a question about the advance of an insurgent group, for example, watch how often the answer starts with something like "Well, the insurgents took another two towns yesterday, so . . ." Don't blame the commentator. TV is designed for fast entertainment, not slow analysis.

Use this image to keep in mind the human tendency to answer complex questions by building analytic stories based on one dimension of a problem drawn from the most recent bit of data, in this case the insurgents' move into two towns. That's a compelling story but disastrous analysis. When you feel the urge to go down this path of least resistance, transitioning quickly from question to data and answer—or when you watch a colleague do so—take a moment out of your day, sit in front of a blank piece of paper, and ask yourself just two questions:

- Whether I think the insurgents are winning or losing, what are the six or eight or ten elements I think I need to understand to figure out how they're doing?
- If I think those six or eight or ten are the key drivers to help me break down and assess the insurgents' gains, why did I just base an answer on only one of them?

––––––

Experts often transition from questions to data too quickly. How confident should I be that Pablo and his girlfriend will vacation in Uruguay? In thirty seconds, I'll give you an answer. The problem with this transition from question to answer is that my mind can't juggle too many variables (our drivers) simultaneously, so it defaults to just a few (Pablo's financial situation, for example), and we reduce a complex problem to improbable simplicity. That's fine for cocktail conversation but not for effective and efficient analysis. We need a step between crafting the question and weighing the data; we need a mind crutch.

Drivers are the crutch, as long as we're careful about ensuring that the drivers are comprehensive enough to cover all the aspects of the problem but not so exhaustive that you're weighing factors that are interesting but inconsequential. After you go through the process of framing your question, just ask yourself: What are the things I need to understand to analyze this problem or decision? And am I really sure I have enough information to understand them?

CHAPTER FOUR

MEASURING PERFORMANCE

The steps you have worked through so far depend on you to practice the kind of analytic discipline that makes the HEAD Game so tough to practice over time. If you don't, the consequences can be devastating. So many analytic mistakes I have witnessed and participated in stemmed from basic analytic oversights, the kinds of mistakes that analysts can anticipate, even if they can't prevent them. Even quality analysts sometimes forget fundamental principles of sound thinking. To avoid the real prospect of shortcutting the thinking process we're practicing in this book, we need a better way to hold our own feet to the fire, beyond just assuming that analysts will try their best to practice good analytic tradecraft. We need a way to begin to measure our performance so we can be confronted with analytic red flags if we head in the wrong direction. Even with the art of analysis, we need metrics that will push us toward personal accountability.

Personal accountability sounds better in theory than in practice. Half of us are below average at everything we do, statistically speaking. We have some profession we practice for a lifetime—at work, at home, on the road—and we think we're pretty good at it. There's no way to escape the fact, though, that a significant portion of the population can (and does!) do what we do better than we do it. Whether you're a parent, a student, an accountant, or a spy, by definition, if you take a large enough sample size, there's a 50/50 chance you're in the bottom half of what you do.

It's simple human nature to sidestep the uncomfortable reality that we're not all above average. Even worse, three-quarters of us by definition don't even reach the grade of "very good," if you define "very good" as those who are in the upper quartile of what they do. But who wants to acknowledge that they're just not very good at what they do during the only life they'll ever live? How many parents would place themselves in the bottom 50 percent of all mothers and fathers? Like opposable thumbs, though, one of the traits that makes us human is our ability to hold incompatible views simultaneously; we're perfectly able to understand conceptually that we might be average, or below, but we can also easily convince ourselves every day that we're the best at what we do. We practice this dual-mindedness without even thinking. Want more and better government services? Yes! We should have them! Want taxes to pay for them? No, lower them, we're taxed too much already! Are analysts fallible? Sure, all the time. Are we among them? No. We're all in the upper half!

To take this further, and to get closer to the purpose of this book, we should add that if we're experts at what we do, we're inclined to assume that we know our areas of expertise better than people who aren't experts. Because we have superior knowledge, then, what we say should pass for truth, and sometimes even wisdom. This logical misstep is where we get into trouble. It's the experts' Achilles' heel, or what I'd call the expertise trap: experts are the best at explaining what is happening today, because they can trace history and current events and put them in context. But they are terrible at forecasting what tomorrow will bring, because they struggle to explain why their views of today will or won't hold true tomorrow.

The past is an anchor for most experts, leaving them trapped in knowledge and judgments about today while they struggle to see how life might change overnight. The expert on Iranian politics might have spent decades watching as the shah of Iran withstood periods of turmoil. Going back to 1979, it's easy to see how analysts who had watched these periods judged that the new unrest would yield the same result. The shah would maintain his grip. Except he fell. The Indian government had the capability to test a nuclear weapon before 1998 and didn't; the nuclear preparations that year would again result in delays. Except India tested. This software company is a great performer and has rebounded remarkably after previous downturns, so its stock is a great buy. Until it plummets.

We need to give ourselves at least a fighting chance to avoid the expertise trap that blinds us to change. To do that, we need a measuring stick, a way to force us to at least consider that we may occasionally be wrong about our area of expertise (because, we should acknowledge by now, there's a good chance we may not be above average). In other words, without a way to measure our judgments, we're all prone to overconfidence.

Think of your brain as a sprinter, preparing for the Olympics. Maybe you're an aspiring Olympian on some tiny South Pacific island without facilities, trainers, or the resources to help you with a training regimen. Nevertheless, you have decided that you're competitive with the best athletes in the world. You practice alone every day, and you've convinced yourself that you're getting better and better, faster and faster. You work hard, and you probably equate hard work with success, but you don't have a stopwatch that allows you to judge how you compare to a hard norm. You then appear for the Olympics, competing against well-trained sprinters for the first time, and find yourself lapped by the competition. Humiliated. Embarrassed.

Sprinters have a relatively easy time comparing themselves to the average, obviously, because they have a clear metric: time, measured not only by how fast they run but by how wide the margin is between their performance and the competition's times. They know when they're in the below-average pool. Can we look for metrics where we, too, can test our judgments, even if we assume that we'll never reach close to the precision of a sprinter's stopwatch?

Many experts, including analysts, resist this kind of test because we think what we do is too hard to measure. We also think that metrics oversimplify what we do, reducing a complex process, such as analysis of a country's political stability, to what appears to be a mathematical precision. As experts, we dismiss metrics that we think will squeeze out nuance and handcuff us to answers that are too black-and-white. Moreover, I suspect that we secretly resist measurement because we're afraid to confront the fact that experts aren't very good forecasters, and that fresh eyes can make seasoned experts sometimes appear to be not so prescient at all. Finally, sometimes we probably just lack the patience and intellectual rigor to set meaningful metrics. Either we don't know how to create measurements for soft subjects—because metrics aren't common in most analytic conversations—or because we are like the trout, unwilling to expend the energy to go out into a current that will make our brains do some serious work.

Those perspectives are understandable, but they aren't defensible for seasoned analysts. We should hold our brains, and our thought processes, to the same rigorous standards used by sprinters who measure success or failure in hundredths of a second. There's obviously no way we can get close to reaching this same level of precision; we can, though, demand the same aggressive questioning, every day, of whether we're performing at a peak standard. If we don't, the analysis we provide will suffer the same fate as a sprinter who thinks he's great but has never owned a stopwatch: he enters an elite competition, and reality intervenes.

This chapter is about forcing ourselves to find metrics, even if we know they're no more than rough measuring sticks that push us to ask questions about whether we're on the right path or veering off the highway.

There are a few initial steps we can take if we want to (or need to) take a hard, unvarnished look in the mirror, holding it up as if we could see an image of our brains and how we think:

- First, we have to take the big step of not only judging but believing that we may not be the best at what we do. After we take that painful leap, we have to accept that maybe we can improve. Further, we have to accept that we will never be perfect analysts, so every new analytic problem is a chance to keep improving. This process never ends.
- Second, we need to understand the expertise trap, accepting the fact that expertise about what happened yesterday isn't nearly the same as analysis about tomorrow. If we are going to try to be experts and analysts simultaneously, we need ways to escape the trap of using our knowledge of yesterday and today as the sole basis for forecasting tomorrow. Metrics will help us measure incremental change and avoid the trap.
- Third, we have to be willing to go through the frustrating step of figuring out how to add measurements to analytic problems and judgments that lack clarity, measurements that will allow us to test ourselves as we attempt to limit bias. And you're guaranteed to find that settling on metrics is highly frustrating and time consuming. That's not an excuse, though, for bypassing this step.

Try this for a first example: How can we analyze the prospects of a revolutionary political movement—say, in Iran before its revolution in 1979—in a country that is witnessing severe unrest? That's a tough question, and analysts typically will refuse to participate in discussions that start not with an assessment of the facts on the ground but instead with the boring front end of what metrics might help add rigor to an assessment. "We're involved in an analytic conversation about soft variables," expert analysts might say. "Adding metrics would suggest a false sense of certainty, a sense that we can put numbers on a highly nuanced social science problem." Or, more likely, you might hear, "I've been watching this country for twenty-five years. Let me tell you how this one will play out: the president will roll out the army, suppress the street demonstrations, and then arrest and imprison the leadership. He'll crush these street protests, just like he's crushed other opposition movements."

Let's translate what these victims of expertise are forgetting with these answers. It may be sunny today; that doesn't mean it'll be sunny tomorrow: that's a good starting point, but it's not a certainty. Just ask the British as the Revolutionary War began. What seemed a certain victory over ragtag colonials yesterday turned out to be a surprising upset against the Redcoats tomorrow. Or look at George H. W. Bush's poll numbers a year before he lost the election to Bill Clinton. Or check up on Hosni Mubarak, the ousted president of Egypt, in 2009 and ask whether he faced much of an internal threat. Ask Lehman Brothers, or Merrill Lynch, or even Major League Baseball, which has steadily lost its sway over America as the marketing beast of the NFL has taken over.

This easy, complacent rhythm of expert analysis, where you can explain tomorrow by referring to yesterday, is how Western observers were struggling in the late 1970s, watching pressure rise against a linchpin of Western influence in the Arabian Gulf: the shah of Iran. If we're assessing the prospects for a revolutionary environment, we can quickly list the drivers that might illuminate our understanding of the nascent revolt. There is no need to be exhaustive; this exer-

cise is simply illustrative of how we can add simple metrics to our
drivers so that we can try to avoid slipping into death by a thousand
cuts—watching a situation change so incrementally that we don't
notice the change until it's too late. We can use the shah's downfall
as the example for how we apply these metrics. Following are a few
of the questions you might have posed at the time of Iran's descent
into revolution:

- How can we judge the shah's stability, and Iran's generally? How is the threat of an opposition takeover
  changing?
- How do we assess the options the US government has as
  policymakers try to change the equation in Iran?
- How would we consider the option of talking to the
  Iranian opposition? How do we weigh the pluses and
  minuses?

Note quickly, when you glance at these questions (and maybe
you've developed your own), that we didn't pose the inevitable yes/
no question that would kick off most of these debates, questions
such as "Will the shah fall?" or "Is the shah stable?" Both, as we've
discussed, are asking for answers that are inherently unknowable,
and they're too focused on yes/no answers that strip away context
or nuance.

Some experts on analytic thinking would call these dramatic
yes/no answers "hedgehog" answers, not "fox" answers. This concept appears throughout one of the most seminal recent works on
analytic thinking and analytic mistakes. It's called *Expert Political
Judgment*, and it's a book that returns again and again to the idea
that experts are not even close to being the best analysts. The author,
Philip Tetlock, conducted decades of research into the forecasting
capabilities of experts over time, and here's what he says:

The intellectually aggressive hedgehogs knew one big thing and sought . . . to expand the explanatory power of that big thing to "cover" new cases; the more eclectic foxes knew many little things and were content to improvise ad hoc solutions to keep pace with a rapidly changing world.[*]

In sum, Tetlock explains, better analysts are defined not by what they know but instead by how they think. They're analysts first, not experts. In our society, though, it's the hedgehogs, with bold, controversial predictions, who often win the day. How many TV talk shows are dominated by foxes? Their more carefully constructed, less colorful study of events and forecasting wouldn't sell on cable TV. Hedgehogs own the airwaves; foxes own analysis.

The hedgehogs also owned the analytic landscape during previous times of analytic crisis, and their big-idea analysis was as flawed then as Tetlock's patient research later showed. Back in the prerevolutionary fervor of 1979 Iran, we would have liked to be able to offer a bold answer on whether the shah would still be in power within six months. Of course, that question is really unanswerable, since no one can predict the future with any certainty. The better option might be identifying characteristics that help clarify whether the shah's troubles are intensifying, and then to watch these characteristics and offer an assessment about whether, on balance, the indicators are intensifying or not. Here's a parallel: none of us knows whether our family car will break down tomorrow. A yes/no answer might provide some illusory comfort because we can pretend a level of confidence we don't have, but even with a brand-new car, there's a small chance that we'll be headed to the shop in the very near future.

---

[*] Philip Tetlock, *Expert Political Judgment* (Princeton, NJ: Princeton University Press, 2006), 20–21.

We might be better off, though, if we assess less black-and-white likelihoods based on metrics. If your car, for example, has more than 100,000 miles on it, if it has experienced an increasing number of breakdowns, and if other cars of identical make and model are heading to the repair shop with increasing frequency, you can begin to forecast that you'd better budget for some big-time repairs soon. Further, if you put together a team of statisticians, you can probably come up with some pretty good forecasts about how likely it is that your car is going to be in the shop before long. You know some of the characteristics (our analytic drivers) that indicate when wear and tear increases your risk of breakdown; you can add measurements (our metrics) that will tell you roughly the risk you face with each of these drivers; and you can then get closer to an analytic answer to a common question: When do I get into the time frame when my car is going to break down more often? And when is the cost of constant repairs (and the hassle of going to the repair shop) going to surpass the cost and hassle of replacing the car with a new one?

Regardless of which question you decide is more relevant—the shah's staying power or your car's staying power—each will lead you to write up a list of drivers. In this case, we're talking about players who will have roles in whether the shah stays or goes. Here's a quick list that fits within that range of roughly six to ten drivers that might be the maximum we can juggle for any one decision-making process:

- The shah himself, and his family
- Senior Iranian military and intelligence officers
- Junior military officers and enlisted personnel
- Elites in the population
- Iranian citizens below the elite class

- The revolutionaries, including Ayatollah Khomeini, the central force behind the shah's overthrow
- Other clerics
- External players (the United States, Britain, France, etc.)
- Iran's business community

For each of these drivers, analysts might consider deciding on a rough measure that will help hold them accountable as they confront change. Let's take just one example: Iranian citizens. Some analysts might argue that street protests don't represent much, or that they're easily containable by security forces. Some might claim the opposite. For this scenario, we're going to sit these debating analysts in the room and step through this process:

1. Our drivers are supposed to be agnostic; any expert would judge that these are the elements you need to understand in order to assess what's going on in Iran. Do you all agree that popular sentiment is important? (The answer had better be yes, in this case.)

2. We might judge that street protests are important or irrelevant. It doesn't matter. Can we agree, though, that an increase in intensity, size, violence, or geographic spread (in other words, the number of cities that are experiencing street protests) might be something we should talk about?

3. Let's take one of those characteristics of street protests: intensity. How often are protests happening today? Now let's give ourselves a thirty-day window into the future. If we saw double this number of protests, should we worry more? If not, what's the right number? Triple? Whatever it is, that becomes our metric. If we decide on doubling, and we see a doubling of protests and the analysts still claim

that street protests mean nothing, we have a good analytic
starting point that's not based on intuition: If they mean
nothing, why did you tell me a month ago that this increase
was worth discussing?

4. We can go through the same exercise for the other characteristics. What increase, or decrease, in the size of protests
   would we consider significant? What level of violence, in
   terms of types of weapons used or number of fatalities,
   should we judge is significant? How many additional cities
   should witness riots before we grow more concerned? Or,
   at the other end of the spectrum, how many cities should
   return to normal?

Quickly, we have transitioned from the intuitive (and dangerous) art of intelligence—an expert pontificating on the future of
the shah—to a much clearer, driver-and-metrics-based conversation that forces analysts to assess change.

If you think this analytic process is too distant from a real-
world exercise, we can spend just a moment reviewing the analysis of this issue that was declassified as part of the countless
after-action "what went wrong" exercises that followed the shah's
inglorious fall. In December 1983, the director of the Central
Intelligence Agency asked one of his advisory boards to look at
how intelligence analysts had assessed Iran before the shah's fall.
Read some of the excerpts below, keeping a simple tally of which
drivers you think the experts looked at and which they paid less
attention to. And then compare the two, circling the gaps. Here's
what the advisory board wrote:

You [the CIA Director] have asked whether there
was speculation that the Shah was finished, and what the
alternatives might be. There was a little speculation in the

estimative* work concerning the Shah, but only in purely personal terms: i.e., what would happen if he died, either of natural causes or by assassination? Up until November 1978, the answer was that the monarchy and political-social structure would survive, held together by the Crown Prince, the Empress, the elite, and the military.

. . . It was not until late November 1978 that the intelligence community considered that the Shah might fall. . . . A military regime was seen as a likely successor, with a radical government based on the religious opposition less likely. . . .

The talking paper [referring to a paper used to brief the Senate Foreign Relations Committee in September 1978] recognizes the substantial but divided opposition to the Shah, explains his reaction, says martial law has greatly improved the situation, and predicts that a combination of reform, political liberty, and armed force will put the Shah in a position where he "will probably meet the challenge." Possibilities for overthrow and a radical regime are not mentioned. . . .

Acquaintance over the years with various US officials who were involved in Iranian relations has brought out, strongly I might add, the point that US views and intelligence were heavily influenced by our long-term ties with Savak [the Iranian security service].†

---

* "Estimative," in the US Intelligence Community, refers to formal intelligence assessments prepared by analysts from various US intelligence agencies, such as the Defense Intelligence Agency, the Central Intelligence Agency, and the Bureau of Intelligence and Research at the Department of State. Most intelligence reports are prepared by individual agencies rather than the interagency groups that prepare Estimates (known formally as National Intelligence Estimates, or NIEs).

† "Intelligence Estimates on Iran, in Senior Review Panel Report on Intelligence Judgments Preceding Significant Historical Failures: The Hazards of Single-Outcome Forecasting," NIC 9079-83/2, 6 January 1984.

This is a classic case of hedgehogs prevailing over foxes, with disastrous analytic consequences. Analysts, at the time, looked at a narrow range of Iranian society, and their data were limited to that range of driver baskets that didn't represent the spectrum of revolutionary players. Further, they appeared to believe that the past would prove to be precedent—that the shah and his surrounding security elites could manage the opposition during the revolutionary ferment of the late 1970s. Let's take this one step further: you can bet that many analysts—and I have been among this group—would have resisted adding metrics to their forecasts: "Our Iran analysis is more art than science," they would have said, "and you can't measure analytic forecasting without squeezing out the human analytic factor." A longtime student of the shah and Iran's politics would not have embraced managers or other analysts insisting on metrics to help judge whether that expert's analysis was faulty or worse, as it proved to be.

You can find classic examples of this hedgehog-driven antimetrics bias unfolding everywhere. Here's another one: hidden in newspaper reports is a minor revolution in how to rate a college's value, and how much benefit students are gaining at different colleges and universities. Traditionally, college ratings might measure admissions selectivity (the acceptance rate for applicants), student-teacher ratio, and judgments by staff at peer-group colleges.

Some rankings now are pushing harder for metrics that are more closely linked to how students perform once they graduate, and to the ratio between the cost to the student and the potential benefits for the student once he or she heads out into the working world. These rankings have problems of their own—for example, schools defined as "elite" by the more traditional measures, are more likely to place students in higher-paying jobs, simply because employers value certain schools' reputations more than others. Still, this newer set of metrics results in surprisingly different conclusions. Queens

College in New York, for example, doesn't appear at the top of traditional rankings, but it does when you apply different metrics.

Meanwhile, and perhaps unsurprisingly, some purists—experts on colleges who've been around for years, and who are comfortable with the soft rankings that are most common today—object to this newer approach. They point out that picking variables to isolate value is difficult, and they share concerns that this approach will devalue how we judge the pure experience of college, beyond the dollars-and-cents value of an education. These critiques make a lot of sense in one regard: they highlight the same point this book starts with—be careful about what question you ask before you go down an analytic trail. Do you want to know what students think of their educational experience? Is that your key determinant in understanding how to evaluate one college over another? Or do you want to know how much students' earning power increases afterward? Your answer hinges on your question. And, of course, the tough part is that neither question is wrong.

Then, too, the purists are also right in their skepticism about which measures (we might call them drivers) fit best into a harder assessment of value that goes beyond traditional college ratings. Do you want to choose students' salaries five years after graduation? Ten? If so, you're introducing bias: my guess is that salaries are driven partly by students' socioeconomic class entering college, by the quality of primary and high school education, and by the types of degrees the university grants. Engineers typically make more than English majors. Still, you can filter out these biases to try to get closer to meaningful metrics.

The purists who squirm at the prospect of tougher metrics to gauge the value of a college education sound to me a lot like analyst purists who might squirm at adding metrics signposts to questions of political stability. Sure, there is art to these experts' analytic judgments. To get to the "art" part of the equation, though—to introduce a human expert's views—it's helpful to start with a common baseline of information that isn't all soft or subjective. In general, the approach in this book should lead you to be leery of experts who resist metrics because they insist that the measures are too subjective, or because the subject matter is too soft to be measured. Remember, we're not trying to predict the exact outcome of the future here; we're just trying to reduce uncertainty in a world where we know there are no perfect answers.

Foxes are OK with that. They like complexity and uncertainty, even if that means they can only draw cautious conclusions and they have to admit they could be wrong. "Maybe" is fine with them. But not hedgehogs. They find complexity and uncertainty unacceptable. They want simple and certain answers. And they are sure they can get them using the One Big Idea that drives their thinking.[*]

If we can't predict the future, we still have to sketch the outlines a little more clearly and explain waypoints that can signal where the problem—the shah's durability, the status of a rebel group, etc.—is headed. Signposts, exact metrics, will help us do that, while also guiding us in the tough decision of whether and when we need to consider course corrections in our analyses.

Think of these signposts as guardrails along a highway. The guardrails don't get you to your destination; you're still behind the wheel, and driving (at least for now) requires a human being to navigate twists and turns in the road, just like analysis. The guardrails do, though, warn you if you're veering off the path that leads you to your ultimate destination. We won't guarantee that we'll arrive at the right destination, but we will try to guarantee that we're not driving all over the map as we get there.

The most significant rule we can establish, as we set off on this

---

[*] Dan Gardner, *Future Babble: Why Pundits Are Hedgehogs and Foxes Know Best* (New York: Plume, 2012), 87–88.

journey, is the understanding that these guardrail metrics are not and should not be designed to force an analytic change. They can only help keep us on track, and we can tear them down if we choose to, to build a different route. We're the ones driving the car, after all, and we're ultimately responsible for the analysis. The guardrails are designed for a more nuanced series of purposes than just forcing us down one route or another.

Another benefit of the guardrails is that they help level the playing field among analysts, so that nonexperts can have more meaningful conversations with experts. Complex or technical problems can prevent outside parties from becoming full participants in analytic conversations. If we're discussing the development of a foreign country's missile system, for example, how can a nonexpert have a meaningful conversation with a group of scientists or engineers? This imbalance between expert and less expert analysts leads to the inevitable "I know more than you know, so don't try to adjust my thinking" mentality. This is entirely defensible on technical judgments—on whether, for example, a liquid-fueled engine is more volatile than a solid-fueled engine. It is less defensible, though, as analytic tradecraft when the question starts not with "What's our technical assessment?" but rather with "Are we thinking through this problem in the right way?" This metrics-based process should allow nonexpert analysts to have more meaningful conversations with a closed circle of experts on whether an analysis is flawed, or whether judgments and assumptions about an analytic problem could benefit from more rigorous thinking.

To underscore this point, let's start with an example of setting metrics for one driver basket in a complex problem, an intelligence question I looked at during the mid-1990s. The case, in a nutshell, involved the timeline for how quickly a certain country might develop an advanced missile system. You can pick Syria, Iran, China, North Korea, Russia, Pakistan, India—the country doesn't matter. What does matter is the process we'll go through to add analytic rigor to the analysis of missile developments.

In this case, the subject of the analysis was a country that was already well along the road to developing an advanced missile system. The question wasn't really whether the country's engineers and scientists would field the missile system. Instead, we were looking at timelines: When might the US government have to face the reality of this emerging missile threat, so that US leaders could plan for the deployment of longer-range missiles?

This question is complicated enough on its face, with variables ranging from whether the country in question had sufficient expertise, money, and facilities to develop the missile, and whether politicians in that country would provide the political backing to continue the program in the face of intense international pressure. In this case, the question grew even more complicated, and quickly. The country in question needed foreign assistance to develop its program, so we had to consider not only the fuzzy variables of how the country was proceeding on its own but also the added complexity of how its missile-development timeline might be affected by fluctuations in the amount and quality of foreign assistance.

I can't remember whether we changed our judgments as a result of the steps we took to add metrics that helped us check our work. I do, however, remember something close to an analytic turning point that happened while we were talking through the timeline one day at a conference-room table. The analysts evaluating this problem were technical experts, typically engineers who spent their entire careers studying foreign missile programs. The engineers around the table could run circles around me, or any other nonexpert who coordinated meetings of analysts from intelligence agencies across Washington.

It wasn't hard to figure out, though, that among the critical variables in assessments of the development timeline for this missile program was the extent of technical expertise our target country received from its foreign partners. You might safely conclude that more foreign expertise would change our timeline. But this wasn't happening: our estimates of the missile program's timeline weren't changing substantially as the level of foreign assistance fluctuated. Every time we received a new bit of data suggesting yet another infusion of foreign assistance, in other words, analysts figured out a way to explain why the initial estimates remained accurate. And I, as a nonexpert, lacked the technical knowledge to ask good questions, much less to challenge the expert judgments.

The issue wasn't as simple as asking whether we were wrong, because the answer, just as simple, would come back: "No, we're still confident of our original estimates." US intelligence analysts had limited data for their assessments, and that data had many glaring information gaps. There was no right or wrong answer. The issue was tougher than that. How could we understand the impact of foreign assistance on our timeline? Were those of us around the table explaining away continued foreign assistance that we should have been considering more carefully? As experts, were we overly wedded to explaining why the timeline we had come up with yesterday remained true? How could we jam new information into our model timeline to explain why the model was still right, even if that information didn't quite match up?

We sat down then and had a conversation about metrics, though I doubt anyone in the conversation would have used that term. The idea wasn't to use simple numbers that reduced the analysis to a mathematical equation. Instead, we wanted to force ourselves to ask harder questions about whether we should adjust our timeline if our indicators about foreign assistance continued to change. You might assume that those metrics could center on one or more of three areas foreign countries could help with: financial aid, technology, or scientific and engineering expertise.

It's worth repeating the mantra that these are only guardrails; they're not hard walls that are designed to force you to take a U-turn in your analysis. The human analyst is the final arbiter. If, for example, we decide that visits of foreign engineers are the most critical variable in assessing the timeline for the country's missile program, we should ask ourselves the $64,000 question: How much might an expansion of assistance alter the time frame within which our country of interest develops and deploys the missile system? This is a question that requires a great deal of human expertise, not just a mechanical analytic exercise. The follow-on question is even more salient for our purposes: How could we add rough signposts that will help us gauge whether we should consider reviewing (not necessarily changing!) our assessment?

The experts will often respond in a scenario like this with something like "No, we'll know change when we see it." If your analysis is that subjective, anomalous information will quickly be seen as somehow invalid, erroneous, or otherwise not relevant enough to affect the initial assessment.

Try to envision a scenario in which this phenomenon of explaining away change happens. It's not hard to imagine an expert group that sees information about an increase in foreign expertise in an adversary's missile development program and says, "Our timeline remains valid. This country isn't getting closer to closing the gap on their development program. The increase in assistance suggests instead that they're having problems, and they need more help." Maybe this explanation is true, but you'd probably be suspicious if you heard it, regardless of whether you had a background in missile engineering.

To ensure that we keep ourselves honest, we're going to ask some specific questions that help us set guardrail metrics for this country's missile program. First, we'll start by setting the rules for our guardrails, so that we avoid fuzzy analytic disputes. How do we do this? At the outset of the metrics-setting process, we can help create the right environment by letting the experts set their own metrics. For example, if the provision of foreign expertise is so critical to this missile program, how significant an uptick in assistance would analysts expect to see to trigger a new conversation about the current estimate? Can analysts offer a rough pair of brackets to capture what they think—if, say, there's an increase of more than 20 percent in the number of visits, is it time to revisit the timeline? What guardrail metrics do the experts suggest?

Remember, we're not looking for a perfect solution that will *guarantee* that we should change our judgment; we're only looking for answers that trigger us to reconvene the expert group to answer some hard questions. Because the experts set the trigger, they shouldn't quibble about being questioned. "Don't worry," you might tell them. "First, you, the experts, get to pick the metrics. Second, you get to make the analytic calls at the end of this process. You're still allowed to stick to your original assessment at the end, even if we hit the analytic tripwires you set. Along the way, though, we're going to have harder, fact-based conversations about whether our judgments are sound."

In the real-world experience I lived with at the CIA, when we considered cases like this, our initial analysis included analysts' judgments that foreign expertise was critical to the advancement of the missile program we were studying. The country developing the missile system just didn't have enough scientific and engineering know-how to move its missile program along quickly and without many failures. As we saw a steady flow of missile technology experts into the country, though, we couldn't find a way to handle the basic question of whether this continued flow should lead us to accelerate our timeline. "We know what we're doing," was the experts' refrain, "and we don't think the timeline is changing." If you're coordinating that meeting at the head of the table, as I was, you might then ask the following question: Doesn't the fact that this outside expertise continues unabated affect what we say about our timeline?

Eventually, the experts agreed that we had reached a point where we needed to talk through whether our previous estimate was too conservative. The reason? The analysts set the metric—consistency in the level of foreign expertise flowing in over a specified period of time—and then watched as the level of expertise hit their metric.

This point is crucial, so stop a moment to review the lesson: had we not set tripwires, the likelihood that we would have been able to escape the expertise trap would have been low. The experts most likely would have simply taken the new data and explained how it fit into the model. And a nonexpert coordinator at the head of the table would have been hard-pressed to challenge them.

Instead, what happened during the conversations at that time forced an analytic turn. At the head of the table for those meetings, as a nonexpert, I didn't even have to press the point; the experts knew they needed to reconsider.

This raises the inevitable question we will turn to throughout this book: the importance of expertise, and the value of leavening that expertise with fresh perspectives. To add new perspectives, this process of setting guardrail metrics—of checking ourselves—argues for the inclusion of newer analysts, or even nonexperts, to ask different questions of analytic teams. This addition of nonexperts seems counterintuitive, because most of us would revert to a simple model as we choose analytic teams: select the people with the most experience, the most analytic expertise, or the most time studying the problem. Think of the painful experiences many of us might have had in elementary school. During recess, or after school, we're going to play a game that requires two teams, and two team captains are charged with dividing up the group. Taking turns, each captain selects players from among the group. At the end of the selection process, when there are only a few left in the group, the embarrassment grows. Clearly, the two captains have chosen those they believe to be the best players, leaving the leftovers to hope that someone else would be selected last.

Transferring this process to the selection of an analytic team, we might default to looking across the workforce within which we work and handpicking only those with the most experience, the best academic credentials, or the best training. We fail to recognize, though, that in contrast to the playing field, where the expert talent of each player is the only variable we might weigh, here we need a combination of experience and freshness. The freshness might give us an opportunity to break out of a pattern that the more experienced analysts are wedded to. A team that combines both long experience and a new lens on a problem might, surprisingly, turn out to be more analytically proficient than a team that includes only participants who are judged to be the most experienced in the room. Think about it: if you know that one of the critical weaknesses of analysts is the inability to see change, even as they stand in the middle of it, how does it make sense to select only those analysts who are most likely to fall prey to this trap?

A county fairground, believe it or not, offers the most storied example of this seemingly paradoxical analytic fact. Put a cow in the middle of a pen. Ask a farmer to guess the weight, and you'll get a good answer. You would think that asking the same question of people who aren't farmers would, by definition, lead to a less accurate answer. Not so fast.

You can read about this paradox in stories all over the Web in relevant literature, but one recent example appeared at the now-famous TED forum. The speaker, Lior Zoref, asks the audience to estimate the weight of an ox. About five hundred responders submit guesses ranging from 308 to 8,000 pounds. The average of the five hundred responses—a sample group that presumably includes very few agricultural specialists—came out to 1,792 pounds. The ox's actual weight: 1,795 pounds. If this seems incredible (and it did, to me), feel free to check out the history of research on this type of crowdsourcing.

METRICS AND THE BOILING FROG

It's steaming hot outside, and you walk into a shopping mall after crossing the black asphalt of an endless parking lot. It's one of those days that's so hot you can see ripples of heat shimmering off the tar. Immediately, a wall of cool air washes over you. If it's blazing hot outside—98 degrees, let's say—the temperature drop could easily be twenty degrees once you step inside the mall. The refreshing wave of air feels invigorating, as long as you're not the mall's operator, worrying about what it costs the mall to keep the thermostat set at this temperature throughout the summer months.

Try another temperature scenario. What if it's 73 degrees outside and you walk into a building with a thermostat set at 72 degrees. What are the chances that you would notice the one-degree drop in temperature? Maybe not high—the change is too small, almost imperceptible. It's incremental—a term at the core of understanding the boiling-frog concept, which we'll get to shortly. Incremental change, such as when popular resentment toward a dictator boils over into violent revolution, is hard to see, and harder to guard against, but it can be the death knell of good analysis. We've discussed incremental change a few times through the analytic process; now it's time to consider this fundamental analytic problem head-on.

Let's try yet a third temperature-related scenario. You step into the mall, entering a big-box retailer that always sets the thermostat at a temperature just one degree cooler than the outside temperature, a comfortable 73 degrees. You walk around this retailer's store for about twenty minutes. Then you walk into a second retailer's store, which is one degree cooler than the first. Then you check out a third spot whose thermostat is set at 71 degrees, one degree cooler than the second store. You might have noticed had you walked from the 73 degrees outside directly into this room. But do you notice after you've already acclimated yourself to the 72 degrees in the first retailer's store? Maybe. Probably not.

But what about after you enter a fourth retailer's store after another twenty minutes? And then a fifth? A sixth? A seventh? Hours later, you hit your twentieth store, with each being one degree cooler than the previous one. Do you notice? My guess is that you would. It's 53 degrees, and now you need a light jacket. Even so, it's not the drastic change that you would have felt had you walked directly from the 73 degrees outside into Store Twenty, with its thermostat set at a chilly 53 degrees. In that scenario, you would have had no adjustment period, and no chance to pass through subtle, one-degree temperature drops every twenty minutes.

This is a version of the boiling-frog concept. The theory is that if you put a frog in cool water and bring the water quickly to a boil, the frog will hop out early on, none too happy to be facing the prospect of a boiling bath. If, by contrast, you heat the cool water ever so slowly, degree by degree, the frog will die rather than jump out because it won't notice the gradual change fast enough.

This phenomenon happens in everyday human life, including yours and mine. How often have you bought just a few small items that, over a few weeks or months, left you with a credit card bill that was a lot higher than you anticipated? How often have you pledged not to have a piece of pie at a party and instead ate ten small bites that amounted to more calories than if you had just eaten a normal slice at the start? Or, closer to our concern in this book, how often have you invested in some sort of stock or business and then explained away occasional problems with the investment, only to confront the fact, as those imperceptible indicators piled up almost unnoticeably, that your investment eventually turned out to be a loss leader?

These boiling-frog scenarios are the same sort of slow-motion train wrecks that Detroit automakers fell prey to more than four decades ago, as they competed against each other for market share among US consumers. While tradition-bound companies such as Chrysler faced down Ford and Chevrolet, the Detroit executives didn't realize that Japanese firms had a better idea: cheap and gas-friendly cars that would capture a market as oil prices skyrocketed. The automaker frogs in Detroit boiled, one GM and Chrysler at a time, until they realized, too late, that their real competition wasn't the other traditional automakers in the Motor City but a new, post–World War II phenomenon: the Japanese economic juggernaut of the 1970s that dominated the market because of Americans' post-oil-embargo demand for small, inexpensive, and reliable cars.

All of us are vulnerable to the boiling-frog syndrome because we want to believe our choices and decisions are right, and we hold onto our beliefs as long as we can, despite contrary indications that should signal us that we're slowly slipping into hot water. So we judge, often without a great deal of thinking, that we should either discount new information—"that's not really important"—or force what appears to be anomalous new data into our analytic line of argumentation: in other words, explaining why everything stays the same until it doesn't. And then we look back and see, painfully clearly in hindsight, all the moments at which you could have noticed that the water around you was warming up, fast.

Let's try a different, tougher example of a boiling-frog problem to drive home this common human vulnerability. Here's a scenario: we are analyzing the capabilities of an opposition group. In this case, the opposition is an armed insurgency, similar to what we've seen in various Middle Eastern countries during this Arab Spring decade. The oppositionists we happen to be studying are fighting against a despot who has tortured, murdered, and otherwise abused his people for decades. Saddam, Qaddafi, Syria's Assad—pick any one of them for the purposes of the exercise. As the scenario begins to unfold, over the course of a week or two, the insurgents take a city. And then they take another. And then they overrun a third. They go on to build up a remarkable six-month series of successes, month after month. We claim, as we're analyzing these insurgents, that their successes mark a significant milestone for the insurgency: they have proven that they can go toe-to-toe with the government and its security forces and win over time. The insurgents have built a track record, and we, as a result, have built our analysis on a judgment that the insurgents will gain yet more momentum, and greater advantage, over time. The despot's days appear to be numbered, an analyst might say.

Whether we like to admit it or not, as analysts we are invested in the judgment of the insurgents' prospective gains. Because we're already staking our intellect and experience in the initial judgment, we now have an emotional bias in favor of the initial vision of how we think the insurgency will unfold. If our judgments prove erroneous, the errors we acknowledge might help us develop the humility to grow as analysts, but they would also undermine our reputations as authoritative experts. How can we expect that any analyst worth his salt can claim both the authority to speak expertly and the humility to accept that he has failed in forecasting change? This is exactly the balance we need to strike, though, between growing the specialized expertise over time and understanding that this expertise anchors us. Time and time again, from the CIA's analysis of the Iranian Revolution in 1979 to analyses of Iraq's WMD program before the Iraq War, change proved to be analysts' implacable enemy. In these painful episodes, many analysts thought that the past presaged the future: that the shah could once again contain unrest, as he had in the past; that Saddam maintained WMD stocks, as he had in the past. As time passed, though, new bits of data and pieces of information slowly accumulated, and the analysts slowly suffered through the experience of the boiling frog.

We should try, then, to find ways, as we have throughout this book, to ensure that we balance the clear expertise we have with methods to anticipate change. As we previously discussed, to keep us honest, we need to look at our drivers from chapter 3, and assess how they might be changed by creating metrics for them that will serve as rough guidelines for conversations about whether we need to adjust our judgments. These metrics will then serve as our rough guideposts, baselines we can use to test ourselves as time passes and the world changes.

Try the example of insurgents who steadily gain territory over time. If we said that the insurgents' loss of three towns within a one-month period would be significant, for example, we would sit down if we hit the three-town/one-month trigger. If we had set that metric early on, how would we explain ignoring it as it came to pass? If you don't set metrics, you can almost guarantee that you will have an easier time explaining away the loss of territory. We could say that the insurgents willingly surrendered towns because they need to replenish their weapon stocks and take a breather while their fighters rest. What if we had set a metric a month earlier, though? If we had agreed to reassess the insurgents' prospects in the event of a three-city setback, we should sit down for a conversation about our estimates of the insurgents' prospects for success. We can still bet on them, or against them. But we can't do so until we come to the table, with our colleagues, and answer the question of why we set a broad tripwire and then, a month later, decided in the heat of the moment that a tripwire set earlier is now no longer significant.

HOLDING UP A MIRROR

You might also think of the metrics process we will step through as a mind mirror, in addition to a set of guideposts. We know that we have to use a real mirror to judge how we look as we dress in the morning, to determine whether a tie is knotted properly or whether it's positioned cleanly up against the collar and lined up straight down the front of the shirt. Who wants to be embarrassed by not noticing that the back collar of a dress shirt is accidentally turned up when you walk into a party? Mirrors help us prevent the occasional wardrobe malfunction.

We don't think about it, but we can also hold up a mirror to our minds, and to the way we think. How? There are a lot of books out there that will help you understand how your mind works and what kinds of tricks it will play on you. Few books, though, will step you through a simple, real-life methodology, based on practical examples, ones that might help you avoid some of these obstacles. If our thinking is like a tie that's crooked, can we find a way to avoid walking out the door with analytic assumptions that need some straightening?

To test yourself, take a position from the opposite perspective, assuming that other people who disagree with you nonetheless have something useful to say. Listen to them, without reference to your own views, for elements of their analytic position that make sense to you. Is it possible that every single thing they say—those who oppose you—is wrong? Or are there bits and pieces of their assessment that either align with what you think or represent some point of view that you hadn't considered? If you start with this approach, you might realize that there is substantial middle ground between what you hear from differing opinions around the table and what you had planned to say, before you conceded the floor to an alternate viewpoint.

We might call this effort to capture the opposition position the "charity proposition." If we're sitting around a table with a group of experts, whether they're stock pickers or football pundits, many of us might go into a meeting prepared to defend whatever position we've staked out. We think this stock is a good call; others around the table don't. We think this football team can beat the Las Vegas odds; nobody else around the table shares this view. Our going-in position is that we're at the table to convert those who don't quite have the expertise, judgment, or intellect to understand our position. We may be in the minority, but despite the odds, we'll hold to our view.

To start a conversation using the charity proposition, flip your personal view on its head and practice a little humility. Begin by noting those judgments or facts from your analytic adversaries you agree with or can't disprove with facts. Then, when you present what you think, start with this common ground. Otherwise, if you go head-on into the battle, explaining that everyone else is wrong and that you represent the only perspective that makes sense, you not only will guarantee that the conversation will turn defensive, but you'll also waste a lot of time while each party at the table states and restates the differing perspectives.

This is not to suggest that you somehow just assume that everyone else is smarter than you, or better at piecing together their analyses than you are. It's instead an exercise in analytic efficiency. By applying the charity proposition, you may be able to more quickly settle in on those core areas that represent real differences among the experts sitting around the table.

———

This measurement process is the only stage during the analytic process when you can check your work with something that approaches precision—beyond waiting for time to tell you whether you're on the right track or not. You may think you've got the right question, the right drivers, and the right judgment about the quality of your data. Thinking isn't knowing, though, and you will be prone to missing key points or overestimating your level of confidence unless you find a way to test yourself.

Think of these metrics as inflection points in your decision-making process. To avoid slowly boiling yourself, revalidate your initial conclusions constantly through guidepost exercises. And when you hit a guidepost, be careful about explaining away how that could happen. Sometimes you've set the guideposts wrong. Sometimes, though, you've gotten so wedded to the analytic avenue you're headed down that you just can't see clearly that you're off course. Stay on course. Try to measure your performance, even when experts around you tell you it's impossible.

We think some despot is stable in the face of demonstrations. We know opposition rallies are more persistent, more violent, and larger than ever before. Do those opposition rallies reflect a growing threat to the despot? Is something changing, or is this a passing phase that government forces can squelch? Unless we've added a few guardrail metrics up front that we can use every time we return to the analytic table, most experts will hedge on the side of writing off the demonstrations.

Finally, don't slip into the trap of thinking that these guideposts will give you clear answers—and don't let unhappy experts explain how their subject matter is too fluid, or complicated, for this technique. It's not. They'd just prefer to be hedgehogs rather than foxes, because hedgehogging is easier. Well, that's true. It is easier. But it's not effective. And it's not analysis.

CHAPTER FIVE

WHAT ABOUT THE DATA?

Many of us go down the path of becoming experts, dedicating ourselves to learning and then continuing to acquire knowledge, because we're passionate about the subjects we spend our lives studying. We like to accumulate knowledge, and we're often paid to take this mass of knowledge and experience, maybe gathered over a lifetime of work, and present it in written and oral form. In the backward-thinking model, though, it's not until relatively late in the process that we look at ways to categorize and understand this wealth of experience and data. Starting with the data is a dangerous approach. Instead, we want to start by building a rigorous analytic framework—by using analytic exercises—before we sort data and then apply our own personal knowledge to the problem or question at hand.

Think of it this way: rather than rushing to the building supply store to buy the items that make a house—lumber, cement, and then interior furnishings—we might instead start the construction process with a clear idea of what the foundation and outlines of our house should look like. In the analytic process we're the architects, and the blueprints of the house represent the time we spend formulating the initial question. We then transition to a detailed architectural plan of our house that includes all the key elements we think are important to executing our vision. This architectural plan includes our drivers; it's the framework for our analysis, for our understanding of the problem. All the preparatory work we've gone through requires patience, and a great deal of discipline, because once we work through our analytic model, we have to reexamine it periodically, using the same methods every time, to determine where our initial judgments remain sound and to judge carefully when our analysis is slipping. At this point in the process, though, after all the work on the key question and its underlying drivers, it's about time to dig into the dirt of real data.

The up-front investment in building the analytic framework might seem irritating, cumbersome, artificial, or wasteful, but it will save you time in the end. More important, it should lead you to a more precise understanding of the problems you face: if you ask a vague question, you'll get a vague answer. This process will help you find a better path to arrange information so that you can mold it into knowledge without finding out at the end that you've missed some key elements that require you to start all over again.

To start the process of looking at your data and identifying those areas where you should be aware of knowledge gaps, separate your data into the driver baskets you've created. For an investment decision, those drivers might be cash flow, debt, capital investment, market share versus key competitors, or whatever else you've decided helps you determine whether the investment is worth your money.

As you do this, you may find some pieces of data that don't fit clearly into any of your six to ten driver baskets (assuming you've stayed disciplined and haven't created more than this). Place that data into an "other stuff" category. Don't try too hard to squeeze a random piece of data into a basket that doesn't seem right; the fact that it doesn't fit might be a clue, later on, that helps you realize that you haven't quite defined your drivers clearly. Don't waste a lot of time at the outset sorting through this "other stuff" pile. When you've finished figuring out your first cut at which data fit into each basket, we'll return to the misfit pile to sort it out.

Before you determine that this extra pile of data is critical, and that you have to add a few drivers to your list, take a minute to ask yourself the hard question of whether the data in this extra pile is really vitally important in the first place. Don't be an information hoarder, in other words. These driver baskets are an opportunity to do the same thing you might do in your closet: when you see an item of clothing you haven't worn for three years, how often do you come up with an explanation of why you have to keep the item? "On a rainy fall day, when the temperature is between 50 and 60 degrees, if I don't want to get wet and I'm meeting friends at a café with a fireplace, this jacket would be *perfect!*" Well, in three years, there hasn't been a single day when that jacket seemed like the perfect option. And you probably have two others that are pretty close to answering those requirements anyway.

For an expert, this extra data pile of loose ends might appear to be interesting, but that doesn't mean that it's critical to understanding what you're studying. Meanwhile, you probably already have too much data in your driver baskets. Do you want more clutter? The answer is easy in theory but difficult in practice: your default should be to toss the excess data. You can store the extraneous data if you want it for some future analytic project, but hold yourself accountable for tossing data that seems interesting but can't pass the "important" threshold.

In rare circumstances, you might decide that the item of clothing, or the random data, really is important. Let's say you're assessing the capabilities of an opposition movement, and you notice that opposition groups are gaining ground in peripheral cities faster than they had been three months ago. When you came up with your initial question, you went on to list a handful of drivers critically important to breaking down the question, drivers such as training, leadership, organization, and equipment. The willingness of the local population to harbor antiregime rebels in those peripheral cities, however, wasn't one of them. In the past, maybe the population was more sympathetic to the regime, and rebel leaders and fighters faced constant problems when their locations and identities were revealed to regime intelligence officers. This now appears to be happening less often, you find; the opposition cells are complaining less frequently about the difficulties of living among the population.

In this case, the accumulation of information on a driver you hadn't considered carefully enough—civilian attitudes in peripheral cities—now merits an additional driver basket. You might call what you've done a sort of "gap" analysis: you didn't know it, but your initial driver list didn't allow you to consider this new element of changing popular attitudes toward the opposition. Without addressing that gap, you would clearly end up with an analytic process that failed to weigh public opinion. By reviewing the leftover pile after you placed your data into the initial baskets, then, you might have stumbled on a clue that will help you continue to refine your drivers.

Serious consideration of whether to add this driver, though, doesn't quite end this story. You will often find that it's easier to create a new basket than it is to discard information that is interesting but peripheral, just as it's easier to come up with a reason to keep an item of clothing than it is to donate it. So be careful about expanding your number of driver baskets too quickly; if you do this, you'll find yourself with fifteen drivers, as opposed to a more meaningful and manageable ten, and you'll be assessing pieces of a problem that are way too far down the priority list to affect the analytic problem you're facing. This shouldn't happen often—your driver process should be sharp enough that you only rarely miss significant areas—so, again, be very careful about defaulting too quickly to adding more drivers.

To keep yourself on track, ask yourself this difficult question when you're considering whether to add another driver: If I have ten key drivers already, and this would be the eleventh, is there a way I can limit myself to ten by eliminating one? If the answer is no, you might want to reconsider the new addition. As we discussed earlier, how many hard problems really require consideration of more than ten factors? Are you adding this new factor because it's interesting, and it seems painful just to leave it on the cutting room floor? Maybe you're adding it because you're an expert, and dropping information at the margins of your analytic debate feels like you're somehow corrupting your professional standards.

Too much data might provide a false sense of security; it doesn't necessarily lead to clearer analytic decision-making. Granted, the ten-driver limit is arbitrary, but it's yet another metric. If we didn't set some sort of standard, all of us analysts, who love to hoard stuff, would find ourselves considering dozens of variables to assess an opposition movement. And at that point, we're mired in a confusion of analytic dead ends, lost in data and focusing on information that's fascinating but maybe inconsequential in answering the original question we worked so hard to create.

As we review the amount of information we've accumulated in each basket, we should return, just for a moment, to one of our opening principles: analytic humility. Analysts want to know everything, but an excess of data will cloud judgment, if we don't control the hoarding instinct that comes with expertise. So when we're pitching our bits of data into our various driver baskets, we should focus on returning to the core principles that are worth returning to again and again: differentiating between what we know, what we don't know, and what we think.

Analysts typically overestimate the first, ignore the second, and confuse the third, taking what we "think" and switching it over to the what we "know" basket. For example, if you need to know about the quality of opposition leadership, you'll obviously need some data. But when you're tossing those pieces of data into that pile, you don't have to toss in every bit. As the baskets grow full, ask yourself: Am I sure this one additional bit of data helps me understand the quality of opposition commanders? Do I have sufficient data already that will help me understand the answer to the question? If I have eighteen reports on the quality of opposition leaders, does this nineteenth add substantially to my base of knowledge?

ASSESSING DATA: ASSIGNING CONFIDENCE GRADES TO DRIVER BASKETS

If you're dealing with an analytic problem that's significant enough to demand this level of effort, you might want to employ another simple method to assess your confidence levels across multiple baskets. This takes a bit of work, but it's not overwhelming. It's not worth the time, in other words, if you're dealing with a casual problem. It's well worth the time, though, if you're boring into something that is high on your list of personal or professional priorities. We can use the red-yellow-green colors of a stoplight to clarify the three basic confidence levels you might assign to the data in your driver baskets:

- **GREEN.** I have such a great quantity of information, you might say, from such high-quality sources, that I can assess the driver with confidence; I don't need to slow down (yellow) or stop (red) to look for more information that would round out this basket and raise my level of confidence. I can say "I know," but I still have to return to the basket periodically to check whether we've received contradictory information, or when we haven't seen any information in a while and thus have to start looking at the information we're relying on as dated. *Warning—more judgments end up in the green category than should be there. Don't jump quickly to green. It's an expertise trap.*

- **YELLOW.** I am accumulating enough information to make a start at assessing this driver. My pile of information has at least one key gap, though, that prevents me from assigning a high level of confidence to my answer. I may have terrific data, for example, but it only covers a limited time period. Or I have a great deal of data over time, but the quality is suspect; my sources of information are secondhand. This data might allow for a healthy "I think" judgment, but it's too thin to support a high degree of certainty (in other words, to be a green). *More judgments should be yellow than you'd like to think.*

- **RED.** I may have bits and pieces of data, but I simply don't have enough quality data, or enough of a baseline of data, to make a good-faith assessment of the driver. At the moment, I should highlight this area as an "unknown." If this basket was critical enough to be on our list of the core six to ten drivers, then the gap is important, and I need to ensure that I clearly mark this "I don't know" in any document or presentation I make to the customer, whether it's my boss or the president of the United States.

Let's say you've identified ten drivers as critically important in assessing your question. You spent that frustrating, labor-intensive time at the front end of your analytic process. Now you start to reap the dividends at the back end of this process by quickly sorting your data into baskets. If you've decided that your assessment of the capabilities of the opposition rebels, for example, requires you to create a driver basket we'll call "weaponry," you're going to put all your weaponry data into this basket. Into this driver basket, you would file all the information you have on rifles, ammunition, rocket-propelled grenades, antitank devices, mortars, etc.

Once you've divided your data into two basic groups—the data that fits nicely into one of your ten baskets, and the data you've decided is interesting/important but doesn't quite fit anywhere— assign yourself a grade. This grade can represent a rough approximation of your confidence in assessing the overall question, just as you assigned a grade for each individual basket. Granted, this grading exercise is less than scientific. We're trying to break down our analytic process into a methodology that takes the art of analysis and turns it into a more scientific, step-by-step process. In this case, though, we need to shift a bit toward the "art" side: there's no hard-and-fast way to determine whether the amount of data you've accumulated into any individual basket is enough to declare victory. Just resist defaulting to green.

Be tough on yourself. Green is rare, so don't grade on a curve, and don't give yourself a lot of wiggle room: if you're deciding between two options (Am I confident I have enough information here to color this green, or is this borderline?) always go with the tougher choice. Even if you're wrong—if you've given yourself too tough a grade on a driver that really deserves a green go light—you can always enjoy the prospect of shifting back up the scale.

Remember that you should assign yourself a time frame on this color-coding. If you have given yourself a green in May on how you assess the opposition's weapons capabilities—meaning that you're confident you have a handle on understanding rebels' weapons stockpiles—you might still want to come up with the date by which you think you should reassess your confidence level. The date becomes its own metric: How often do you have to reassess a confidence level, to determine whether the story has changed?

Over time, new information might reinforce your confidence or cast doubt on your conclusions, or perhaps a gap in information forces you to drop your confidence grade. If you're confident in May, how quickly might the picture change so that your assessment is out of date? A month? Three months? A grade of green in May might quickly become a grade of yellow in August. No problem—this is part of the dynamic business of analysis. Just don't let yourself fall victim to the passage of time. Set up a schedule that forces you to reexamine all your confidence levels periodically. If your information sources have dried up, and you've lost a bit of confidence in your judgment—maybe because you don't have the same access to the rebels who imported weapons that you had in May—have the humility and analytic integrity to admit it. Shift a green light to yellow. Or a yellow light to red.

CAREFUL WITH THE COLORS!
THE RISK OF ASSESSING INTENT

You want to pay special attention to one especially problematic set of driver baskets: capabilities versus intentions, or metrics designed for a measurable question (how many tanks the opposition has captured) versus a soft question (how opposition commanders are thinking about using those tanks). If you want to look at the history of ugly analytic mistakes, look no further than this divide.

Let's take the issue of India's nuclear test in 1998 as a quick case study. The drivers we might be interested in would include the level of activity and preparedness at the country's nuclear test site, the engineering capability of Indian scientists, and the scientists' access to material for a nuclear device. This isn't a comprehensive list, but note one critical aspect of each of these drivers: they will help you understand the country's *capability* to conduct a test, or whether the country has the material and know-how to explode a device.

These are metrics that lend themselves to hard facts and figures. At the test site, preparations are accelerating or decelerating, or they're stagnant. Scientists have the academic background and experience to develop a program. Or they don't. The country has fissile material sufficient for a weapon. Or it doesn't.

You may not know the extent of the country's fissile missile stocks, but the amount is certainly measurable. Someone somewhere probably knows it. These hard measures tell you something about what the country's leaders can do. Capabilities estimates, though, do not tell you anything about what the country's leaders want to do—what their intentions are. Intentions are in someone's head—the head of the prime minister, the president, the defense minister, or others. Unlike capabilities, intentions are impossibly hard to measure with any certainty, sometimes because the players themselves don't know what they'll do. Unlike capabilities, intentions might simply be unknowable. Saddam can develop WMD; does he want to? Egypt can invade Israel; do Egypt's leaders want to? Any American can run for president; does he or she want to?

In many cases, from assessing a potential investment to studying national security problems, this distinction between capability and intent is critical. Capability is much easier to measure, and therefore easier to assess. Do you want to know a country's military power? Count tanks, guns, aircraft, or personnel. Do you want to know if India has sufficient nuclear material to build a device? Figure out how to penetrate the country's nuclear infrastructure.

Intent, though, is both inaccessible and quickly changeable, which makes it difficult or impossible to assess. If an opposition group has a hundred tanks they've captured, the condition of those tanks might be such that a fair percentage aren't serviceable, but that's measurable, too. If the head of that group tells a US intelligence agent repeatedly that he has no interest in using those tanks aggressively against a rival group, analysts have very little way to assess the veracity of what that leader says. Suddenly we're skating onto thin ice. Is he lying? What are his motivations? Who are the other decision makers in the group, and how might they be influencing him? Will he wake up tomorrow with different ideas about whether the neighboring country represents a threat?

Once again, before you jump to decide that this is some sort of national security distinction, understand that capability versus intent appears frequently in analytic assessments. Let's say you're assessing a company as a possible investment opportunity. The company is turning over increasing profits, and the company's managers have a lot of cash on hand. This cash represents capability—a capability you can measure, based on a balance sheet. It does not represent intent. The company's CEO issues an annual plan that indicates the company will use this cash for dividends. This statement is a measure, and only one measure, of intent: the company's managers intend to use their cash to pay out dividends, but this intent is a long way from an ironclad assurance that the company will do this.

You can't take this problem of assessing intent and break it down so that it's easier to grapple with. People are hard to predict. In my old world of intelligence, informants lie, cheat, and steal. People also change their minds, as the world shifts. All of us listen to advice that sways us. Or we simply make bad decisions that don't make a lot of sense in hindsight.

To review, here are the points you might consider when grading your drivers:

- First, make sure you separate capability from intent as soon as you look at your driver baskets. A firm you're interested in investing in might include managers who have the financial flexibility to pay out a dividend next year. Those same managers say they want to pay a dividend. The first is a capability; the second is an intent. Keep them separate.

- Second, question your data aggressively. If we're counting tanks and come up with a figure of five hundred, we need to attack this number with healthy skepticism. Is there another hidden hundred somewhere? If we're asking what an insurgent wants to do with those tanks, and the answer is "nothing," we should be far more aggressive in questioning how heavily to weigh this bit of data. Counting tanks to measure capability, in other words, likely will yield far more reliable data than assuming that what the group's leader says is true when he talks about how he intends to use those tanks.

- Third, be careful of analysts, especially longtime experts, who tell you that they understand the intent of those you're trying to assess, whether it's a friendly company or an unfriendly, nuclear-capable adversary. Consider the way your own thought processes work, and reflect on a few of the major decisions you've made in your life, from buying a car or a house to choosing a vacation location or even settling on a spouse. If you'd been asked about your thoughts a month before your decision, you might well have offered a clear-minded explanation of where you were leaning. Did you change your mind? Were you influenced later by factors even you, when you're the decision maker, could not have anticipated? Before you judge that you have a high level of confidence in the data in baskets that represent intent, think of how often you don't even have a full understanding of what you intend to do. Then discount your confidence by half.

A CASE STUDY IN COLORS:
IRAQ, SADDAM HUSAYN, AND THE NO-FLY ZONES

We can apply this red-yellow-green approach to an intelligence problem we faced among a group of analysts I managed during the late 1990s. It wasn't a front-burner issue, but it clearly shows how you can take a question, add a series of drivers, and sum up where you have confidence, where you don't, and what you think as a result. Once again, the problem was our perennial thorn in the side, Saddam Husayn. In 1999 and 2000, I was managing an analytic group at CIA Headquarters in Langley, Virginia, a talented group of a few dozen analysts who were responsible for helping US government decision makers understand Iraq's economy, politics, and military. It's the Iraqi military we will discuss here—in this case, the Iraqi Air Force, which was then restricted after the First Gulf War from flying in large swaths of territory in northern and southern Iraq. The air force was permitted to fly in the central part of the country, but the northern and southern no-fly zones were off-limits, clearly delineated areas that were established to prevent Iraq from striking its own citizens or threatening neighbors.

Nonetheless, through the intelligence data we were collecting, we at the CIA would often see incursions into the no-fly zones by Iraqi fighter aircraft. These aircraft weren't particularly threatening—they didn't stay in the no-fly zones long, and they didn't enter the zones in significant numbers. But US policymakers were interested in Iraq, and CIA analysts were supposed to give them a heads-up, with some context, when we saw something happening in Iraq that we thought was noteworthy. So often, on mornings when the military analysts would note another incursion by one of Iraq's dated fighter fleet into one of the zones, we'd talk among ourselves. Is this something we should write about for Washington decision makers? What's the significance of this? What are the patterns? Is something changing?

As discussed in the first chapter of this book, we might formulate our questions and answers in two different ways:

- Left to right (wrong). A descriptive explanation of Iraqi incursions, with a bit of context added in. What are the Iraqis doing?
- Right to left (correct). An interpretive analysis that includes the information about the incursions and an explanation of whether they suggested any change in the threat from Saddam, whether he was potentially threatening his own restive population; neighboring states; or US and allied forces. In other words: How do the actions of the Iraqi Air Force change our understanding of the threat to these potential targets, if at all? Might the actions reach a point where the United States would feel compelled to respond?

In the first instance, if we provide a simple descriptive analysis of what Saddam's air force is doing, what's the policymaker supposed to do with that? For example, we might say that two aircraft flew into the no-fly zones for fifteen minutes. Why does it make a difference? More fundamentally, why would anybody care, if Saddam wasn't doing anything that was threatening? Was he just testing whether we were paying attention? Were pilots on a training mission? Was the air force testing whether US pilots would react, or maybe over-react, which might give Saddam an opportunity to regain the stage in front of an international community that had lost interest in Iraq?

To understand the right-to-left question, in this case, we'd have to break down the problem into a series of agnostic drivers that would detail the kinds of things any analyst would want to know, whether he thinks the incursions are significant or not:

- Depth of incursions. Was the air force going deeper into the no-fly zones?
- Frequency. Were we seeing more incursions?
- Location. Are we seeing a change in the pattern of incursions? More in the southern no-fly zone? More in the north?
- Type of aircraft. Are we seeing the same aircraft? If not, how should we understand the change?
- Blue team. What are US and allied forces (known as the "blue team," as opposed to the "red team" Iraqis) and allied forces doing? Have they changed behavior in ways that might have led Iraq to change its own operations?
- International events. What's happening on the global scene that relates to Iraq? Might the incursions somehow relate to a broader message Saddam is trying to send?
- Response. How are US aircraft responding to the incursions? When they respond, are Iraq's pilots doing anything that's different from past behavior?
- Intent. Why are Iraq's commanders doing this? Are senior commanders involved? Is Saddam involved? If so, what do their orders mean?

If we run quickly through these drivers, to assign our red-yellow-green grades, we can quickly see echoes of the themes we've covered earlier in the book. First, we can assign hard metrics to a good number of these drivers. We can be confident that we know how frequently the Iraqis are flying into the denied zones (green), where they're flying (green), what types of aircraft they're flying (green), and how US pilots are responding (green). Sit back and note the following clearly: each of these represents a "capability" driver—what the Iraqis can do, and what they are doing. Not a single one of these offers much indication about intent—what Iraqis (the pilots, their commanders, or Saddam) are trying to accomplish, or what they're thinking. Their goal might be as mundane as a change in training cycles, or a new commander might have decided to alter flight patterns. Or a change in behavior might be as significant as Saddam testing to see whether he can push harder to provoke a reaction. Maybe the explanation is even simpler: a poorly trained Iraqi pilot wandered off course from his assigned flight path.

Let's look at another part of the intelligence ledger, the "intent" side—anything that might tell us not *what* the Iraqis are doing but *why* they're doing it. Reviewing our list of questions, you should expect to see a line of reds on this intent side of the ledger. In this Iraq scenario, we probably wouldn't know whether Saddam had issued orders related to air operations or whether a local commander had simply taken some independent initiative that led to a change in Iraqi tactics. We wouldn't know whether we were seeing a training blip or an indicator of some deeper intent. And we wouldn't, therefore, have a good answer to whether we should judge that the threat was up, down, or unchanged. The red-yellow-green grades tell the story. Here they are:

- Intent—red. We don't know what Iraqi leaders think. We don't even know whether they had anything to do with an increase in incursions.
- International events—red. Obviously, we know what's happening on the world scene. But we have little to no idea of how regime insiders view these events, and how they might view no-fly zone violations as an element of their response to international events.
- Blue team—this is a curveball. On the surface, you'd judge that we could give this a green, meaning that if the blue team represents what US and other friendly

forces are up to, we should have perfect insight into their activities. This judgment would be correct. But the quick assignment of a green grade to this driver basket misses a critical question: Do we know how the opposition views US activities? Is there any chance that Iraqi officials are concerned about some US training activity we view as benign? Might they be miscalculating? Are we assuming that they have any insight into our intent? If not, we should be careful about assessing blue team (allied) activity. We may think some accelerated training among US pilots is just that—accelerated training. What if the Iraqis misread us, assuming that we're gearing up for something?

Before we close, think how much different this ledger would look if we just changed the question and used the same data. If we're supporting a military commander responsible for US operations in the no-fly zones, we might provide decision advantage by answering something like this:

- How confident are we that we can track any Iraqi aircraft entering the no-fly zones, and that we would see any significant incursion shortly after the aircraft left an airbase?

Here, we're less focused on intent than on warning: we may not know why Iraqi leaders would launch an air assault, but we certainly would know quickly if something unusual was happening at Iraqi airbases. This is a classic example of the "Garbage In, Garbage Out" principle: If you spend the energy to ask a good question at the start, you may generate a helpful answer at the finish. But if you ask a bad question at the start, you're almost guaranteed to generate a bad answer at the finish.

Red-yellow-green will help you avoid a few critical analytic errors in these situations. First, as you've seen, it will help prevent you from focusing only on what you know and force you to acknowledge what you don't know. This tool gives you a fighting chance to acknowledge the importance of the unknown in your analysis, and to spend more time studying whether and how you can close gaps in those areas.

The technique also exposes the crucial difference between assessing things we can count and things that are inherently unknowable—often those within the broad category of how other people think and act. Think of your final analysis as an iceberg. If you're on a ship looking at the tip of the iceberg, you might have one perspective on how big it is, and what threat it poses to your ship. But if you're assessing the real risk, you're worried about the unknown: what lies beneath. You shouldn't need much help with assessing the tip of the iceberg; you can see it. Beware of what you don't see.

INTENT ANALYSIS AND RED-YELLOW-GREEN: A TERRORISM CASE STUDY

I remember being called to the White House National Security Council in the early 1990s to discuss a concern that had escalated quickly that month: whether one of America's embassies was facing the heightened threat of a terrorist strike from a country that had been hostile for decades. The intelligence reports we analysts were receiving at the CIA seemed as clear as they were ominous. Intelligence officers from that adversary state had received orders to surveil the local US Embassy, at a time of high tension in the region.

On the surface, this seems like a straightforward intelligence case. If tensions are high and an adversary steps up surveillance of a US Embassy, you can presume that the risk of some sort of terror event is increasing. This is particularly true when analysts are assessing a hostile country that had been involved in sponsoring terror attacks in the past, as was the case in this scenario.

Before we take that analytic leap to step up the terror threat, though, we have to weigh the driver variables we are considering. We know tensions are high in the region and important, so we'll list "international/regional environment" as a driver to assess. We should examine this particular driver more closely before moving on, however, mainly because it is so potentially confusing. On the surface, we might quickly grade our understanding of this driver as green, meaning not that the environment seems peaceful but instead that we're confident we understand the level of tension, maybe just by reading newspaper reports.

In retrospect, the grade we should have given this driver, though, is near the opposite end of the spectrum, toward red—meaning that we should assume we have almost no understanding of the international/regional situation. But how can this be? We're reading newspaper reports that hostile rhetoric is clearly on the rise, and that particular part of the world looks like a tinderbox. The problem with this simplistic analysis is that the rationale for the tough red grade centers on the old problem of intent. We are not simply taking the temperature of a public diplomatic row in the region. We're trying to understand a few different questions about which we know little to nothing.

- First, how do the leaders of our adversary country view this environment? Why should we be confident that their views are even close to ours? Are we assuming that they think like we do, an old analytic problem known as mirror-imaging?
- Second, even if we guessed that they shared our views, why would we jump to the conclusion that they would

take the step of sponsoring a terror attack in response? Do we know this? Or do we think this? What are our insights into how they're weighing their options— assuming they are even considering options?

- Third, why do we assume that what they say closely approximates what they think?

Now that we understand the complexities of assessing even superficially simple drivers, we can move to a longer driver list. We can start with this first issue, the thorny problem of intent and the international/regional environment, and then move on:

- International/regional environment. How tense is the region, and what is the US role in that tension? How much have the levels of tension changed in the recent past?
- Access. How much difficulty would the adversary face in gaining access to a US target, whether it's the US Embassy building or a softer target, such as a van transporting employees to the embassy through city streets?
- Weapons/explosives. How hard would it be for operatives from the adversary country to get their hands on weapons or explosives?
- Operatives. How difficult would it be for the adversary country to put in place operatives who could conduct such an attack?
- Context. How does what we're seeing in this country of concern compare to or contrast with what we're seeing elsewhere or have seen in the past? Is this kind of surveillance common? Is it an anomaly?

Half of these problems are about as easy as it gets in the fuzzy world of intelligence analysis, where nothing is quite black-and-white. The drivers we're looking at on the capabilities side of the equation—access to operatives, weapons or explosives, and targets—are far easier to assess than the first intent driver we looked at. In other words, judging that an adversary can train operatives, bring in a cache of weapons or explosives, and surveil a potential target—such as a US Embassy—should not be difficult. These elements of terror attacks are easy to add together.

Remember, this is a real case, though, and the soft intent side of the equation isn't anywhere near as easy as the more measurable capabilities side. Yes, anybody can get their hands on some explosives. But do we have any idea of why they would want to do this? We might jump to the conclusion that we know. Why would they want to store explosives if they weren't planning a terror operation?

Not so fast. If you think this, believe me, you are not alone, even among experts. I thought this too when this scenario unfolded, as did many others who had a lot of experience in this field of counterterrorism. When we dug down, though, over the course of a few days and weeks, questions that now seem so basic were nowhere near evident.

Let's go back to the "context" driver. How does what we are seeing in this one particular country, where we think the embassy might be facing an imminent threat, compare with what we're seeing in other countries around the region? Only later in this analytic process did we step back to assess these kinds of contextual questions, believe it or not. And the answer turned out to be critical, maybe more important than any other single driver we looked at. Here's the story of what happened.

We discovered that this adversary country had sent out identical directives to every single office it had throughout the region, at roughly the same time—not just in the area where the embassy was. The order to their officers in the country we were concerned about wasn't unique at all, we found. They got the same directive everybody else did. Adding this to our mix of information, you might start to reconsider fundamentally your initial concern, in a world of vague and conflicting information. Maybe some kind of threat is brewing here, but could we instead be seeing some sort of bureaucratic exercise, such as a routine headquarters order to collect information about US Embassies to keep old files fresh?

We then uncovered another clue: urgency, or lack thereof. If this was a unique order, issued because of some special interest in surveilling one single US Embassy as a prelude to a terrorist operation, you would expect the adversary's field operatives to move with some swiftness. Well, they didn't. Not in the least. They seemed to treat this directive as yet another in a long list of priorities from their head office—headquarters orders that might have to be completed sometime, but certainly not in any hurry.

I am obscuring some of the details here that would make this case even clearer, but suffice it to say that we shifted from high concern one day to a toned-down level of concern during less than a week of intense analysis. We had started with knowing very little, in retrospect, but assuming a lot: some hostile operative has been asked to collect information on an embassy. But then, after a little digging and a few good questions, we realized that our first judgments had resulted from huge leaps in our assessment of intent. The adversary's activities were still worth watching, to be sure. We were not nearly certain about what was going on, the same sort of intelligence riddle an analyst would face watching modern-day North Korea, Iran, China, or Russia. But we also weren't near a fever pitch of concern that should have galvanized a group of presidential advisers.

This scenario helps outline analytic principles, but it did not have a profound affect on America's security. Prewar intelligence on the Iraq invasion of 2003 did, and it would be hard to conclude any discussion about analytic errors, and particularly the question of understanding (or misunderstanding) intent, without taking a look at intelligence on Iraq before the war.

In this case, we have two diametrically opposed sides, Baghdad and Washington, each misreading the other. With Saddam, years of sanctions and intrusive UN inspections persuaded him that he would never escape the cloud of harsh UN resolutions hanging over Iraq, particularly given US pressure on the international community to maintain sanctions on Iraq's imports, oil exports, and military activities.

On the US side, Saddam's games to evade UN sanctions for years had persuaded analysts and policymakers that Saddam would never comply with the requirement that he explain what had happened to Iraq's WMD stocks, which we will go into shortly. Before we look at this intelligence case, however, keep in mind the problem of hindsight bias, or looking back at how events developed and assuming that any decent analyst could have forecast these events beforehand. We unknowingly suffer from hindsight bias all the time, but it's a classic analytic mistake to keep in the back of your mind as you consider this scenario.

To summarize the complex problem of misreading intent, and how deeply ingrained our biases about intent can be, start with one of the thousands of bits of information about Iraq and WMD that influenced analysts over time. The incident we'll discuss below dates all the way back to 1991, more than a decade before the war in 2003, but many of the analysts assessing Iraq after 9/11 had been working on the problem for years, and events a decade prior would have been well known to them.* The following is from a declassified study of Saddam's WMD programs in the 1990s:

------

* All the material in this Iraq section is drawn from a declassified study, published in January 2006, of intelligence analysts' assessments of Iraq before the invasion in 2003. See *Misreading Intentions: Iraq's Reaction to Inspections Created Picture of Deception*, 5 January 2006. The declassified document appears in Appendix C.

In April 1991, for example, Iraq declared [after its retreat from Kuwait and its defeat in the First Gulf War] that it had neither a nuclear weapons program nor an enrichment program [for nuclear weapons material]. Inspections in June and September 1991 proved that Iraq had lied on both counts, had explored multiple enrichment paths, and had a well-developed nuclear weapons program.

Baghdad destroyed rather than revealed items, attempting to make its inaccurate assertions of no programs correct in a legalistic sense. . . . Decisions to destroy much of the paperwork that could have verified the destruction exacerbated Iraq's inability to later extricate itself from being viewed in the "cheat and retreat" paradigm.

With that disturbing backdrop of deception in mind, an analyst might hold two opposing views, simultaneously, about the now well known errors of assessing Iraq's WMD before the war in 2003. The first is that analysts had good cause to suspect Saddam before the war; he had lied repeatedly. The second is that analysts failed to see how Saddam and Iraq's WMD program were evolving over time, and how analysts' judgments about intent, colored by these experiences of deceit a decade earlier, proved so tragically wrong. Here's the rest of the story, drawn directly from the declassified study of how the US intelligence analysts misread Iraq's intentions:

Key events and Iraqi behaviors that shaped Western perceptions include:

- An early established pattern of "cheat and retreat." Iraq concealed items and activities in the early 1990s, and when detected, attempted to rectify the shortcomings, usually secretly and without documentation. Those coverups were seen to validate analytic assessments that Iraq intended to deny, deceive, and maintain forbidden capabilities.

- Shocked by the unexpected aggressiveness of early UN Special Commission (UNSCOM) inspections in 1991, Iraq secretly destroyed or dismantled most undeclared items and records that could have been used to validate the unilateral destruction, leaving Baghdad unable to provide convincing proof when it later tried to demonstrate compliance.

- We [US intelligence officials and those assessing Iraq's WMD after the invasion] now judge that the 1995 defection of Saddam's son-in-law Husayn Kamil—a critical figure in Iraq's WMD and denial and deception (D&D) activities—prompted Iraq to change strategic direction and ease efforts to retain WMD programs. Iraqi attempts that year to find face-saving means to disclose previously hidden information, however, reinforced the idea that Baghdad was deceptive and unreliable. Instead of helping to close the books, Iraq's actions reinvigorated the hunt for concealed WMD, as analysts perceived that Iraq had both the intent and capability to continue WMD efforts during inspections.

- When Iraq's revelations were met by added UN scrutiny and distrust, frustrated Iraqi leaders deepened their belief that inspections were politically motivated and would not lead to the end of sanctions. As Iraq turned its political focus to illicit economic efforts to end its isolation, eliminate sanctions, and protect its dual-use infrastructure, these actions increased suspicions that Iraq continued to hide WMD.

———

A large portion of this chapter boils down into warnings about traps that we all fall into from time to time. The red-yellow-green approach gives you at least a chance to avoid these traps. Here they are:

- First, there's the trap of believing we know more than we know, and blowing through the bright line that separates what we know and what we think. By pushing harder to differentiate between green and yellow and red, we might be able to highlight areas where we've blurred what we know and what we think.
- Second, analysts typically emphasize their areas of expertise and knowledge, downgrading areas in which they suffer from knowledge gaps. This is like looking at a few pieces of a puzzle and guessing what the completed whole will look like when 90 percent of the pieces aren't in place. By pushing harder to identify key drivers that are yellows and reds, we have a tool that helps us identify gaps.

More than likely, when you come out on the other side of the exercise, you will find that you know less than you think you did, and that your knowledge gaps are a larger part of the picture than you expected. If you play the HEAD Game fairly, then, you'll find that your confidence level through this analytic process decreases. Don't worry. That's the goal. Remember, this process is about trying to get closer to analyzing like a fox, looking at a lot of bits and pieces that don't fit together neatly. If you end up killing the hedgehog in you that wants to force the pieces into a neat, coherent picture, we are already much closer to success.

Data is the bane of analysis, if it's used or understood properly. Too many experts equate more data with better analysis, maybe living with the illusion that more information necessarily results in sounder conclusions. Eighteen months before a national election, polls will give you data on which candidates are emerging, suggesting that this group of early leaders somehow might be representative of who's on the ballot a year and a half down the road. But how about the data on how many polls eighteen months out predict the final contenders with any accuracy? That's a different question, and a different data set. If you start with data, at some point in your analytic career, you'll end up with horrendous results.

When you reach the data stage in your process, give your brain some assistance. Have you ever tried to make a complicated recipe by forcing your mind to remember the ingredients and quantities without a reference? You'll remember some, but not all. In the days before GPS devices, how often did you take a wrong turn when you tried to remember a complicated route leading to an address you'd never visited before?

We do this all the time in the workplace, stepping through complicated analytic decision-making without a way to judge data, maybe because we've been the experts in a certain profession for decades. Even doctors who've performed the same surgery a thousand times make mistakes. So they have checklists, which have proved to be surprisingly effective in reducing error rates. Try to be as consistent when you look at your own problem sets, and your own mounds of data. Sort the data into your driver baskets. Assign a confidence level to it, to uncover your key gaps. And then return to reevaluate your data, time and time again.

CHAPTER SIX

WHAT ARE WE MISSING?

We have stepped through what can be an exhausting analytic process up to this point. If you apply this right-to-left methodology to difficult analytic problems, you should become more efficient, over time, in making assessments, but not without pain. One challenge through this process will be maintaining humility at the end: with all the work we've invested up to this point, we might expect that the end result is as good as it gets, in the analytic world. And then we'll look back, after the next analytic mistake, and almost certainly utter the same words every analyst utters after a major error: I should have seen that coming. Pushing toward this constant questioning and constant humility is an everyday analytic challenge, and we need to spend more time focusing on one of the most important questions every analyst faces (and avoids): What is it that I don't know?

"I don't know": three words we struggle with every day. Those three words shouldn't be that hard to say, but, as many studies on our thought processes show, humans have a very hard time swallowing pride. These same books also describe the mountains of research on how poorly experts perform when they try to forecast the future— often, they're no better at forecasting than they would be if they flipped a coin. This is not a wholesale indictment of experts: as long as expert mistakes aren't the result of immodesty—boasting, or an erroneous belief that an analyst somehow knows all the answers—pride in producing quality work is something we should accept as a positive.

Unless and until, of course, false pride prevents an analyst from acknowledging that he might very well be wrong about tomorrow. Any analytic conversation about a complex problem has to include a segment about what the analyst doesn't know. If a Wall Street analyst opens with the statement "Let me tell you how the markets are going to rally this year," without adding a cautionary note about market volatility, he's presenting analysis that suggests that somehow he has solved the riddle of predicting the future. Acknowledging gaps, in other words, should feature as prominently in analysis as acknowledging where analysts can bring knowledge advantage.

The combination of expertise and pride is the scourge of experts. To combat the human tendency to trust our own judgment too quickly, we have to embrace gap analysis—understanding holes in knowledge and data—as a basic step in the analytic process. No analyst can afford to focus on knowns (the greens on your driver list) without paying the same attention to the unknowns. For all of us, overemphasizing what we know, or what we think we know, is a lot easier than assessing gaps.

Let's start with a test of how we can conduct gap analyses. Think of it as embracing a Copernicus moment, when experts anchored in the judgment that the Earth was the center of the universe refused to accept the arguments of a more scientifically based analysis. As good analysts, we might have tremendous success over time: we could be on a two-year—or a ten-year—hot streak. Joe DiMaggio, the legendary New York Yankees baseball player, got a hit in fifty-six straight games in 1941. But he failed to get a hit in the fifty-seventh game. Many experts believe his record never will be matched; still, he wasn't flawless, and his streak came to an end. It's a safe bet that after that fifty-seventh game he asked himself some version of the question we all need to ask to prevent overconfidence. What can we do better? Where does our work have holes? For DiMaggio, which pitch was it that he might have hit more squarely in that fifty-seventh game? We can't expect perfection, and we shouldn't. We can, though, insist on daily exercises that test the limits of our knowledge and expertise.

ANOMALY ANALYSIS: HOW TO USE DISCORDANT DATA

There are simple ways to test judgment and humility. We've already gone through a few, such as the charity proposition. Try another one: anomaly analysis. We can start by looking at a notional problem that we might have studied for months, or even years. Using the process we started in chapter 1, we have defined the question properly, and we have settled on a mix of six to ten drivers to break the problem down into constituent parts. We then sort data into baskets that correlate to these drivers. Over time, the accumulation of data might help you look at your problem from different angles.

First, as we've discussed, there's a good chance we will find at least some pieces of data that don't fit easily into any basket. These could be indicators that we haven't thought clearly enough about our baskets. If there is critical information that doesn't fit anywhere, does that tell us that there's another basket we need to weigh? Or are we learning that we're gathering data that we initially thought was important but now can discard, because it doesn't relate to any key basket? Second, and perhaps more important, we should look at anomalies to test judgments and assumptions. Anomalies shouldn't be discarded because they don't fit an analytic construct; they're potential canaries in the coal mine, maybe warnings that something is changing. If we've developed an analytic line that Saddam is hiding WMD, what do we do with the fact that we haven't actually seen a chemical weapon in Iraq for years? Is this because Saddam is so good at hiding weapons? Maybe. If we're not wedded to yesterday's analysis, though, we might use this data as a starting point for a conversation about alternative analysis that starts with a simpler explanation: maybe Saddam doesn't have chemical weapons anymore. Before we discard this option—and analysts, time and time again, will routinely discard simple explanations like this, in favor of more complicated explanations that support their long-held views—take the anomaly and build a case around it. How compelling is the case? Does the anomalous data stand alone, or are there other bits and pieces that support a new, seemingly anomalous, conclusion?

Some aspects of Iraq's WMD program, and US analysts' struggle to assess the program, offer a forgotten but telling example of anomaly analysis and its role in developing alternative scenarios. Analysts' mindsets about Saddam, back in the late 1990s, were guided by a few basic elements. If you look through a few foundational pieces that helped shape the analysis, it's hard to argue, even in retrospect, that we should have been certain Saddam was clean on WMD. Here are some key points that would have made you suspicious:

- Saddam had surprised the United States with the extent of his WMD apparatus at the time of the First Gulf War, in 1991 and beyond.
- Saddam had used WMD (chemicals) against his own people, the Kurds of northern Iraq.
- Saddam had repeatedly lied to UN weapons inspectors about Iraq's former WMD arsenal, issuing a series of updated "final declarations" about Iraq's WMD stocks as UN inspectors uncovered more information.

- In years of cat-and-mouse games with UN inspectors, Saddam's security services tried to keep inspectors at bay, creating a large Iraqi concealment bureaucracy that appeared to be at the core of a massive WMD shell game.
- Saddam had a deadly rivalry with Iran, Iraq's neighbor to the east. The Iran-Iraq war of 1980–88 had left many tens of thousands dead, and WMD featured in that war. Saddam lived in a region where WMD was standard.

One final point before we go on. By the invasion of Iraq in 2003, the United States hadn't had an embassy in Iraq for years, and weapons inspectors also hadn't been on the ground for several years. Glance through those key points above, and note the dates. Compelling as the story of Saddam's interest in WMD might have been, the UN and the United States hadn't actually laid eyes on Iraqi WMD for some time. Analysts' near certainty that Saddam had a WMD program was a judgment, not a fact, especially when what the US Intelligence Community knew was so dated.

Into this tragic drama walked the now-forgotten Husayn Kamil, Saddam's son-in-law and a senior Iraqi official in his own right, who defected to Jordan in the late 1990s. (Husayn Kamil's defection was temporary; he made the monumental mistake of returning to Baghdad after defecting, and he was murdered soon thereafter.) Over the course of several weeks in Jordan, Kamil underwent intense intelligence debriefings, many of which pertained to the enigma of Saddam and Iraqi WMD. What he said was disturbing at that time, partly because it was so anomalous: this former senior Iraqi official and member of Saddam's family, with better access to Iraqi leadership than anyone else US intelligence officers had access to, said he knew of no weapons of mass destruction.

If you were a longtime WMD analyst reading what Kamil

said, you were, to say the least, perplexed. Many analysts had been steeped in Iraq's WMD program for years, schooled by the memory that Saddam had surprised the United States before and had designed an elaborate concealment apparatus to dupe inspectors. With those memories, an analyst might readily dismiss the anomaly of Kamil with a perfectly reasonable response:

A. Husayn Kamil is lying; or
B. Husayn Kamil wasn't part of the WMD concealment apparatus in Saddam's regime, so he wouldn't know about a highly compartmentalized program.

This, of course, is exactly what happened. Added to this fixed mindset, developed over the course of years, was the problem of time. When the drumbeat of war grew louder in 2003, analysts gathered at the CIA to look again at Saddam's WMD program. They didn't have much time, though, because the White House was already in the midst of making the case for war in Iraq, and White House officials wanted a consensus analysis from intelligence analysts quickly. Because of this rush, it would be a stretch to say that the analysts started fresh. They compiled what they had done up to that point and published a new National Intelligence Estimate, the premiere publication of the US Intelligence Community.

Before leaping to the conclusion that these analysts got it wrong, it's worth one last reflection on the contradictory information they were dealing with. The picture was murky. Add to this picture alarming new information from an Iraqi defector shortly before the invasion who (erroneously) described aspects of Iraqi WMD. To argue that no one looking back on the Iraq WMD analysis today would have made the same mistakes is just plain arrogant, and wrong. The analysts doing the work were professionals. If you met them on the street, you'd be impressed.

There were, though, key anomalies, including the Husayn Kamil case, that probably should have sparked a more serious effort at alternative analysis. One anomaly was Husayn Kamil himself. To look at his statements from a new perspective, managers would have had to assemble a separate analytic team. This point is crucial, on a couple of fronts. First, if you asked mainstream analysts then to look at anomalies about Iraq, they would have found (and did find) ways to discount the information. It's the old problem of past experience and accumulated expertise shading how analysts view new information, and it's human nature. In addition to compiling anomalies for closer study, here are a few ways to deal with this challenge.

RED TEAM ANALYSIS AND ALTERNATIVE THINKING

Putting together a fresh group of analysts to review old problems gives analysts a way to attack anomalous information that might be dismissed by mainstream experts. We can think of this new team as the "red team," as opposed to the "blue team" traditionalists. Since they're bound to face some opposition from the blue team (and maybe even hostility), the red team will need a senior sponsor to shield them. Further, they may need help ensuring that they benefit from a level playing field: if they need access to senior experts or sensitive information, the sponsor can open the door.

We should also keep in mind that this fresh team has to play by the same rules as other analysts, so they can't be accused of taking shortcuts. The red team doesn't get to cut corners just to achieve the greater good of presenting a different perspective. To be taken seriously, the final analytic product from this team has to be comparable to the original, traditional product. In this case, the team would have the same key data points at their disposal as the mainstream analysts, such as access to all the secret reporting about Saddam's concealment programs and the debriefing reports from

Husayn Kamil. They would have to present their alternative version of how to interpret this information with the same rigor, and using the same style, as the original, mainstream analysis.

This red team likely will lean heavily on gap analysis, in addition to anomaly analysis. The intentions of decision makers they're assessing—Saddam Husayn, in this case—should fall into the "gap" category: In a perfect scenario, the analyst might know everything there is to know about Iraq's nuclear *capabilities*, from the inner workings of its facilities to its scientific and engineering successes and failures. But the alternative team should ask hard questions: What do these capabilities tell them about the *intentions* of Iraq's leaders, particularly Saddam? Any suggestions that analysts *know* this should pop up immediately as a red flag. Even if the CIA had recruited Iraq's defense minister as a secret informant, the analysts should not assume that he has all the answers about the innermost thoughts of the key players in this decision.

As you're setting up your red team—think of it as a "clean" team, free of the analytic anchors that might hold back mainstream analysts—set one clear ground rule for the project: we're not talking about what is known as "devil's advocate" analysis, or analysis that simply takes whatever the mainstream analytic position is and turns it on its head, arguing the opposite position. In other words, you think football is America's most popular sport? Let me find a way to prove otherwise, regardless of whether my position is analytically sound. You're welcome to try this devil's advocate approach, but we're not going to cover it here. In my experience, over the course of a short period of time analysts who use it might prove valuable once or twice, but they lose credibility over any longer period.

To start with, alternative analysis red teams should be looking at the same question as the mainstream team. The red team has to identify the drivers they think are important. Better yet, if you've come up with a strong set of drivers already, they can just use the drivers you've identified. This is one reason the "agnostic" test for drivers helps: if any team assessing the question would agree that the original drivers are the ones they'd use, this new red team should be able to use them as well. The drivers aren't weighted in favor of the mainstream judgment.

There are a few verbal clues to how resistant you or your blue team of analysts might be if confronted with alternatives. More generally, these clues will help you quickly evaluate whether you're dealing with the kind of analytic maturity that marks a seasoned expert who's become an analyst. The clues center on one concept: Does the analyst view himself as an independent arbiter of information—so much so that he's prepared to question judgments as new information comes in?

You can watch analysts' use of simple terms to determine how wedded they are to a position and whether they will embrace, or even listen to, a red team approach. Analysts who use words such as "my argument" or "my case" or "my position" are suggesting that they are dug in, and that they are more likely to argue their views than to engage in a conversation that might lead them to adjust what they think based on new information or new perspectives. Similarly, analysts who talk about "defending" an analytic position are already on the defensive, more likely to prepare arguments about how they're right and you're wrong than to walk into an open-minded conversation.

Look instead for analytic presentations that include, early on, explanations or assessments of what the analyst doesn't know, and judgments about which future signposts might suggest that his or her analysis is on the right track, or going off track. Also, look for analysts who avoid point predictions about the future—in other words, don't allow analysis that offers certitude about what will happen tomorrow—and who don't attach themselves to sweeping conclusions, such as that the stock market is "guaranteed" to hit 20,000 in the near future or that capitalism will be dead in twenty years. These analysts are hedgehogs, and they are almost guaranteed to be wrong. The foxes, who will be less colorful in their analysis, are not as likely to be heard, but they're more likely to be right. Pick hedgehogs for TV. Pick foxes for red teams.

Once the red team has settled on drivers they think need some testing—and it makes the process much easier if they simply rely on the drivers you've used in the main assessment, so you're comparing apples to apples in your two assessments—the analysis they present has to apply the same rigor you applied initially. They have to take the information at hand and determine whether there are vulnerabilities in how you judged your data. For example, you identified ten key variables, or drivers, that are leading you to make a "buy" recommendation to clients for a certain stock. The red team looks at your drivers, analysis, and gaps, and assesses that your general analytic line is sound but that you've overstated your level of confidence in one particular area, such as the quality of the management team at the company in which you're investing.

Don't expect immediate revelations through this red team process. It is unlikely to lead analysts on the mainstream team to agree to an analytic U-turn. Even with great red team analysis, if the core group that produced the original assessment includes seasoned pros who know what they're doing, you're in for a dog fight if you cram a red team's view down their throats. In most cases of red team analysis, the alternative view might instead slowly lead to doubts about flabby mainstream analysis, forcing analysts to at least begin to accept that some of their work has gaps or blurs the line between what they know and what they think.

Before you dismiss the red team process as too labor-intensive or theoretical, remember how often even seemingly unthinkable alternatives have become reality. In politics, early in the presidential election cycle, who expected victories by unknown candidates such as Jimmy Carter, Bill Clinton, or Barack Obama? In national security, who anticipated that Saddam Husayn didn't have weapons of mass destruction? Who thought in 1977 that the shah of Iran would be out in two years? In business, who foresaw the decline of Lehman Brothers or Merrill Lynch? How many people thought about the prospect of an economic meltdown in 2008? How did grim predictions about oil shortages in the late 1970s turn out to be so flawed? Again and again, experts will sit at the table and offer forecasts about a world in which change happens in a straight line. And again and again, life changes far faster and more profoundly than we expect. We have to accept that change is a constant, and our analysis has to have ways to shake us out of our analytic torpor and confront change.

FRESH PERSPECTIVES: BUILDING ANALYTIC GROUPS AND A RED TEAM OPTION

When we pick analysts the way we pick kickball players in sixth grade, which we all too often do, we're confusing two analytic talents that we should keep completely separate: first, the ability to use a wealth of expertise and history to explain today's events, and second, the ability to step out of those shoes and see where these patterns might change tomorrow. The two are related—let's not go so far as to judge that an expert on Peruvian politics doesn't bring a great deal of value to a conversation about the evolution of Peruvian politics—but they are not twins. Not even close. The first is an expert; the second is an analyst.

So when there's an analytic question on the table, take three steps that might help open up the conversation, even at the expense of irritating some of the more experienced members of your team. Pay closer attention than you think you should to the nonexpert players who sit amid the team of seasoned experts. The experts will want to dismiss them, and maybe they should, nine times out of ten. It's the tenth time, though, where experts bogged down in yesterday and today miss broader changes that are taking place. And it's your job, if you're managing these analysts, to change this expert-only dynamic.

Here are steps you can take to build a team with this mix of expertise, experience, and fresh perspectives:

- First, differentiate between current events and future forecasting. The two types of analysts are different.
- Second, supplement your expert analytic teams with relative newcomers, and give them a chance to speak. Ask them in particular about anomalies other analysts might explain away, and ask them about the big assumptions that other analysts might be making. All of us old-timers believe Saddam has WMD. What do those with a fresh perspective see? Where do they see assumptions that are masquerading as facts? Where do they see groupthink? Where do they see the more experienced hands explaining away significant facts?
- Third, guarantee these relative newcomers the chance to ask questions and make statements that might be dismissed out of hand by others at the table. To do this, there's a good chance you're going to have to ask a manager to sit at the table, at least at the outset, so that the experts don't dominate the discourse. We're all familiar with the psychology of this kind of mixed group: in that closed culture of experts, the new questioners (especially if they're younger, or newcomers) will quickly become ostracized. Give them the cover and space to overcome this.
- Fourth, having just one fresh set of eyes on the team

might not help. We're all familiar with this herd mentality: the one juror who doesn't want to fold feels so much
pressure—without anyone else to lean on for support—
that he eventually changes his vote. So you'll need at
least two of this type of questioner at the table to help
make this work. When one newcomer feels compelled to
ask tough questions of the experts at the table, he or she
should have a lifeline to reach out to in the herd.

If you're sitting at the head of the table encouraging this type
of conversation, there are a few meeting-management lessons you
might employ to tease out the right questions. These easy tools are
designed to prompt participation among participants who might
feel uncomfortable speaking up unless you create an environment
in which different ideas are welcome. Without this key step, if you
later ask how participants view the trend of the conversation ("Does
anyone else have a different perspective?"), many participants, especially that large proportion of analysts and thinkers who are intro-
verts, will see this as a rhetorical question that is not directed at
them personally. The analytic line you've taken earlier in the conversation is clear and represents a herding majority; nobody wants
to be the one to offer an alternative, particularly if they fear offend-
ing more senior analysts by questioning their judgments or offering
a different view.

Nudge the participants forward along this uncomfortable
path of nonconformity by being the first to present a different
perspective. Start the conversation with a question that assumes
the mainstream analytic position is incorrect. Rather than asking
whether everyone agrees with the going-in judgment, start at the
other end. "There's a good chance we're missing something here,"
you might say. "Nobody's perfect at figuring out what's going to
happen down the road. Let me offer a few guesses about where

we might be off track, or where we might be weighting something too heavily or too lightly. Then I'd like to go around the table and ask each person to lay out a few guesses." In this scenario, you've tried to rule out the chance that participants are starting with the mainline judgment, and you've opened the door for anyone who wants to test an alternative without seeming to attack the expertise of others.

If you do this, give the participants around the table fair warning. Surprising them won't help, because there's a chance they will freeze in the face of countering the prevailing wisdom, or they won't have enough time to come up with a thoughtful alternative idea. It's an easy meeting-management fix that will signal that unsuspecting person on your left that, in three minutes or less, she'll be on the hook to say something. And she'll know that the something she should say has to relate to a question about the initial analytic line. She doesn't have to stick her neck out questioning the experts, not when everyone around the table, starting with the chair, is required to do the same thing.

Also, if you're at the head of the table, you're welcome to ask the general question that might typically kick off this kind of conversation, something like "So, what does everyone think about this?" At one or two points during the discussion, though, go around the table and ask every single participant for his or her individual view: What do *you* think? The psychology of some participants will lead to silence if you don't direct questions at each individual. Some people around that table won't believe you're really soliciting their input when you ask the entire group a question. It's the experts who are supposed to answer, not me, they might think; he's not really asking for *my* opinion. But if you go around the table and ask each individual for thoughts, you will find that a surprising number might offer insights that you would have missed if you'd just asked the group collectively for their views.

A HEAD GAME PRACTICE EXERCISE:
THE CASE OF INDIA'S NUCLEAR TEST

It's 1998, and Washington is facing a new, relatively unknown cadre of political leaders in New Delhi who are riding a surge of popular support that swept them to the prime ministership. These new, nationalist leaders have made India's nuclear policy—more specifically, whether India should join the exclusive club of nations with a declared nuclear weapons capability—part of their electoral platform, and they've now got to determine whether to act on their pledges. How will they decide? And when?

Already, by asking just a few basic questions, we have a few red flags that should signal that we're on analytic thin ice. First, we are dealing with sudden change (an unprecedented electoral victory for populists), with the prospect of more change in sight (a radical turn in India's nuclear policy). We know that analysts struggle to see change; this is a classic example during which analysts cannot expect to see all the twists and turns that will define the future. Second, we are dealing with intent, how Indian leaders whom we do not understand will think about whether to test. We know as analysts that intent is somewhere between difficult and impossible to assess with precision.

We should be heading into this period of Indian government decision-making with a healthy dose of humility, even trepidation. So once the core analytic team of analysts delivers its assessment, the red flags we've already noted should spark a conversation among analytic managers: Should there be a separate analytic team (a red team, in contrast to the team that conducted the mainstream analysis, the blue team) to try to look at this problem through a different lens? Should we assume our core analytic line is somehow vulnerable and put together different analytic lines—looking at the same drivers and using the same data—that will challenge us? We know we will be surprised somewhere in the future; we'd better do everything we can to anticipate the surprises that will come with any change this profound.

For the sake of practicing the red team process, we can look at India's decision to test a nuclear device in 1998. We can start with a quick list of the drivers we might have considered at that time:

- The domestic political scene. How would India's populace react to a test?
- The international environment. How would the international community respond?
- The traditional adversary. How would Pakistan, India's adversary since the two countries won independence in 1947, answer an Indian test?
- The engineers and scientists. Does India have the capability to conduct a successful test?

Those of us who were assessing this problem of India's stance on testing weren't working in an information vacuum. In fact, we knew quite a bit. I say "we" because I was among the many analysts watching this problem unfold in 1998. We all knew, for example, that Indian scientists and engineers had stepped up activity at the country's well-known nuclear testing site in the western Thar Desert. And we knew that the question of whether to test was a topic of discussion within the ruling nationalist party, so it wasn't as if we were asking an academic question. If decision makers among the elites in New Delhi were discussing a test, did they mean to take the next step?

The story we told wasn't analytically groundless, despite the fact that it turned out to be so mistaken. Indian government insiders were telling US officials that nuclear testing was on their agenda— after all, the newly elected politicians had raised the testing issue during the national election that had catapulted them to power. Those elections resulted in an unprecedented victory for these staunch Indian nationalists, their first-ever opportunity to take over the prime ministership of the world's largest democracy. Secret sources were saying the same thing. Party leaders would consider a test, they said—there was no question that they might eventually declare India as a nuclear state—but they were in no rush to judgment. Their policy process to decide the nuclear question would be deliberate, they told the Americans.

Meanwhile, US government intelligence specialists looking at activity around India's desert testing site made a few observations. India had the capability to test, without question. The country had conducted what was called a "peaceful nuclear explosion" at the same desert test site in 1974. By 1998, twenty-four years later, who would argue that India's advanced scientific and defense community had lost their nuclear know-how, or that the Indians somehow lacked the equipment and nuclear material to build another device?

This uncertain period in 1998 felt like a rerun of sorts. There had been stepped-up activity at the desert site during the mid-1990s, activity that was clearly visible to American satellites watching the well-known test area in the vast desert wasteland. That earlier activity had occurred under a previous Indian government that had been less nationalistic than this newly elected party in 1998. During that earlier period, armed with declassified satellite images of the activity, US officials had threatened international ostracism if the Indians proceeded with a test. Well, whether they listened or not to international pressure during that earlier period, that government didn't test. Here we were again, a few years later in 1998, badgering a new government about this same old issue using the same diplomatic pressure points.

That's a quick summary of some of the forces at play in the pretest period. Let's go back now to our driver baskets:

- **DOMESTIC POLITICS IN INDIA.** Yes, Indian politicians acknowledged that they thought the global nuclear club was discriminatory—big powers (the United States, France, Britain, China, Russia, etc.) had nuclear weapons, and these same governments told everyone else in the global club of nations that this exclusive club was closed. This understandably rubbed Indian nationalists the wrong way, especially when they lived in a neighborhood with nuclear-armed China to the north and nuclear-ambitious Pakistan to the west. We don't believe in the discriminatory international nuclear control regimes, they said.

- **NUCLEAR TEST SITE.** Yes, there was intensified activity at India's isolated desert test site. But our experts asked an interesting question. If the Indians, with one of the world's most advanced scientific communities, were going to bother to absorb the international criticism and sanctions that a test would trigger, why not add the kind of extensive diagnostic infrastructure at the test site to allow specialists to capture as much data as possible? Wouldn't we see more cabling around the test shaft? Wouldn't we see more diagnostic equipment? Wouldn't we see more of what we'd expect to see from any major nuclear test?

- **INTERNATIONAL SITUATION.** Yes, international pressure sometimes works, and threats such as sanctions could force politicians to realize that India's economy might suffer as a result of the political gesture of a test. India was slowly emerging as more than a Third World regional power, and India's emerging economy would suffer under post-test sanctions. Wouldn't the Indians try more diplomatic groundwork before a test, to see if they could limit the economic blowback? Wouldn't this new Indian government view the potential threat of sanctions as seriously as its predecessor had?

The flaws in this analysis are glaring, all these years later, just as they were glaring on that day when we first heard the news of the test at CIA Headquarters in Langley. I remember hearing the initial media reports and wanting in those first hours to believe that we weren't wrong, and that the news reports were somehow mistaken.

Even knowing today how we erred, I'm confident that we could not have arrived at a perfect answer in that sea of disinformation, misinformation, and contradiction. Despite what appears to be a simple analytic problem in retrospect—of course the new government was going to test to prove its nationalist credentials to a huge domestic audience—there was too much noise to be confident about that option. In retrospect, the Indians had the capability to test; popular opinion was wildly in favor of a test; and the inherently inward-looking, nationalistic party that had just won elections didn't much care about international repercussions. This analysis-in-hindsight sounds easy, but reality just wasn't that cut-and-dried. The answer that analysts (including me) offered at that time, before the test, wasn't as simple (and mistaken) as "No, they won't test." It was more, as I remember it, "US officials might have more time to press the new government against a test. It doesn't look like they're ready to test a device now, though they are thinking about it."

The differences between these judgments—test now or maybe test a little later—may seem subtle, but they aren't. Remember the early chapter on how to ask good questions: the correct question here, and in other similar cases, isn't a yes-or-no, black-or-white "Will they test?" The analyst's role in helping to narrow uncertainty for decision makers is much more subtle: If we can't honestly provide a clean yes/no answer, can we provide any sort of decision advantage? How about this question as an alternative:

- How much time do US policymakers have to work on this diplomatic headache? Where should this be on Washington's list of urgent priorities?

It's not worth belaboring this example. We all know what happened in India. The new nationalist leadership figured that they could cement their electoral gains quickly by testing, because the popular opinion they so craved was wildly in favor of India's entry into the nuclear club. The international opinion we analysts weighted so heavily—because we spent too much time thinking the people we were watching shared our worldview—was an afterthought for the new government. The constellation of US intelligence agencies, with their armies of analysts, was castigated for missing the test, and we went through blistering criticism in the media and on Capitol Hill. One primary reason we failed was classic: we fell prey to the old analytic trap, mirror-imaging. At least some of us judged, even without knowing the bias in our mindsets, that our thought processes about how we would weigh a test seemed so transparently logical that they should represent how India's new leaders were thinking.

The intelligence errors I've witnessed and participated in, including India's test in 1998, have at least one common characteristic: the errors do not stem from missing one little clue that was lost in the noise of bigger, less subtle clues. They stem from fundamental oversights in critical thinking. We didn't miss the placement of an extra cable at the test site, or some late-night political meeting in New Delhi at which Indian leaders suddenly changed direction. We missed the fact that a new party didn't much care about what the Americans thought, or what the blowback would be. Simply put, they meant what they said during their election campaign, and they saw no reason why Western powers should decide their nuclear status. They didn't state their immediate plans openly because they didn't want to hear all the grief they'd get, and many of the officials who spoke with US diplomats about the new government's plans probably didn't know what the inner circle was thinking anyway.

Here's what happened, looking at history through the lens of an analytic process. Here are our drivers again, this time reviewed in the 20/20 hindsight of knowing what the Indians ultimately did:

- **DOMESTIC POLITICS.** As it turned out, popular opinion was overwhelmingly supportive of testing. Among most Indians, entering the nuclear club was (and is) viewed as a national right. Further, the new nationalists held power for the first time, and they wanted to trumpet their nationalist credentials and differentiate themselves by playing the nuclear card. They also simply acted in a way that showed they were serious when they spoke of challenging the global nuclear status quo during the election campaign, though perhaps on a timeline that was different than they led outsiders to believe. The cresting wave of support for the party's decision after the test proved them right.

- **SENIOR LEADERSHIP.** Many party officials were telling US diplomats before the test that their decision would be studied, taken after careful consideration. We might have asked about this squishy issue of measuring the new party's intentions: Did the officials who were speaking to American diplomats have access to the insider decision-making process? And if they had this access, did they open up about the party's deliberations? The answer to both questions turned out to be equally simple: no. So, in short, those who pretended to be knowledgeable weren't, and those who were in the extremely tight decision-making circle didn't reveal their plans, no doubt partly because they didn't want a stream of foreign governments lining up to hammer them in advance of the test.

- **INTERNATIONAL PRESSURE.** Assuming that somebody else shares the same worldview as the United States might lead you to believe that the Indian leadership—perhaps like you and me—would be sensitive to international opinion, and to the prospect of international sanctions. The previous Indian administration had been; intelligence analysts had to presume that this pressure was one reason they'd backed off a test a few years earlier. Well, it turned out that the game had changed. The new leaders, the nationalists, were more inwardly focused, and far more interested in cementing their domestic base than in responding to global players who wanted to exclude them from a nuclear club that seemed discriminatory. We thought the new government would worry more about international sanctions and global censure. They didn't. Case closed.

- **TEST SITE PREPARATIONS.** There was substantial activity at the nuclear test site. This wasn't hard to see; the test site was well known, and it was out in the middle of the desert. So it was not hard to tell, in the middle of nowhere, when more equipment showed up. But the primary question the Indian leadership faced wasn't whether the amount of diagnostic equipment was sufficient for the scientists and engineers to take full advantage of the test. That was our own judgment. But it wasn't a fact, and it turned out that the Indians were far more focused on making a political point with a test than on gathering diagnostic data. In retrospect, we might have overemphasized the activity at the site as one of our drivers. If the Indian leadership wanted to test primarily for domestic political reasons, why should we have been so confident that technical considerations would be a critical driver? Furthermore, the United States had showed the Indians satellite photos of the test site a few years earlier, to prove that we knew they were heading down the testing road and to pressure them against conducting a test. The Indian leadership knew full well we'd watch the site; why, if you're intent on testing, increase international pressure against a test by signaling to the satellites that you are on the verge of exploding a device?

- PAKISTAN'S REACTION. Any expert watching South Asia at that time would have been concerned about a nuclear race between two old rivals, India and Pakistan, that had been at war three times since gaining independence in 1947. Why would you roll the dice by testing and potentially sparking an arms race, or worse? The new nationalists who took office in New Delhi despised the Pakistanis. They simply didn't care. They threw out old models. The thinking of US analysts, by contrast, was still shaped by old models, and old assumptions.

A team charged with alternative analysis might have stepped through the process in parallel as the mainstream analytic team made its judgments. Rather than simply reconstructing the entire analytic process, this second team might have started with a simple question. Not whether the initial analysis is correct—that's too easy, and it's unknowable. Try this:

- Some analysts think we have more time to press the Indian government. How confident should we be of this judgment?

With that as a start, the team might consider the key drivers that analysts already have assessed—with a hard-nosed team leader at the head of the table who won't be cowed by experts but will be swayed by facts. Here are just two of the key drivers we've already studied, with quick-and-dirty assessments of how an alternative team might have assessed each one:

- **ENGINEERING AT THE SITE.** Yes, we have a lot of data about what is going on at the site. But it tells us almost nothing about India's intent, beyond suggesting that somebody made a decision to upgrade the site's readiness. Further, we don't know whether the testing procedures that the engineers at the site follow look anything like what we're familiar with. Some experts might look at the mounds of data and make a quick decision that India isn't close to testing because the site preparation still has a way to go. That's a guess, though; it's not a fact. A red team might reach a different conclusion: Why are we confident we understand what the site preparations mean? This is at best a yellow light, and possibly a red.

- **SENIOR LEADERSHIP.** Some senior leaders talk about testing, but only as a process the new government will step through over time. Some experts might look at this and (understandably) draw a simple conclusion: this makes perfect sense. India's new leadership is heading in this direction, but they're going to ease their way into it, preparing foreign governments and the general population over time. Why are we so confident, though, that what we've heard reflects senior leaders' views? The comments we've heard come from officials below the prime minister's office. And when the prime minister spoke, during the election, he talked about joining the nuclear club. Again, with all the data we have here, based on countless conversations with pundits and politicians in India, we might give ourselves a green under leadership intentions. It's a red, though. We know what some officials say. We don't know whether what they say matches what they think. And we don't know whether either of these matches what the prime minister thinks.

This process wouldn't have predicted an Indian test. It might have led to greater circumspection in the final analysis, though, just as reviewing what we really knew about Iraqi WMD before the war, contrasted with what we thought, might have led to less certainty about Saddam's programs. Red teams often can't and shouldn't change analysis. They can, though, add a set of fresh eyes that helps analysts understand where they're overconfident, where they're ignoring gaps, and where they're explaining away anomalies.

———

In hindsight, major analytic errors look so basic. Of course the Indians might have been closer to a test than we thought. Of course the prospects of the shah's fall were higher. Of course Saddam's WMD program might have been a mirage. You would think that the analytic mistakes I've experienced and described suggest that the analysts who made up those teams were somehow inexperienced, or fundamentally flawed, or not that bright. Or not even analysts. Not true. In each of the cases I witnessed, the expertise around the table was superb, in terms of experience and knowledge but also in their relentless questioning of the data. Still, they missed, just as I missed.

These failures underscore a key point: no matter how good you are at the game of complex analysis, you need a set of checks and balances to hunt for flaws, biases, and levels of confidence that aren't merited by the underlying analysis or data. Whether you're going through the frustrations of red teaming, with an outside group checking your work, or simply looking for where you have yellow and red lights, you've got to have a way to hold up a mirror. Just look at the litany of analytic mistakes you've read about before you dismiss this rigor with a wave of the hand. "I wouldn't do that," you might say. "Yes, you would," I'd respond. "Just wait."

In Appendix B of this book, you will find original source documents from the world of intelligence that give you insights into how analysts made mistakes. Read the documents with one thought in mind. Before you dismiss the errors as the work of people who didn't meet a basic standard of analytic expertise, think again. They did. And they still erred. Learn from their mistakes.

CHAPTER SEVEN

THE FINISH LINE

We have gone through a handful of basic steps that comprise this simple analytic methodology, from trying to understand the needs of a decision maker through crafting good questions, deciding on drivers, and assessing data. In each chapter, examples highlight how these principles play out in real life. At the finish line, we should bring these threads back together, to outline all these practices in one place so that you can take an analytic problem and practice, using this chapter as a one-stop guide, and a refresher when you'd like to apply these principles without reading again through the entire book.

Think about this finish line as the horse-racing test. We are analyzing a race, and we know that we can't predict a winner. But we can look at a key question (How can I understand the characteristics of these horses in a way that gives me a greater chance of success?) in a way that summarizes the concepts in this book. So let's start there.

In contrast to its prominence in decades past, horse racing in America is not a spectator sport many Americans would rank among their primary pastimes today. Except, that is, during the Kentucky Derby: put your outrageous party hat on, find some outlandish clothes, and muddle some fresh mint to mix a few traditional mint julep cocktails. Then, if you haven't overindulged in the juleps, sit down to watch the ponies. The Derby, of course, only lasts a few minutes. It's the party-time ambience that counts. That, and the hours and days of lead-up during which tens of millions of us pretend that we understand horse racing well enough to place a few bets.

We might be among the tiny horse-fanatic fraternity that actually grades the horses based on some serious analytic work using the *Racing Form*, the standard compilation of horses' performance that looks like the stock market pages of your daily newspaper. If we're among the vast majority of the population, though, we might make a barely educated guess about the outcome. Better yet, we might simply pick a horse based on the color of the jockey's racing silks. Who needs a complex formula to pick a horse when you can just place a bet based on whether you like pink or blue?

When we pick that horse, we are making a point prediction, someplace between a guess and a sophisticated, fact-based analysis about which horse will win. When we decide, as we're assessing an ongoing insurgency, whether the government or the revolutionaries will win, we're doing the same thing, passing judgment about the precise trajectory of the future. But whether we're picking winners among horses or revolutionary insurgents, we're taking a step that is inherently speculative. We're assuming that because we are experts, or pretend experts, we have not only the capability but the responsibility to predict a precise outcome, from the name of the horse to the outcome of the insurgency. If you have spent a lifetime studying insurgencies and someone asks you who will prevail in Syria, what do you say? "No comment, I'm busy assessing this"? Or "I don't know"? If we are advising the president on the prospects for an insurgency where America has an interest, shouldn't we feel compelled to explain which outcome we anticipate? Who we think will come out on top? Which horse we are betting on?

We might offer this kind of precise answer, but we don't have to: we can provide a different answer, and base that answer on an analytically sound process, even if we don't take the step of taking a shot at a point prediction. As we have discussed earlier, experts are the worst at predicting tomorrow; they are anchored in the past and therefore challenged to explain how the picture they drew to explain the past can change to explain tomorrow. By providing point predictions, especially when we are talking to nonexperts who think our expertise gives us a crystal ball, we risk offering to the decision maker a false sense of certitude and security that we shouldn't pretend to offer. We don't know which horse will win the Kentucky Derby, any more than we know with certainty during an uprising whether it's the insurgents or the government who will win. Unfortunately, because we're supposed to be the pros at picking the horse, or the winner in the insurgency, the decision maker might reach the conclusion, falsely, that our predictions are likely to be true. As history shows, again and again, they're not.

In real life, of course, there is a point at which we will have to make choices based on predictions. Are we going to buy a stock or not? Is the company a good investment? Or, for the publisher of this book, is the book worth investing in or not? Yes or no? Make a decision, you might say; we can't dawdle forever.

That final decision, though, shouldn't be confused with the analytic process we undertake to try to reduce uncertainty before we make the choice. The analytic process helps squeeze a little uncertainty out of the choice; the choice itself, though, still leaves us betting on a future outcome that we can't really predict.

We can look at drivers to assess whether a company has the characteristics we want in a potential investment, maybe judging that we're 60 percent confident in the pick. We may still buy, but not because our analytic process gave us a simplistic, bold prediction that guarantees we're right. Furthermore, because we're dealing with uncertainty, we might attach metrics to our "buy" choice—if we don't see an increase in profits within twelve months, for example, maybe we should take another look at the investment—to ensure that we ask whether that 60 percent confidence was too low, or too high.

The process we undertake, then, gives us both the confidence to understand that we're making the soundest analytic choice we can and the humility to know that the choice we've made is never going to be based on perfect knowledge.

In sports, you might equate this to a coach who prepares a team in each aspect of the game but can't guarantee that the preparation will ensure success. Instead, that coach tries to ensure that the team has developed skills in those aspects of the game that are most critical to success. Even then, though, that team might lose, just as you might work through a difficult analytic process to assess a stock or an insurgency and still find that you have to make major adjustments along the way.

Success lies in reducing uncertainty—in subtracting elements that are extraneous and focusing on those areas that are most important, including areas that represent gaps in your knowledge. Practicing these exercises will become part of your success; training your mind through this analytic path will help you analyze problems more clearly than you could by applying a less organized, more intuitive approach based only on expert knowledge.

Above, I selected the coach/team example for a reason. John Wooden, one of the most legendary coaches in the history of college sports, preached the importance of preparation and process. He led UCLA's basketball team to eighty-eight consecutive wins during one stretch, and eleven national collegiate titles during the 1960s and early 1970s. Here's what he said:

We live in a society obsessed with winning and being number 1. Don't follow the pack. Rather, focus on the process instead of the prize. Even during the height of UCLA's best seasons, I never fixated on winning—didn't even mention it. Rather, I did everything I could to make sure that all our players gave everything they had to give, both in practice and in games. The score will take care of itself when you take care of the effort that precedes the score.

———

It will be hard to stick to this taxing, time-consuming analytic methodology over the long term. Let's face it: you're almost certainly not going to read this book again, and trying to remember these steps even a week after finishing the book would be difficult for just about anyone. To me, the steps have become second nature, but that's only after decades of work—first learning ways to think as a result of successes and failures, and then applying those lessons by building a simple series of steps that only took shape over more than two decades as a professional analyst and manager of analysts.

We can close, though, with a shortcut that might give you a fighting chance of applying these lessons, and maybe even absorbing them so that you don't have to refer back to this book to remember. What follows is a sort of cheat sheet, a quick checklist that you can use to guide you through an analytic problem. We'll go back to the beginning of the analytic process that started the book, thinking backward and then working through drivers.

First, let's return to the complex question of terrorism, a subject that defined American foreign policy—and drove debate on domestic policies from civil liberties to taking off your shoes at airport security checkpoints—during the first decade of this century.

We should begin with a question that you might have asked before you started this book: Should we worry about terrorist attacks in America? It's a question we used earlier, and we're returning to it here to prove a point. It's not the right question, but neither is it a bad start; there's nothing wrong with kicking this one around when you're talking with friends. We should begin by thinking backward, using this question as our starting point. We have to keep working on it, though, because it's a classic yes-or-no, black-and-white question that doesn't allow for much analysis. Keep going: break the problem down in a different way, but not until you pause for a moment and answer the question yourself. What do you think? And why?

Spend a minute reflecting on where we should start. Then break away from the exercise, clear your mind, and try to come at the issue from a different angle, adding the context of everything else you think you should worry about in everyday life. You might be concerned about terrorism. Who wouldn't be? It's an issue that once dominated my life. Maybe both of us think (and we're not wrong) that terrorists murder innocent people with a randomness that is chilling. Terror incidents dominate the airwaves whenever terrorists strike in the United States, regardless of the extent of the attack. Terrorists attack without warning, and with brutal and bloody consequences, including loss of life and casualties among innocents that are hard to stomach, much less understand. This phenomenon of terrorism might have already affected a few of us personally.

As we analyze the problem of terrorism in our own lives, we might go back to the original principal of analysis: What kind of decision advantage can we gain through the analysis? For this question, the decision might be something like the following: Is terrorism an issue I think I should spend a lot of time worrying about? Is it something that should decide my vote on election day? How heavily should the government weigh counterterrorism programs when Congress and the White House negotiate budgets? How does terrorism stack up against education, health care, roads and bridges, and conventional defense against long-term threats such as China? These are times of budgetary shortfalls and tough decisions about where to spend federal tax dollars. Many among Washington's national security experts wonder whether we overinvested in counterterrorism programs during the first decade-plus of the global counterterror campaign.

One thing is certain: in answering the question, the first instinct of many citizens might be to pull out whatever is foremost in their brains, or whatever (sometimes the same thing) appeared most recently in the news. This isn't wrong; it's how the human brain is wired—it's the old problem of availability bias. Somebody might wonder: How, then, could the answer to our question be anything but a firm "yes"? The proof for that quick answer might be as follows.

- The FBI still breaks up terror plots pretty regularly in the United States.
- We're vulnerable because we can't secure everything in a free society, as we witnessed in the Boston marathon bombings in the spring of 2013.
- There is still a lot of extremist activity around the world, from Asia through Africa and into Europe—with much of this activity, along with its core ideology, directed at America.

These may not be the reasons any respondent would cite directly in answering the question, but it's a safe bet that a substantial number of respondents would quickly answer, "Yes, I should worry quite a bit," based on a cursory review of factors like the ones listed above. That's a rapid, gut-feeling thought process, though; it's not an analysis. Further, the respondent who answers this way, because of a bias embedded in the emotional content of the question (How could you argue anything but that the killing of innocents is a serious threat?) might be equally confident in challenging anyone who would judge differently: How can you say this isn't a huge issue? Don't you care about the children who have been killed and wounded? By allowing a yes/no question, you give the advantage to a respondent who wants to play the emotion card.

It's important to point out, as we start this final practice exercise, that handling this question with a colder analytic approach might appear to be inhumanely unemotional. This is a false argument. You can say, analytically, that the loss of a hundred, or a thousand, children to an influenza epidemic doesn't have a significant impact on the economy, population growth, or the well-being of the general population. This is true. This analytic judgment, though, has nothing to do with the human tragedy that follows the loss of a child, and the resources we might spend to prevent the loss of life of even a statistically small number of children. The two, analysis and emotion, are clearly separate; in this case, emotion rightly wins, even if analysis tells you that the flu isn't a major cause of death in America.

With that in mind, let's go back to the question we started with. Should we worry about terrorism in America as much as we do? First, you should be saying that this violates the yes/no principle. Just adding the word "how" to many questions results in more open-ended, less yes/no, analysis. Here's the switch: How much should we worry about terrorism? How should we rank it among our list of concerns? Already, we're into a format that allows you to respond beyond the simplistic "of course" answer you might give to a yes/no "Should we worry about terrorism?" question. Rather than simply look at our first gut reaction to the terrorism question we started with—of course terrorism is a threat!—we're onto something more analytic, and subtle. How much should we worry? How should we rank this problem, beside all the other stuff life throws at us?

The framing, though, still isn't perfect; it's too vague. What does "worry" mean? Worry about the United States and its vulnerability to another catastrophic attack? Worry that some one-off terrorist might shoot shoppers in a mall? Worry that one single innocent

American somewhere around the world might die in a random strike sometime this year? Or worry, at a personal level, that you or your family might be at risk? This framing-the-question business is a pain. It takes a lot of effort to whittle away until we arrive at a good question that adequately captures whatever is at the heart of our concern. But remember the example of the road map: if we don't invest more time in figuring out where we're going, we're going to waste a lot of time getting to our final destination.

Let's say you've just seen cable news reports of an attempted terror attack on an airliner halfway across the country, and the reports have sparked fresh concerns in your mind about how vulnerable you feel. You're worried, maybe, because terrorists are still present in America, and they can clearly attack at random. They're persistent, and they represent an incomprehensible and odious ideology that not only contemplates but embraces the murder of innocents for some vague political purpose. So there's a start. Rather than a general question about whether terrorism is a threat to society, what about asking the following: How much should I personally worry? As we step through the exercise, note how quickly we can change the question in a way that would lead to a fundamentally different answer. Side by side with the original question, consider another: How much should I worry if I live in lower Manhattan? Frame the question carefully. Even minor adjustments might alter your conclusion markedly.

We'll use this as a starting point, or a reference point, through the checklist that follows in Appendix B. You can try to envision a scenario in which you're running through your own personal views and analysis of what you think about this question. The checklist is meant to be your guide for any type of analytic problem you're facing, but applying it to this question of ranking the importance of terrorism may help you anchor these questions in a real-world problem that makes sense of the list.

Have some fun with these exercises, and have fun as you try to apply this methodology at your workplace or in everyday life. Play around with simple questions first, from why you like a certain house or neighborhood to what kinds of cars you find attractive. Try it on more personal questions. What kinds of people do you find attractive, and why? What cities do you like, and why? Once you feel you're gaining a little confidence in defining questions clearly and breaking down those questions into driver categories, you can shift to harder questions, maybe questions you're facing at the office.

Finally, don't get discouraged. Remember the exercise book that is supposed to help tone your body: you can read it again and again, but when you go out and apply the exercise principles, your body hurts. Your muscles ache. You want to stop. You think the program might be helpful for somebody else, but not you. The same holds true for your mind. You'll want to stop, to slip back into the easier expert analysis you used to live with. Keep the faith, though. This will work, with patience. That patience also will come with the understanding that you'll never be perfect, and you shouldn't even try. Tomorrow is unknowable, and to think that we can see change happening with clarity is a myth.

When you get discouraged, remember part of the foundation of this book: the mistakes of assessing Saddam and WMD; the mistakes of election prognosticators who missed the rise of presidential candidates; the lack of vision of statesmen and politicians who couldn't imagine another world war; energy experts who predicted the end of cheap oil, again and again and again; and experts who insisted that the sun revolved around the earth. Even the most talented people make mistakes. What you have now, though, is a tool that will give you the only answer there is after these painful failures: *I tried my best. I trained my mind, and the world just turned out differently.* Go back to the drawing board and try again; this is a process of self-improvement that never ends.

WHERE ARE THE TRAPS? THOUGHTS ON BIAS

Think of yourself slowly working your way through a crowd at a friend's cocktail party, meeting a few people you know along the way and occasionally stopping as you're stalled in a human bottleneck on the way to the bar. You strike up a conversation with a stranger. "Are you a friend of the host?" you might ask. "Yes," comes the answer, "we became friends after working together for a few years. We both research how humans might respond to prolonged travel in space." *Whoa*, you think to yourself. *I started a random conversation on a trip to the bar and I stumbled on a guest with a fascinating story. This almost never happens!* You immediately pick up on the conversation. "That's really interesting," you respond. "What are you learning in your research?"

You're anticipating that you'll get to hear a specialist's unique insights into a field that might mushroom in years to come, if humans choose to invest in space travel beyond the moon. Instead, what you get is some form of the following: "What we are learning is mostly how much we don't know. We don't have a good way to conduct experiments. We don't have any methods by which we can look at historical precedents. We don't have a sample size that's meaningful." In other words, we know a lot about what we don't know.

At this point, you might quickly decide that, in contrast to your earlier hope that this might be a great cocktail conversation, you'd rather try to reach your original destination, the bar. *That's it?"* you ask yourself. *I was prepared for insights into interplanetary travel and I get a detour into everything this person doesn't know?*

The analytic point here is that when we spend our lives on a subject, whether it's space travel, counterterrorism, or anything else, we want to weave a narrative that adds context and sense to the facts we have at our fingertips, regardless of whether these facts fit together analytically. You want to know about why the stock market reacts as it does? Ask a stockbroker, and you'll likely get a detailed answer that suggests a high (and maybe misleading) level of confidence in understanding stocks. You want to know how to treat some form of cancer? Ask a cancer specialist, and you'll likely hear an extended explanation of new research, drug patents, and potential cures. But you would have to ask pointedly about knowledge gaps to hear an answer that exposes areas about which these same experts lack knowledge. Human beings engage, as a default, in what we might call "dependent" analysis: they take whatever bits and pieces of information they have, and they build an analytic framework, or an entire narrative, that depends on this limited pool of information. This sort of analysis is the expert's equivalent of an oyster building a pearl around a bit of sand.

There's great analytic risk in the overstatement of knowledge, because it will lead us not only to overestimate how much we know, but also to overestimate the level of confidence we have in the conclusions we draw from our limited pools of knowledge. If you're living the earlier cocktail party scenario, you might be disappointed that the expert reveals such a limited understanding of a fascinating topic. If you're in the midst of an analytic exercise, though, you should be energized by the chance to grapple with the unknown. Analysts have to watch out for what we might call the illusion of knowledge. Some of this illusion is avoidable, if we're conscious enough about the games our minds play.

We're all illusionists in some part of our lives. Think of fad dieters. If someone told you that you could stay in great shape and eat whatever you want, without ever having to work out or diet, what would you say? It would be like living with the kind of metabolism you had back during your teen years, when calories meant nothing. An all-you-can-eat diet, with all the benefits and none of the pain of conventional diets, sounds like a terrific deal. It's not realistic, though, and we should know that anyone trying to sell us this kind of pain-free weight loss program is fraudulent.

As smart as we humans are, however, we let our minds fool us every day, and there are a lot of people out there making untold millions by cashing in on the vulnerabilities of the human mind. Even when we *know* we're being fooled, we still take the bait. At one and the same time, we can understand that a flashy diet plan is too good to be true but also buy into the silver-bullet sales pitch that is at the heart of the endless series of diet books. Deep down, we know the truth—that only pain equals success in losing weight and maintaining fitness—but we persuade ourselves that maybe, just maybe, this diet is the one that produces pain-free results. And then the new diet book we just bought falls off the *New York Times* bestseller list and into the discount remainder bin at the bookstore when the next perfect diet solution hits the presses.

Fake diets that allow us to think we can lose weight without real discomfort are just the start of it. The height of absurdity is the mental game we play on the Las Vegas Strip. We know that the casino has an advantage over us when we walk to the blackjack table, but we also secretly think that we are the ones who can beat the house and win. This hope is all well and good, if you're hoping for that special one-night run that is not statistically relevant. This hope is not fine, though, as a general rule, unless you're a card-counter. Try translating your one-night run into a full-time job and six months later you'll find yourself joining Gamblers Anonymous. Have you looked at the opulence of the hotels that host gambling casinos? And the cash flows they generate? Where are we supposed to think that cash comes from? All of us! The same grandiosity of the Vegas Strip that attracts us also screams out that we are falling for a scam, and yet the human mind still allows us to believe that we're the lucky ones. Doublethink, it's called, or the uniquely human ability to hold two contradictory views at the same time.

Our minds, in other words, play tricks on us if we're not paying close attention, and we're sometimes vulnerable even when we know full well that we're being misled. If we learn to shift these tricks from the unconscious into consciousness, we can at least be aware of the devil of mind traps, even if we don't ever fully exorcise them.

AVAILABILITY BIAS

We can open with one of the most common challenges. It's a good starting point because if you keep this one in your mind for just a day or two and listen to your friends or co-workers talk, you are guaranteed to see examples of this bias everywhere you turn. Experts on thinking, psychology, and human behavior call it "availability bias."

When we face a problem, our minds naturally turn to the first available piece of information we can access so that we don't have to spend a lot of time sorting through the cluttered attic of our minds, whether we're working through a complex problem or choosing which restaurant to visit tonight. If this sounds a bit too simplistic for this book, it's not. Not because you somehow lack the will, or the talent, to avoid bias, but because this particular version is so deeply ingrained in who we are as humans that we can't help but fall into its trap.

Before we get into a complex problem, we can look at the question of how we choose restaurants and come up with an example that will drive home the concept of availability bias. It's a Saturday morning, and you're reading the weekend section of the local newspaper, with its pullout section on concerts, first-run movies, plays, outdoor activities, and, of course, restaurants. There's a feature on a new Italian place not far from where you live. You and your friends are planning on dinner that night and begin e-mailing about where to meet, and you, having just read about the Italian place, mention it right away. Why? Well, one reason might be that the review was great—fresh pasta, maybe, and superb clams. The restaurant might be convenient for the group, centrally located.

Another reason you default to the restaurant is that it's the first available option that pops up in your mind, which goes through its freshest memories of restaurants and comes up, without spending a lot of energy, with the last restaurant memory you stored. There is, of course, the alternative of taking additional steps to pick the perfect place. You could sit down for a few minutes, run through your mental Rolodex of every place you've eaten in the area, think about which places match the interests of the group (price, location, decor, noise level, style of food, etc.). You could also get on the Web and search this year's reviews from the local food critic. The bottom line, though, is that all of these burn mental energy; if we want the easy option, because we're anxious to close out on this decision and head off to run the day's errands, we might well turn to the first thing that comes to mind. We're biased to what our minds serve up, which is typically going to be the first available memory. That's availability bias.

This bias isn't, of course, limited to weekend dining. We make these kinds of quick decisions every day, without going through the pain of serious thinking.

At work, too, when we're faced with either focusing on what

we know or scratching our heads and highlighting where we lack enough information to make solid judgments, most of us will stick with the former. If we're experts on the stock market, for example, leading a conversation about how to play the market by starting with the market's vagaries and the unknowns in stock-picking might well result in muddled decision-making—if we don't know much, how in the world are we supposed to make choices? That in turn would lead to a generally depressing professional life. We'd be concluding, day after day, that after a lifetime of building expertise, we just don't know enough about our supposed area of expertise to make any sound choices.

The same might hold true for national security analysis. If we are studying the intentions of North Korea's reclusive leadership, we might look at the limited statements they have issued and come up with perfectly valid conclusions that are based on that minimal sample size. These public statements are readily available to you, but they don't say much about what the leaders actually discuss when they meet in closed sessions. In circumstances where our range of information is limited, we should watch out for availability bias: because we want to make sense of the world, we focus on the information that is immediately available, without spending much time on the huge slice of the pie that's beyond our reach. We have at our fingertips a few statements by the North Korean leadership, so we'll use them as the basis for analysis of Pyongyang's intent. Why do we think these statements are representative? They may not be, but they're what's easily available.

There's nothing wrong with this, as long as we spend a fair amount of time thinking about the areas about which we know nothing, and then reflecting this in our written or oral analyses. Think of this as looking through the meager groceries in your refrigerator and designing a minimalist menu versus visiting a gourmet grocery store and surveying all the opportunities for extravagant menus: there's nothing wrong with making dinner from leftover noodles and canned tomato sauce, but you shouldn't pretend that the menu you come up with, based on the available ingredients, is the best menu. It isn't. It's just what's available at that moment.

We faced this at the CIA every day, especially in the early years after 9/11, because we had significant gaps in our knowledge about an adversary that was consuming the entire US Intelligence Community. Some of this huge knowledge gap closed in the spring of 2002, when the CIA captured, detained, and interrogated Abu Zubaydah, at that time by far the highest-level al-Qa'ida member we CIA interrogators had been able to talk to. Every day, CIA analysts, as they had done for decades, assembled a collection of intelligence articles for the president and his advisers, focusing on events as diverse as drug trafficking and global population trends. In the post-9/11 years, that compilation of intelligence articles known as the President's Daily Brief was heavily oriented toward al-Qa'ida, and I helped manage the office that produced al-Qa'ida analysis. So when Zubaydah started talking, we knew that we had an Oval Office readership who would want to know, in great detail, what he said. We did terrorism all day, every day, and terrorism was on the front pages of every newspaper in America for years. We had to fill up the PDB.

This is all well and good, except that the laser focus on that single thread of available information—the Abu Zubaydah interrogations—by definition leads to analysis that lacks perspective. There's a catch here, though: we didn't have the option of saying that despite Abu Zubaydah's revelations, we still suffered from huge knowledge gaps that prevented us from making sound judgments about al-Qa'ida's activities, particularly if you're skeptical (and who wouldn't be?) about the truthfulness of a detainee's revelations. So we depended on the bane of all intelligence analysts: single-threaded analysis, or analysis that is dependent on only one source. We stuck with what was available, on issues such as al-Qa'ida threat plotting and the status of the group's hierarchy, because that's what we had. As long as you know what you're getting into, this is fine—after all, can you imagine saying, in that heated environment, "Hey, we think we'll wait a year or two to assess what Abu Zubaydah says, so we can gather enough additional context to put his comments in perspective"? Just be sure to remember that you're working under the influence of the availability bias.

SAMPLING BIAS AND ANECDOTE BIAS

If you believe that sample size is some theoretical problem that only statisticians have to worry about, think again. You only need to consider about a day's worth of work or personal experiences to come up with examples that will highlight the pervasive effect of what we might call "sampling bias" on analysis. We tend to take statistically small, or even irrelevant, numbers of examples and use them to claim that they prove some sort of rule, and that they represent a sample that's valid enough to reach a conclusion.

The classic example goes something like this: "Both my grandfathers were heavy smokers, and both of them lived well into their nineties." Now, without saying as much, what does this statement imply? That a lifetime of heavy smoking might not shorten life, and that a sample size of two helps prove the point. In reality, however, all it proves is that two men beat the odds—the same way you might beat the odds, for one night, in Vegas. The sample size of two might make for interesting cocktail conversation, but it has no place in analysis. It's statistically irrelevant.

We fall victim to this in our personal lives, too. If you visit the northeastern United States during the cool fall months, you might experience the beauty of brilliant leaf colors and crisp, bright blue skies. If you visit South Florida, however, you're more likely to experience hot, humid weather and temperatures that will shift between vaguely uncomfortable and downright scorching. While running in this humidity with a friend once—as I was enjoying an autumn visit to my hometown of Coral Gables, Florida—my visiting friend asked an interesting question: Is the incidence of hay fever lower in the damp air of South Florida than it would be in drier, northeastern air? Might the humidity help eliminate the air of the tiny particles that cause hay fever and that might circulate more widely in dry air?

I don't know the answer now, and I didn't then. My immediate reaction, though, was to fill the void with an answer based on family experience: my sister had horrible allergies, and we lived in South Florida during her childhood. I almost offered this answer, but even in that split second, the analyst in me took over. It's fine to keep the conversation going by explaining my sister's experience, I thought, but what the heck does that sample size of one (my sister) say about allergies in humid zones? Anecdotes like this are part of the bread-and-butter for great everyday conversation. How would we live without them? But for serious analysis, it's important to recognize that this unconscious willingness to cite one or two episodes as sufficient for drawing a conclusion is analytically nutty. Watch out for this. We're all victims.

Maybe you're still not convinced of how prevalent this sampling error is in everyday life. So let's go to a more sensitive question that consumed America after the debacle that was the start of the Affordable Care Act. Before we begin, let me assuage your concerns: this isn't about whether you like this law or not. Instead, it's about the analysis of the law that we witnessed on air every day for seemingly endless weeks after it went into effect in late 2013. Flip on the TV to a congressional hearing during those months and you'd often hear comments that might go something like this:

- "Here's a letter from a constituent who tried for three days to get access to the Obamacare website and failed every time. And here's another letter from a constituent who is going to suffer lost coverage as a result of the law."
- "Here's a letter from a constituent whose family now has affordable insurance because of this law. And here's another letter from a constituent who had a preexisting condition that previously prevented him from getting insurance."

Each of us, you and me, reacts to these comments with some sort of righteous indignation, depending on which side of the fence we find ourselves on. That's the point: whichever member of Congress is reading these kinds of statements is trying to tug at our heartstrings—that's what they do, after all—to elicit a human reaction. Subtly, though, they're also trying to suggest that these individual letters represent the whole story. And that might be true! But there's just no way we can make good analytic judgments based on a sample size of two letters, like it or not. You can have your heartstrings pulled by these kinds of everyday events. Just be conscious that you have to distinguish between your heartstrings and a defensible analytic judgment.

These two issues—how we react to problems and whether our reaction is analytically sound—are mixed up every day. We might refer to this as the "anecdote bias."

A thousand anecdotes might pile up to become a statistically relevant observation, but one or two anecdotes don't amount to more than an interesting side note that, at best, might possibly merit further study. The reason should be pretty evident by now. These anecdotes mix valid emotions—what happened to one family might be tragic, or outrageous, or simply unacceptable—with more statistically valid analysis, which typically can't be based on just one incident or example.

This problem with sample size isn't limited to nonexperts who aren't comfortable with statistics, though. Following is an excerpt from one of the leading experts on analytic thinking, Nobel Prize winner Daniel Kahneman, whose book *Thinking, Fast and Slow* offers a comprehensive look at different ways your mind will mislead you:

The risk of error can be estimated for any given sample size by a fairly simple procedure. Traditionally, however, psychologists do not use calculations to determine sample size. They use their judgment, which is commonly flawed. An article I had read shortly before the debate with Amos [Kahneman's research partner] demonstrated the mistake that researchers made (they still do) by a dramatic observation. The author pointed out that psychologists commonly chose samples so small that they exposed themselves to a 50% risk of failing to confirm their true hypotheses! No researcher in his right mind would accept such a risk. A plausible explanation was that psychologists' decisions about sample size reflected prevalent intuitive misconceptions of the extent of sampling variation.

The article shocked me, because it explained some troubles I had had in my own research. Like most research psychologists, I had routinely chosen samples that were too small and had often obtained results that made no sense. Now I knew why: the odd results were actually artifacts of my research method. My mistake was particularly embarrassing because I taught statistics and knew how to compute the sample size that would reduce the risk of failure to an acceptable level. But I had never chosen a sample size by computation. Like my colleagues, I had trusted tradition and my intuition in planning my experiences and had never thought seriously about the issue. When Amos visited the seminar, I had already reached the conclusion that my intuitions were deficient.*

This error is so common that you can listen to conversations almost every day and find evidence of it. "I talked to two people who said he's a jerk," you might hear. Or "Somebody told me that's a great city to visit." Both are valid conversation points, and both are valid data points to consider when you're making a decision. But neither represents a valid statistical sample, despite our inclination to weigh these kinds of anecdotal observations as if they were valid, statistically relevant data.

PERSONAL OBSERVATION:
THE SAMPLE SIZE OF ONE

The most prevalent pitfall we fall into is the belief that what we have experienced or observed in our own lives somehow merits greater consideration than other sources of information that might be more statistically relevant but less colorful. Even if we have some idea that small sample sizes skew analysis, we can easily become victim to the sample size of one: while everybody else's opinion is interesting, ours is somehow particularly telling, and statistically relevant.

This tendency is perfectly understandable. First, we all like to think that we're good observers of humanity. We think our experiences have inherent value, simply because they come from a trusted, highly observant reporter—us! Second, what we experience firsthand doesn't come from impersonal reports, studies, or polls. Our

---

* Daniel Kahneman, *Thinking, Fast and Slow* (New York: Farrar, Straus and Giroux, 2012), 112–13.

experiences are more vibrant because we experienced something live, saw it with our own eyes and heard it with our own ears, and what we experienced is therefore (at least for us) more compelling than something we only read or heard about.

If executives in your investment firm are weighing whether to buy stock in different companies across West Africa, for example, one of the executives might fly to Lagos, Nigeria, for a tour of a few regional capitals. When he returns to the office, we all know what happens next. Someone at the investment meeting to discuss prospects in West Africa hands out a package of information about political stability in the region, levels of violence across different countries, infrastructure shortfalls in possible areas of investment, tax and regulatory issues that limit foreign investment, and so on. These are perfectly legitimate factors to weigh, of course, even critical ones that any thoughtful organization would have to consider as its leaders conduct due diligence leading up to an investment decision.

How many times, though, does the one executive who recently returned from the region then start the next phase of the conversation with "When I was there . . ." On the one hand, interjecting this personal commentary into the conversation might be useful—there could be unique observations related to the region that only firsthand observation can offer. For example, if the company has settled on a few key potential investments, personal meetings with their senior leadership might offer a sense of whether potential partners with impressive paper backgrounds seem as impressive in person.

In looking at broader observations, though, such as political unrest or economic conditions, the bias of the one-person sample size is worth watching out for. I remember visiting Baghdad not long after the Iraqi invasion and heading to a noted Lebanese restaurant downtown (with a security escort!) for dinner. My personal observation was that the capital seemed remarkably peaceful, and I didn't

get much of a sense of unease. Contrast that single personal experience with the tragedy of Iraq since, and you have a compelling
example of why the bias of one can be helpful in limited situations
but harmful in most analysis.

Think back to the discussion about sample sizes. The sample
size error is compounded when it's coupled with the personal experience of someone you know. You pass a longtime friend on the
street and start talking about movies. "I just saw a terrific film,"
she says. "You should see it." Her opinion influences you because
you've known her for years. Nonetheless, she's a sample size of one,
passing judgment on a subject—the quality of a movie—that is a
matter of personal taste. Sure, go see the movie. Just be conscious
of how your personal bias is playing into your decision. Would you
choose a restaurant based on a website that had one diner's review?
I hope not.

HALO EFFECT

When you look through the collections of new wall calendars at the
start of each year, you're guaranteed to see a fair number that play
on common themes. Puppies and kittens are always popular. So are
waterfalls or other water scenes—beaches, lakes, rivers, streams.
You'll also see sunsets and flowers, and beautiful natural vistas, from
the Grand Canyon to maple leaves changing to gold in Vermont.
And, of course, you might see funny pictures of babies. Because,
we all know, everybody likes infants. Who couldn't? Everything
they do is adorable. Unless they are screaming, walking around in
droopy diapers, or waking up for another feeding at 3 a.m. Even
then, we write off the negatives because babies are so darned cute;
on bad days and good, babies are adorable. This is the positive side
of the halo effect.

This same halo phenomenon affects almost everyone in high

school. What happens after the initial awkward dancing around before you admit that you actually like each other? When you're in the moment of that budding high school romance, the halo effect is mesmerizing. Every action is cute, loving, and precious, and somehow fits into your concept that this is the perfect romance with the perfect person, and that the relationship will remain perfect for the near future and beyond.

Until some habit that initially seemed precious becomes so annoying that you can't stand it anymore. If you haven't gone through this, when the perfect quirks of a new crush turn into fingernails on a chalkboard, you no doubt know others who have. Similarly, those of us who are fans of a particular professional sports franchise might feel some wellspring of support for our hometown team, regardless of the fact that our favorite team hasn't shown a sign of life in five, ten, or twenty years. Betting experts will tell you to avoid wagering on your favorite; you're inclined to downplay the team's weaknesses and overplay its strengths. The halo effect, in this case, might have you betting with your heart, not your head.

These are fun ways to characterize the halo effect, but we shouldn't dismiss this common human analytic weakness as purely humorous, or limited to grandparents and first crushes in high school. During debates about the invasion of Iraq, it's safe to assume that some sophisticated and experienced policymakers around senior decision-making tables in Washington thought that the Iraqi people would welcome US forces with open arms. In some ways, our perceptions of Saddam Husayn were colored by a reverse halo effect: there was nothing he could do that wasn't borderline evil. No doubt he was an evil man—he gassed his own people, after all, using chemical weapons.

If we allow the emotional response we might have to his most barbarous actions, though, we fail to allow for an unvarnished, unemotional analysis that would put Saddam in context: yes, evil. But when we make our side wear white hats and characterize the other side as black hats, we risk transferring our emotional investment in a problem into our analytic judgments. This division is harder in practice than it is in theory. It requires us to set aside moral views and substitute a colder, less judgmental analytic lens that will help us see the world through different eyes.

Here's a classic description of the halo effect in action, drawn from the genre of modern-day detective fiction. In this case, Commissario Brunetti, a well-regarded detective who features in a series of novels by Donna Leon, is reflecting on one of the characters who appears in the case he's investigating:

> As he read the newspaper articles, all purporting to be neutral presentation of fact but all tinted by the political affiliation of the particular paper or journalist, Brunetti realized that he was colouring the articles with the hues of his own memory. He had known, or at least heard, about Moro [a figure in a murder Brunetti is investigating] for years, and as he tended to share the man's political leanings, he knew he was prejudiced in the man's favour and that he presupposed his honesty. He knew just how dangerous this sort of thinking was, especially for a policeman, yet Moro was hardly a suspect: the totality of his grief excluded him from any suspicion of involvement in his son's death. "Or else I've never had a son; or else I've never had a soul," Brunetti caught himself whispering out loud.*

Returning to the example of Saddam Husayn might reinforce this concept. In a society with competing ethnic and religious

---

* Donna Leon, *Uniform Justice* (New York: Grove Press, 2003), 69.

groups, he provided public security that was lost after the US invasion of Iraq. A lot of Iraqis didn't like Saddam, but some might now trade the freedoms they enjoyed after his ouster for the security he provided in everyday life.

To be clear, this isn't a political judgment, nor is it an argument that the invasion of Iraq was a good or bad idea. It's just a real-world example meant to underscore a point about halo effects: if we harbor strong likes, or dislikes, about the subjects we are considering, even the best analysts run the risks of looking at the problem through a rosy (or, in the case of Saddam, a dark) lens. You can do this. Just don't confuse it with hard-headed, objective analysis that should weed out this kind of bias.

SUPERIORITY BIAS

We all tend to highlight the strengths of our own analysis, just as often as we discount or forget the weaknesses of it. But when we evaluate the work of competing analysts, we focus immediately on their weak points, often without even considering whether there's something worth thinking about. Frequently we only highlight the strengths of someone else's analysis because his points echo what we believe. "That's absolutely correct," we might say. "He thinks the way I do!"

The process of identifying drivers should help eliminate the assumption, or bias, that whoever disagrees with us is wrong. With that in mind, we should always fight the inevitable urge to go on the attack. Discounting an opposing view might be the right answer in the end, but the initial default of a good analyst should be the opposite direction: this person with a different perspective is studying the same problem I'm looking at, and coming out in a different place. What's the chance I'm wrong? Are there factors she's considering that I should have considered?

ANCHORING BIAS

When we start down an analytic path that lends itself to numbers—
such as assessing a stock price, or determining whether a certain
adversary has enough missiles to constitute a threat—we have a tendency to focus on the numbers, because they're easy to count, and
easy to assess. For example, if you walk into a room of investment
analysts who are assessing a stock, they might set the figure of $50
as the "sell" target. But if you walk into that room with no knowledge of investing and no background in analyzing the company,
that $50 target figure will play tricks on your mind. Let's say the
stock hits $55. Without even knowing the basics of the company's
performance recently, you might grow nervous. "Fifty was our target figure," you might say. "We're already well beyond that!" You're
anchored to that figure, regardless of whether you even know what
it's based on. Another analyst with more experience, using different
investment criteria, might see $60 as a far more suitable target to sell
the stock, but you don't know that. If you'd started with that $60
figure, though, you might just as quickly have said, still knowing
nothing about the stock, "We need to hold for a bit. It would make
me nervous to sell now—we're below the target." In other words, we
start paying more attention to some arbitrary number instead of the
data that is actually driving the numbers.

This happens to you every day in life. Think about walking into
the grocery store. What do you want to pay for cereal? When you
walk down the cereal aisle, you see a sale: one box for $4.79, two
boxes for $8. The marketers for the cereal company have hooked
you with a common anchoring bias tool. They've planted the idea
in your head that $4.79 is a fair price for a box of their cereal. So
$8 must be a steal. You win! Well, hardly. If your family needs two
boxes, you'd be silly not to take the two-box deal. But the first hook
that captured you wasn't whether $4.79 is a fair price. It's the fact

that $4 for one box is less than $4.79. Maybe a fair price for that box is really $3.50; how would you know?

We also struggle with the simple challenge of dealing with numbers. Most of us aren't particularly comfortable with serious math, and handling numerical problems therefore falls to the bottom of the list of what we'd like to do on a Saturday afternoon. Consider this, though: whether we like it or not, every day we define problems in terms of numbers, and we use numbers to grade what we think of particular problems. It's wintertime and the temperature tops 70 degrees? Where most of us live, this is remarkably warm. If it's August, though, we automatically judge the temperature against another norm: 70 degrees is cool. We don't judge the temperature as a stand-alone number, but instead anchor our judgment in the range of normal temperatures for that time of year.

Let's try this with a more complex problem, though, such as the stock market. In this modern era of individual retirement accounts, many of us scan our accounts frequently—maybe even daily—to determine how much ground we've gained or lost that day. When we do this, we habitually fall prey to anchoring bias that takes that tactical, daily performance out of context. For example, if the market has gained 15 percent over eight months, which would be a strong rise by most standards, we'd say that we're comfortable, both because our account is growing and because we're beating inflation by such a wide margin. As soon as the market stumbles and we lose some notable amount during the course of a week—let's say 3 percent, for the sake of argument—we immediately grow concerned that the market and our IRA are doing poorly. Maybe they are, and we might look at this drop as a potential indicator that leads us to ask tough questions about whether the market is in for a correction. But we should also keep in mind that the account didn't lose 3 percent during the course of the year; it gained a substantial amount, probably more than you would have expected at the beginning of the year. Again, by virtually any measure, you've benefited from a gain that should lead you to think about popping a bottle of decent champagne.

You shouldn't have a hard time catching this one. Watch for numbers, at home and in the workplace. When you hear a number, run through a quick validity check. Are you working with an absolute number (such as the amount of money in your bank account) or an anchored number (this stock started the year at $10, and it's now at $20; this can of tuna costs $1.50, and two of them sell for $2.50)? Somehow, our brains are wired to treat numbers as facts. They're not. In a grocery marketing game, they're a way to play with our wiring. Go ahead and buy the two-for-one tuna; just know that the store might have priced the first can higher than it should have been. They anchored you in the elevated $1.50 price. Because we're all susceptible to this bias, it works.

VARIABLE BIAS

Most of the biases discussed in this section are common features in analytic studies, but "variable bias" is not; it's a name I made up for something I've seen all too many times in analytic work. An expert is confronted with a complex problem. That expert owns the room— as the expert writes and speaks on his topic of expertise, every listener feels compelled to accept his version of life. In many settings, though, from boardrooms to CIA Headquarters, you will find that those experts often focus on just a couple of variables as they lay out an analytic judgment. The need to simplify complex problems for a nonexpert audience drives variable bias, the push to take problems that may revolve around a half-dozen or more constantly changing variables and jam them into one- or two-variable boxes.

This bias stems partly from our inability to juggle and explain too many variables at once, and it's one reason we need to step through an analytic process systematically, so that we consider a mix of variables that will drive us to a more complete view of the problem. You'll note that the range of six to ten drivers we've used in this book limits you so that you don't try to evaluate so many variables that you're considering elements that don't really have an impact on the answer. But that number also pushes you to consider more variables than you can accommodate mentally without careful consideration. For many problems, it's not sufficient to juggle just two or three variables; we default to that mental limit because we either don't want to spend the energy adding more complexity or don't believe that our customer will be able to understand a more advanced explanation.

PREDICTIVE BIAS

I saw the problem of predictive bias all the time at the CIA, and you no doubt hear this bias every week, when pundits predict everything from the scores of football games to where the stock market is headed. Those pundits are experts, too, which typically means that they know some subject well enough to expound on it endlessly.

As we've seen, however, deep expertise leads us to assume that we can predict the future. It's this confusion between expertise and the ability to see tomorrow that we need to avoid. Throughout this book, the emphasis has been on narrowing uncertainty, not guaranteeing certainty. If you feel yourself slipping into the bias of believing you're a better predictor than the next guy, just remember: even the best TV weather forecasters never tell you what's going to happen tomorrow. They hedge their predictions—there's a 60 percent chance of rain, or a 30 percent chance of snow—so that they can help you make better decisions about whether to plan a picnic, or whether to delay your visit to the beach. They don't guarantee the future; they give you an advantage that helps you make better decisions about your own future.

POST HOC ERGO PROPTER HOC

You remember waking up in college after a particularly ugly fraternity keg party. Ten horrible 16-ounce beers and you feel like you've got a railroad spike hammered into the center of your forehead. "Never again," you tell yourself, even if you know full well that you're going to the biggest fraternity keg party of the year the following Saturday. When the weekend comes around, you conveniently forget the hangover and head out to the party, quickly slipping into the inevitable. One beer, two beers, three beers . . . it's pretty clear what's going to happen here. Once that first beer goes down, you start to lose your self-control, discipline goes out the window, and it's off to the races. Later, at 10 p.m., you pop three Tylenol. "It's a miracle cure," you tell yourself, in a haze.

You wake up. You're not feeling great, you're not ready to run a marathon, you're maybe a little fuzzy in the forehead, but you certainly aren't suffering from the railroad-spike effect. Why is that, you ask yourself? And like a lot of us, or maybe almost all of us, you'd go back to the Tylenol. "I have the miracle cure," you tell yourself. "Next time, I'll do the same thing. Three Tylenol at 10 p.m. and I'm good to go."

Not so fast. You're heading down the rabbit hole of a classic analytic error: you decide that what you felt after the Tylenol no doubt happened because of the Tylenol. This is an easy answer, but it's not necessarily the right one. Think of all the other variables that might come into play here. What did you eat, and when did you eat it? Might your food intake have had an impact on how your body absorbed an excess of alcohol?

Try a few more questions to get at how your experience differed from the previous weekend's. What exactly did you drink, early in the evening and through the night? How much water did you put down as you went through glasses of beer? Might your water intake have influenced whether you fell victim to the railroad-spike effect? What was the weather like? If it was hot and humid, you might have perspired heavily. Were you at all dehydrated that first weekend? If so, did that mean that your alcohol intake had a more significant impact, because you didn't have enough water circulating in your system?

We have a tendency, to a fault, to want to find simple explanations for what happens in life. I don't feel well? Must be the bad air circulating in that long flight I took yesterday. The Syrian opposition took a major town yesterday? Must be because of the new weapons stocks they just received. The French generally are less obese than Americans? Must be the red wine they drink.

This search for easy explanations is particularly prevalent when there's no control group to compare your own experiences against. If you're testing a new headache medicine, for example, you won't be able to truly confirm your results unless you have one group of chronic headache sufferers taking a placebo while the other gets the real medicine. In most of what we do—assessing the Syrian opposition, or determining why we feel worse today than we did yesterday—we can't create a test environment that includes a control group. This is all the more reason to watch out for the after-therefore-because-of argument.

Before you dismiss this problem of after-therefore-because-of (post hoc ergo propter hoc, as it's known in formal argumentation), you should watch how often it crops up in everyday life. You may see, for example, an article that says something like this: "People who take this or that vitamin live an average of 1.2 years longer than those who don't." The implication, of course, is that if you take that vitamin, you'll live longer, when in fact the research may show nothing of the kind. What if people who take vitamins (choose any vitamin) typically are the same people who look out for their health generally? They exercise more than the general population, for example, and they eat healthier foods. Is it then the vitamin that led to greater longevity, or is it some combination of other characteristics? Without a control group, drawing any sort of conclusion here would be analytically faulty.

The word "because" is often your clue. "I fell asleep early because I had a tough day at work," you might say, not realizing that you actually slept two hours less last night than you think. You fell asleep early because your sleep patterns were disrupted; you just leapt to conclusions because you didn't want to think through the problem analytically, and you didn't even know you had a huge data gap (your sleep patterns the previous night). To avoid spending too much energy assessing questions, we slip into an analytic game that allows us to wrap up questions with simple bows: "My team lost because we have a quarterback who played poorly." Well, maybe your team lost because the coaching staff isn't too good, and the management team that selects players is inexperienced. The quarterback is playing with a team that can't win, but he'd excel elsewhere because he's actually pretty good—he just has no support.

CONFIRMATION BIAS

We want so badly to be right, especially when we're defending a judgment in an area of expertise for us. If we're fans of a particular basketball team, we may, deep down, believe that this is their year. They then proceed to lose more than half their games. "I was right," we might think, "but it was the injuries that devastated the team. Without those injuries, they would have been great." Taking this a step further, we might look at debates about global warming and changes in weather patterns. If we think global warming is a reality, we'll take a bit of data—the slow melting of glaciers, for example—and use that data to confirm what we already believe. If we think global warming is bunk, we might point to the rises and falls in global temperatures over hundreds of thousands of years. There have been cycles of ice ages and warming periods, we might say. This is another of them. Either way, you have a heartfelt belief, and you will take whatever happens and manipulate that data point to confirm your belief.

The Indian nuclear test provided a classic case of confirmation bias. Who wants to believe India will take this step into the nuclear club? We'd rather believe they would succumb to pressure and eventually see the good sense in standing down on their nationalistic tendencies. So when Indian leaders said they would be deliberate in their actions, we weighed their words against other indicators (such as the accelerated activity at the nuclear test site) and confirmed the position we started with: India may test. Their words, however, only confirmed our (reasonable) view that they can take their time, and meanwhile we can press them against becoming a declared nuclear state. We knew what we wanted to believe—that they'd act according to our definition of reasonableness—and we took the bits of data that confirmed this view as evidence that we were right. Only we weren't.

Let's go back to the first half of the twentieth century for one of the most painful experiences of confirmation bias—and reasonable-man thinking, which we'll discuss below—the world has ever seen. If you had witnessed the devastating death toll of World War I, particularly the loss of life that resulted from trench warfare, you might have judged that nobody in his right mind would risk that kind of warfare again, particularly less than a generation later. That's certainly how British prime minister Neville Chamberlain felt when he watched the rise of Adolf Hitler and Nazi Germany's moves into neighboring countries before World War II. In one of the most storied events of the twentieth century, Chamberlain traveled to Munich to meet Hitler in 1938, returning home with an agreement that appeared to be a path to "peace in our time," as he announced to the cheering throngs that greeted him.

One way to look at this—and there are a lot of analytic missteps in Chamberlain's approach—is that he suffered from confirmation bias. He believed that his counterpart and future adversary had to be rational enough to want to avoid a replay of World War I. Any sane human being would not want to subject Europe to another such horror. When Hitler agreed to a pact, then, Chamberlain no doubt viewed this as confirmation that Hitler had at least a few reasonable bones in his body, and that he would not want to take steps that might plunge Europe into another world war. Meanwhile, Hitler himself fell prey to confirmation bias during that period: he took Chamberlain's acceptance of his earlier territorial conquests as a sign that Britain had no stomach for another brutal war. Chamberlain's agreement to the fiction of "peace in our time" in Munich served as confirmation for Hitler that his assumptions were correct.

Just as intelligence analysts might place what the shah's advisers told US diplomats into an analysis that confirmed the analysts' own views—that the shah could and would hold on—both Hitler and Chamberlain used the Munich exchange to confirm what they wanted to believe. Analysts struggle with this problem when they use the pick-and-choose method of analysis: take the data I think works with my hypothesis and weight that data heavily; take the data that is anomalous and discard it, or downgrade it. One exercise can help: rather than explaining away the anomalous data, put it into a separate pile and then construct an analysis based solely on that data. How compelling is your story now? If it's at all coherent, you might want to consider your original analysis, because you've just confirmed that it might not be true.

REASONABLE-MAN BIAS

We all have our own lenses through which we view the world, with each person's lens shaped by personal experience, study, reflection, physiology, and probably a thousand other things, from whether you ate a good breakfast to what your mother taught you about keeping a clean house. Despite the uniqueness of our lenses, we also (most of us, at least) hold the belief that we're reasonable, and that if we're given a problem—how to deal with a domestic spat, or how to manage the economy—we'll come up with a solution that makes sense. We might take one step further: since we're reasonable, and we are good problem solvers who are smart enough to come up with sensible solutions, other people might take the same reasonable steps to arrive at the same solutions. Voilà! The reasonable-man bias—the view that because we individually or collectively think in a certain way, somebody else must think that way as well.

The problem is that our version of reasonable isn't a universal definition of reasonable. Take Saddam and WMD as a case study. Saddam wasn't crazy. Quite the contrary; in the world he lived in, he was quite reasonable. It's just that his reasoning process differed from ours. His environment was so fundamentally different from ours that he came up with solutions that we failed to understand. Any reasonable man, some Western observers might have said, would come clean with the United Nations on WMD, because cooperation with the UN would allow Iraq to escape an oppressive economic sanctions regime and, more broadly, the international isolation that had choked the country for so many years. The fact that he's so evasive, then, must show that he's hiding something, because otherwise his actions don't make sense to us.

Saddam's actions turned out to be perfectly reasonable, just not the kind of reasonable many US analysts would have applied to the WMD decisions he made. You'll remember the explanation from earlier in the book: he reasoned that Iran was a greater threat than America, and coming clean with the UN would show Iran that Iraq lacked a WMD deterrent. What might Tehran do then? Who knows, but Iraq's experience during the devastating war with Iran in the 1980s was a fresh memory for Saddam. His reasonable approach was to rank Iran first and the United States in second place, with tragic consequences. We assessed that he wasn't a reasonable man; in fact, he was, just not in a way we understood.

Anyone who's ever been in a romantic relationship knows how hard it is to understand a partner's decision-making, day in and day out. There is no couple that doesn't compromise, at some level, because we're all different. We have different goals, moods, interests, and personalities. When we're in a work environment, we seem to forget this. "The only prudent thing for the management team in this firm is to agree to bigger dividends this year," you might say. Why, though, is your judgment of prudence the same as theirs? It's not; you're assuming that your judgment is reasonable, that their judgment is reasonable, and that therefore they will do the same thing you might do in the same situation. And then they don't. They act reasonably, and rationally, but their reasoning is different than yours, and their world is different. It's not unreasonable to think they'll act the way you would. It's just wrong.

In analytic circles, assuming that the entity or individual you are assessing might think or act as you would is known as mirror-imaging, and it is among the most common mistakes you will see in analysis. The idea is as simple as it gets: I see the world in a certain way. It's sensible, and it's logical. Therefore, other people no doubt see the world the same way. You've already witnessed this error multiple times in this book: If I think international pressure would make me uncertain about conducting a nuclear test, so must the Indian leadership. After all, aren't they trying to integrate more with the global economy? So international pressure that clearly shows that a test would isolate them internationally must work. Well, it didn't. Because they're not a mirror image of who we are. "They"— whoever it is that we're assessing—don't necessarily think like us.

Saddam Husayn can again provide a good case study. As the drumbeat of war grew louder, I suspect, many of us sat back and asked ourselves a question: Doesn't he know we're serious? Why doesn't he give up the WMD he has, because he's risking a US-led invasion if he doesn't? Further, the fact that he doesn't give up what he has shows how committed he is to retaining these weapons. The story, as we all now know, was even simpler: he was more concerned about regional neighbors—particularly neighboring Iran—than with the distant Americans, and continuing the fiction of Iraq's WMD program (he thought) would keep his enemies at bay. So, in the end, he didn't think like we did, though his thoughts, in retrospect, were eminently logical.

REVERTING-TO-THE-MEAN BIAS

Not surprisingly, given the relatively modest achievements of most Americans in the realm of mathematics (I'm one of the math-challenged), very few of us know much about, or are even comfortable with, statistics. To think through tough statistical challenges, though, you don't have to be an expert, and there are certainly no statistical analyses in this book. But you at least have to be cognizant of where your blind spots are, even if you can't fully avoid them. Like sample sizes, reverting to the mean is something you should think about when you're in the midst of coming up with an assessment with heavy statistical factors.

It's baseball season. Deep into the playoffs in October, one of the best players for your team has gotten twelve hits in his previous twenty-five at-bats. That's a prodigious batting average of .480. For those readers who don't follow baseball, this is outrageously high.

The last time a player averaged more than four hits per ten at bats (a .400 average, in baseball-speak) was many decades ago. During the two games that follow, this player on a hot streak goes to bat eight times and comes up empty. "Oh no," you lament. "He's gone cold. He's in a slump." Wait a minute; I wouldn't be so sure. Let's add the two sums together, putting us at twelve hits in thirty-three at-bats, when you include the zero-for-eight stretch we just witnessed. That's still an average of .364, more than one hit in every three at-bats. That batting average, if he could maintain it for a season or two, would result in an astronomical contract, and it would make him the best hitter in baseball during most Major League seasons. That player, then, wasn't necessarily in a slump; he was simply reverting to the mean, or heading back out of the stratosphere to a batting average that fits within a baseball norm.

————

Most major analytic mistakes I have witnessed don't result from tiny tactical errors—the failure to factor in one report, for example, or the miscalculation of one figure. They result from far more fundamental mistakes, such as lack of rigor in stepping through how we weight various factors that feed into a decision, or a lack of humility in understanding how deeply biased our minds can be, even those who are steeped in understanding how bias affects analysis. It's one thing to be aware of these biases, and maintaining a list of them beside your desk might give you a chance to step through a mental checklist when you're in the midst of an analytic exercise. But the red team process can help here, too. Some biases are so hidden in what we do, because they are subtle, or because we simply do not understand how we think, that we can't discern them without help.

So remember bias every time you break down a problem. And then hand your solution to somebody else, opening the door from the outset to the chance that you've unconsciously failed to recognize some flaw in your thinking. You might consider requiring an answer that identifies some appearance of bias, even if the outside red team has to struggle to pick apart your work. Open with a few sentences like these: "This was a complex problem, and I'm not sure I'm seeing it clearly. Can you please point out an element or two of my analysis that seems weak, or reflects some sort of bias?"

A PRACTITIONER'S CHECKLIST

SUMMING UP: A PRACTITIONER'S CHECKLIST

After all these pages of taking the complexities of decision-making and laying them out into a simple, repeatable analytic process, we can close by boiling down all that work into this checklist. If you read through the first six chapters, without this simple guide, you'd forget half the book in a day, and the rest during the ensuing month. Returning to the principles of the HEAD Game, two months later, you might decide that applying them is too hard; you have to flip through a half-dozen chapters again, sorting through the examples and principles in your own mind.

If you practice, and then practice again and again, you should find that these principles are not that hard to apply, even if they can require patience and discipline. Like your physical exercise routine when you start getting into shape, the more time and effort you invest up front, the more you will feel rewarded when you arrive at an analytic conclusion. But you've got to repeat the process, to build your brain's muscle memory about how to go from right to left. You don't have to refer back to the book's chapters. Just scan or photocopy the following few pages; they're an easy reference. And then start living right to left in your everyday life, at work and at home. It's more efficient than tackling every problem anew, without a framework for handling it. It's the HEAD Game.

PLAY THE HEAD GAME

What is the decision maker or audience trying to accomplish?

What is the decision-making goal?

How might my knowledge help the decision maker reach his goal?

How can I limit uncertainty for the decision maker?

Am I trying to provide a point prediction? Or am I narrowing the problem to make it more manageable?

Have I started to answer the problem of how to put terrorism into perspective by looking at a few recent incidents, or a few major attacks, and moving on to assess the problem based on those data points? Or have I tried to focus on where I want to end up—with a question that helps frame the problem so that I can make a better decision about how much to worry? Did I start left—with a summary of information about terror attacks or recent arrests—or right, by spending time on understanding exactly what question I needed to answer?

QUESTIONS

How can I avoid a yes/no question?

Would a nonexpert understand the question? Have I tried the "Call Mom" exercise?

Can I summarize my question in one sentence of no more than three lines with only one dependent clause?

Is the question inclusive—broad enough to cover what I
think we'll need to cover, but narrow enough to provide
a useful answer?

Does the question reflect the decision maker's needs? Am I shading the question to reflect more of what I'm interested in?

How clearly did I build my terrorism question? Can I capture
it easily, in one sentence? And despite the emotion attached to
the problem of terrorism, have I avoided words that are emotionally loaded (words such as "bad" or "good" that are inherently
emotional)?

DRIVERS

Have I created a driver list that appears to cover what I need
to cover?

Does every driver link directly to the question I've asked, or
have I added items that are interesting but peripheral?

Have I limited my drivers to a manageable number—say, no
more than ten? In fact, despite the importance of the issue, do I
really need more than half a dozen?

Are the drivers agnostic? Would anyone attacking this
problem—even people who don't agree with my viewpoint—agree
that these are the factors any analyst would have to consider?

METRICS

How can I set a few metrics that will help me understand
whether I'm on the right track?

How can I come up with at least one rough metric for each
driver?

When I set metrics, can I attach a time frame to them?
    If I'm confident today, when should I reconsider this
    confidence?
Have I clearly defined the line between capability and intent
    metrics?
Are the metrics measurable? In other words, can I judge
    with some certainty when we've hit one of the metrics—
    when we've brushed up against a guardrail—or am I still
    working with soft measures?
Who set the metrics? Have I created a process that allows
    the expert analysts to own the metrics process?

Can I find signposts that would help me understand whether I should adjust my views—maybe the incidence of attacks in America, or whether my city seems like it would be a high-priority target, or whether the number of arrests in America suggests that this threat is growing, or declining? Are those metrics clearly designed to help me understand the specific question I've asked?

DATA

Have I divided my information into baskets that correspond
    with the drivers I identified?
Am I aggressive enough in distinguishing between what I
    know, what I don't know, and what I think?
How many of my baskets have I graded green? Am I too
    confident in what I know?
Have I differentiated between hard drivers and soft driv-
    ers, or between capability and intent? Do I understand
    clearly enough where I might be vulnerable to overconfi-
    dence in assessing intent?

Have I focused on the gaps in my knowledge? What is it
about this problem that I don't know, and are there ways
I can address those gaps?

How will I present my knowledge gaps in the final analysis
or presentation?

Is there data that does not clearly fit into one of the driver
baskets? What have I done with that data? Have I discarded too much data because it's anomalous? Have I
considered too much data because I don't want to take
the time to discard information?

How much information do I have? If I'm making judgments based
on a few attacks, or a few arrests in my city, how confident should I be
that this data shows a clear trend line, or that the sample size is sufficient to make a clear judgment? Should I give my data a yellow—some
data, but not enough for a confident judgment—or a red or green?

CONCLUSIONS AND PRESENTATION

Would a nonexpert understand the conclusion? Can I summarize it in one sentence, with no more than three lines
and one dependent clause?

Have I practiced the conclusion using the "Call Mom"
exercise?

Are the key drivers clearly articulated somewhere in the
presentation?

Did I highlight somewhere what I do not know, and how I
intend to address gaps?

Do I assign future metrics to my judgments—what signposts I'm looking at to determine whether I need to
adjust the analysis?

Does my analysis have a clearly defined time frame
  attached, a date at which I think we should reconsider
  the question?

When I stand in front of the mirror to explain what I think, do
I shift back to my emotional response to this question (Of course
terrorism is a threat!) or do I base my answer on how I assess my
drivers? If I were talking to a friend over dinner tonight, could I
summarize what I think in one clearly articulated sentence, without
emotion words ("good" or "bad," for example), and could I explain
what I looked for to make my assessment (drivers and data) and
what metrics I'll use to assess whether I need to adjust my thinking?

PITFALLS

Did I include a few fresh voices in the analytic process? Did
  they have the opportunity to talk, without facing undue
  pressure from other experts around the table?
Did the analytic process turn up anomalous data? How did
  I weigh this data? How quickly did I dismiss it?
Did my analysis trip any of the metrics triggers? If so, what
  did I say about the metrics? Did I attempt to explain
  away shifts in analytic thinking? Did I set new metrics?
What am I including that distracts from a central focus that
  can help a decision maker? Did I include too much?
Do I have a regular schedule for reexamining the question?
When the team meets, do they factor in the passage of
  time—whether a driver basket that was once yellow now
  should shift to red?
Am I attempting to explain, or defend?
Did I differentiate clearly between what I know and what I
  think? How about considering the significance of those

areas that are gaps? Did I focus only on knowns and sidestep unknowns?

The toughest analytic mistakes are usually fundamental mistakes. They're not all correctable—perfection can't be a goal when we're trying to understand what might happen tomorrow—but we should at least be alert to basic pitfalls as we chart a course. Did we discard information because it didn't fit our model? More significantly, how much time did we spend ensuring that we didn't confuse what we think with what we know? Throughout this assessment of pitfalls, keep a few simple thoughts in mind.

- We usually know less than we think we know.
- We usually spend less time than we should in figuring out where we have gaps in knowledge and understanding.
- We often look back on mistakes and realize that it was the most basic pitfalls that undermined analysis; often, it's not the little things!
- Finally, if you make a mistake, start over again. Pick yourself up and learn. You can even find a silver lining in these failures that helps you grow as an analyst: humility, or the understanding that we can always learn, always improve, and always find somebody who knows more, or who knows how to think more clearly. Nobody who ever amounted to anything succeeded every time.

To reinforce this thought that you have to keep trying, even when you make a mistake, take a page out of the book of one of the most famous athletes of all time, the basketball star Michael Jordan:

I've missed more than 9000 shots in my career. I've lost almost 300 games. Twenty-six times, I've been trusted to take the game winning shot and missed. I've failed over and over and over again in my life. And that is why I succeed.

———

This list of questions is clearly too long for any analyst to step through every day, or even every time you're stepping through an analytic exercise. But it's the outline of a framework that gives you an easy way to test yourself, a measure to judge how far you've traveled from intuitive expertise to analytic judgment. Experts will expound on what they know all day long, sometimes with bold bumper-sticker judgments that aren't based on a painstaking analytic process. Analysts are less bold and less colorful, but more systematic and more open to understanding both the risks of expertise and the challenges of understanding change. They're more apt to understand, too, the gap between what they know and what they think.

LEARNING FROM MISTAKES— ORIGINAL DOCUMENTATION

ADMIRAL JEREMIAH NEWS CONFERENCE

2 June 1998

Thanks very much. I'd like to open my remarks with a report that we have had no advance warning that Ginger is leaving the Spice Girls and George Tenet is forming another commission to take care of that problem for us.

George Tenet asked me to conduct for him an independent evaluation of the actions taken by the Intelligence Community leading up to the Indian nuclear test. I was assisted by a number of individuals within the IC and by one of my associates at Technology Strategies and Alliances. The IC provided full cooperation across the board. We solicited and received comments from all relevant agencies and anybody who wanted to come in and ask us questions or provide information. The report and recommendations, obviously, are my responsibility.

The identification of the Indian nuclear test preparations posed a difficult collection problem and a difficult analytical problem. Their program was an indigenous program. It was not derived from the US, Chinese, Russian or French programs. It was totally within India. And therefore, there were some characteristics difficult to observe. In addition, they took pains to avoid any characteristics that they may have learned were of value to us, and the test preparations they made in 1995/96. And as you and your colleagues have reported, apparently only a limited number of senior level political and government people were aware of the tests within India. So, as a result, our policymakers, and in fact the Intelligence Community, reported back that there was no indication the Indians would test in the near term.

I suppose my bottom line is that both the intelligence and the policy communities had an underlying mindset going into these tests that the BJP would behave as we behave. For instance, there is an assumption that the BJP platform would mirror Western political platforms. In other words, a politician is going to say something in his political platform leading up to the elections, but not necessarily follow through on the platform once he takes office and is exposed to the immensity of his problem.

The BJP was dead serious and to some degree I think they were motivated by the fact that the last time they were in office they were only there 13 days. And so they were ready to move as fast as they could this time given that they were in a 14 party coalition to execute their objectives that were stated in stuff you guys all read on the web. So, first of all, we had a mindset that said everybody else is going to work like we work. Why would anyone throw away all the economic advantages associated that they would lose with testing, why would they hazard all that stuff when there is no reason to do that? And we don't think like the other nation thinks. What drives them, what are their national security requirements, what does their national pride and psyche drive them to do? And second, I think that you'll see through the recommendations that I have made to Director Tenet, a requirement for a better need to integrate all of the capabilities that we have within our Intelligence agencies so that they focus better on certain kinds of problems and cross feed and tip off each other so that we get a coordinated attack upon the problem.

I have provided recommendations that are intended to improve the process recognizing that no process will be perfect in the art of intelligence collection. These recommendations are in several broad categories in the areas of analytical practices, collection processes, manpower and training and organization. Obviously the security classification is going to prohibit me from talking about a lot of these recommendations, and in fact, to cite and provide a full range of my recommendations. The recommendation—and that will tend to bias the balance in the report, so put that in the back of your head as you go through these recommendations.

First, analytic. More rigor needs to go into analysts' thinking when major events take place. Two mechanisms would help: A) bring in outside substantive experts in a more systematic fashion, so that we work against this "everybody thinks like us" mindset. And B) bring in experts in the process of analysis when the IC faces a transition on a major intelligence issue, like the BJP election, and like other things that you can think of. Look at establishing effective mechanisms to guarantee stronger integration of the analysis and greater collaboration and coordination of intelligence agencies and disciplines. So that instead of looking up at each of these stovepipes, we look at the product and the interaction between the stovepipes.

Realign collection priorities so that high-priority issues within individual countries compete more evenly with the rogue states, which we collect against across the board—there are issues such as weapons of mass destruction that we want to provide the same priority to.

We have an imbalance today between the human skills associated with reading photography, looking at reports, understanding what goes on in a nation, and the ability to technically collect that information. In everyday language, that means there is an awful lot of stuff on the cutting room floor at the end of the day that we have not seen. We need to realign the priorities so that we have more ability to provide analysts depth and that those analysts have an opportunity for training so that they can improve their skills. They need better tools to allow them to course through that data more rapidly.

Within the Organization category, there needs to be a community manager with the authority to demand accountability to in carrying out the DCI decisions, directives, and priorities. Right now that only exists at the DCI and DDCI level.

There needs to be a management structure to integrate the collection systems so that we task collection as a "system of systems" rather than each of the individual pipelines and we need to look at the specific problems particularly in today's context of collection and analysis in South Asia, and specifically, the weapons of mass destruction problem.

The organization needs to be scrubbed and I am talking about the IC organization, not necessarily the CIA, to improve the clarity of the structure, to fix responsibilities, to resource the staff with appropriate tools and to inform the organization once that review has taken place.

And I would like to conclude by saying when you look at reviews like this, it always spotlights and makes more egregious problems that in retrospect might appear obvious to everybody. And, in fact, these events took place within a milieu of other events, all clamoring for attention and for increased resources and collection.

But at the end of the day, senior-level attention needed to get on the process and the problem earlier. Leadership should have been focused on critical intelligence requirements even at the expense of the traditional livelihood of Washington of looking at resource allocations and regulatory issues that tend to dominate our structures today.

To some degree, that means senior levels, and I am talking about the levels right under the DCI—the people who have been in this organization and understand the processes, know what the requirements are, know how you do it, know what the decision makers need—that level needs to be able to do a little more risk taking in order to pursue the things that need to be done. With that, I think I'd like to close my remarks and move forward to questions.

Q: Senator Shelby has said in his words that this is perhaps the worst intelligence failure of more than a decade. What is your reaction to that?

A: Well, this is not Beirut, this is not Khobar Towers. There were things that should have been done. I've ticked off some of them. We should have been much more aggressive in thinking through how the other guy thought. When the BJP party came to power, we could have looked harder at our intelligence systems, to make sure that we got as much coverage as we possibly could, even at the expense perhaps of coverage in other areas. But at the end of the day, no one was killed as a result of this decision—correction, as a result of this event. And, so, you can draw your own conclusions. I think it was a serious problem and I don't think anyone is going to walk away from that but it is also true that this is an art. This is not something you do. And if you put x and y in, you will always get z out. Things change.

Q: Sir, saying the IC needs to be scrubbed is a pretty powerful statement, and I wonder if you could expand on that and perhaps talk about the priorities for this scrubbing in a different way. We have been through a number of exercises where people have proposed moving boxes around, moving lines of communication around, and what we come up with often is a problem with talent, of people, of human brain power. Would you speak to that a little bit?

A: The talent is here. The organization has had a startling number of successes I think over the years, and probably those successes have caused the exception to be such a glaring apparent problem. The question is organizing talent so that everybody is pulling on the same set of traces, and I believe that can be done. I think Director Tenet will address that later in the day on what he plans to do, certainly he'll have to address that aspect when he speaks to the Senate. But I think the talent is here and all of the agencies around town to cause that to happen. And we don't want to go through another four year study on how to reorganize anything. That is not the objective. The objective is what are we really trying to do, who is in charge, take charge, make things happen, report back, and move on down the road, and that can be done.

Q: Admiral, if I am hearing you correctly, it seems as if you are suggesting that there is too much compartmentalization within the process. And, of course, many people in the security field will tell you that that is the way you maintain security. Are these two things working against each other? How do you get less compartmentalization and still maintain your security?

A: I think that compartmentation is an important issue. It is a requirement if you are going to continue to maintain your sources. But the issue really is how do I use this particular intelligence system to collect the data that allows me to target that system on a particular objective? And that coordination across the INTs, is the phraseology, has not been as clear and as clean as it should be. And I think that is the issue we want to try to get at.

Q: May I follow-up to that please? I also hear without you using the word. I hear you suggesting that perhaps on some levels there was some complacency in place. Am I choosing too big a word?

A: I don't think that is fair. Complacency says no one is paying attention to the problem. There is a good deal of reporting, there is a good deal of activity inside the Community on the nuclear issue but it was working against the criteria that you would expect for our systems, not necessarily the way they went about doing it. And it was ameliorated a little bit by the feedback coming back from the Indians. And nobody is required to tell us the truth. But it was ameliorated a little bit by their responses that laid out for instance this business about establishing the National Security Council and then subsequently I think we had some evidence that suggested that not all the leadership knew what was going on, and therefore, were not able to deal with it.

Q: Admiral, other than the failure to react to public statements during the campaign, were there any clues that intelligence analysts overlooked or did the Indians successfully hide all their preparations? In retrospect, was there something on the ground that should have given it away.

A: I am going to deal with that in the retrospect part. We put 10 analysts on a problem for about five days with three supporting personnel for the same period of time. And in doing that, we reviewed everything we could see about the areas. And when you do that retrospectively you can begin to piece together things that might have brought you to the conclusion that something might be going on. If that were in isolation, that in of itself would say, got something. But this is part of a history that goes back to 1974. This train left the station twice in a quarter of a century. Once in 1974 when they tested and again in 1998. There was, many of the things that took place in 1995 and 1996 took place before that in the early 90s and through the rest of the decade until today were taking place. So there was activity and it was a question of identifying the degree to which it was unusual in the last few days before the test.

Q: So, Admiral, to what degree was this an intelligence failure, and to what degree was it a success on the part of India in keeping it a secret?

A: About equal. I'd like to say that—I guess I'd rather not say that it was a success on the part of anyone in keeping secrets from us. But, in fact, that happens and some of that occurred here. And some of it was not putting enough assets against it and the competition for assets to deal with other things.

Q: There were ramifications beyond the Indian test; it has ramifications for ensuring compliance with the vast range of arms control agreements by the world. What do you propose in terms of ensuring that we, the United States intelligence, takes action that would better ensure monitoring and verification of a broad range of arms control agreements and proliferation problems?

A: I think that many of the recommendations that I have made to Director Tenet will address our ability to do all of those things and do them more effectively. I don't promise that it will do it a 100 percent, but more effectively.

Q: When you say that you put 10 people on this with three assistants, how many were on it at the time this was going on in real time?

A: Less.

Q: And does that reflect a failure on the part of somebody up the chain of command to task people based on very strong indications that were coming out of India?

A: A, I don't agree with the premise that there were very strong indications. As a matter of fact, to the contrary, they were counter. Their public statements were that we will not test, we will create the National Security Council, and so on and so forth. But there were indications. I don't believe that that is a failure, I think that that is a question of how do you allocate resources in a time of scarcity.

Q: As a follow-up, Admiral, was there only one person on duty at the time of the test as has been reported and the rest of the analysts were at home asleep?

A: At the time of the test? I don't know that. There is one analyst who is regularly assigned to the task.

Q: Can you explain the word scrub—what do you mean by scrubbing the organization?

A: I mean scrubbing the organization as with a wire brush and going out and kind of polishing it up to find out—to make sure it works right—that everyone understands what their responsibilities are, that somebody is in charge of certain areas and that they have a reporting mechanisms and authority.

Q: Somebody in charge specifically of cooperation and coordination?

A: Somebody in charge of the allocation of assets, generally speaking of collection assets across the spectrum of requirements so that you get as much from our collection systems as we can.

Q: Admiral, the CIA, the NRO, the NSA and DIA are all involved here. How would you allocate responsibility and was a lack of cooperation between these agencies?

A: It was not lack of cooperation. It was an absence of coordination to some degree. And I wouldn't propose to allocate across because I was looking at it as a Community—I wouldn't try to segment out who did what to whom—tried to look at the whole context of the problem.

Q: Two things. First of all, you talked about the preoccupation with the rogue nations and the focus of the Agency was diverted. And secondly, you seem to exonerate the DCI and place the blame one level below.

A: No, I'm sorry, I don't mean to do that. George wouldn't tolerate that, if I did say that. What I am saying is that there needs to be more aggressive activity by the old hands in the organization in stepping forward and taking some risks and doing what is right and not waiting to be told to do things every time.

Q: Can you focus on rogue nations, sir? The preoccupation, I guess.

A: My impression out of this report and also of my prior experiences—when a unified commander is engaged, has troops on the ground, we throw assets at him—and we make sure he has got everything that is required to deal with his problem. In some cases, we give them far more coverage and more assets than the demand requires, particularly in the context of theater assets that are available to them. I think there is some balancing—let me put it in my own terms that you would understand. It is a classic allocation of carriers—we've only got so many deployed and we've got to deal with the Persian Gulf, Eastern Mediterranean, and Western Pacific and how do you get all that covered. Somebody has got to make a decision, and that is the kind of issue, that we have here.

Q: Admiral, will anyone be held accountable for this and when Congress, as they usually do, call for a head on a platter, what recommendation do you make? Is there any punitive recommendation?

A: I think George Tenet would step forward and say I'm accountable and so is the Community. We are responsible for our actions. I would say that is correct. They are running a very fine organization, the best in the world, and we do not have anything here that, I believe, is serious enough to require that kind of activity.

Q: At the press conference yesterday, members of the Pakistani government, the Parliamentarians who were here, said that they had warned the US explicitly that they were preparing a test like this.

A: Since about 1974, I think.

Q: The Pakistani ambassador went so far as to say that India deceived the United States and that was now evidence in State Department memos. Would you go so far as to say that it was deception?

A: I would certainly say that they had an effective denial activity.

Q: Admiral, could you talk a little bit more about this mindset of the IC some sort of basic assumed that we didn't have the same sort of mindset associated in this country? How did they arrive at the conclusion that they would be thinking?

A: It wasn't just the IC.

Q: And the policymakers?

A: And us, and I've talked to several other nations and this was not on their scope. But, you know, you begin to fall into a pattern. You operate the way you expect things to happen and you have to recognize that when there is a difference and you could argue that you need to have contrarian view that might be part of our warning process, ought to include some diversion thinkers who look at the same evidence and come to a different conclusion and then you test that different set of conclusions against other evidence to see if it could be valid. I think that is what we are looking at here, a different set of analytical techniques that would compliment, and you'll get analysts in this building who will tell you we did precisely that, but at the end of the day their answer came out the way data and the answers have come out over the last decade or so.

Q: Were there any analysts in this building, during your investigation, that were saying that we need to look at a different way, was there anybody or were there any memos or anything that you can talk about?

A: I think we came to that conclusion predominately based on the material that we read. But there is sporadic evidence that there were people who were looking at things differently.

Q: Admiral, along those lines, is there a lack of understanding in this building and with other Intelligence agencies of the different cultures in India and how Indians react to certain problems or behave in certain ways, and if there are not people here in this building, are you out to get some people like that or if they are here, just not heard from or ignored maybe?

A: One of our recommendations is when you have significant events in countries like this, you seek outside sources which would include those who have spent a good deal of time in India, including Indians, or whatever particular nation that we are interested might be to bring more to bear. I know when we started in Somalia, for instance, it was very difficult to find anybody who had any background or understanding of Somalia. Ambassador Oakley came into the process because of his longstanding background and experience there, but he was one of the few that we had.

Q: Admiral, what about human intelligence. There was comment after this episode that it underscored the idea that there simply were no solid sources inside India, and that pointed to a larger weakness in the human intelligence community.

A: I think that generally across the board without being specific to India that I think we could say our human intelligence capacity is seriously limited. It is limited because of the tremendously expanded coverage that we are required to deal with in today's world. We are no longer looking at Russia and China as sort of the key places—we now have to be able to look at almost anywhere in the world for that kind of problem.

Harlow: We have time for just one last question, please.

Q: Admiral, how confident are you that the United States is in a good position to assess the continuing tension between India and Pakistan?

A: I think that you, we, are going to have to be quite careful in understanding what it is going on there and it will require probably significant amount of diplomatic interchange to understand what they really have in mind.

Q: One last follow-up—two points really. There were published reports suggesting India had essentially fooled the US intelligence community by creating a diversion with some missile tests that it really wasn't planning to do—diverting our attention. Would you comment on that? And generally just when the US had confronted India in the past with evidence that it is prepared to conduct nuclear tests, did that, in fact, give them an edge in terms of giving some insights about how to better defeat US efforts to monitor what is going on there.

A: With respect to the missiles, I wouldn't give too much credence to that report. With respect to the disclosures—in part from our Ambassador and in part from press reports, I think that whenever there is an opportunity to look at what someone else is looking at in your territory it gives you some insights into what you would want to do to cover that and that is all I would conclude from that—we probably did suffer a little bit—that is going to happen though because the value of intelligence is not keeping it inside a building somewhere—the value of intelligence is using it to make and achieve national objectives. In that case, we believe that we, I believe, probably averted a test in 95 and 96, and you could argue that it was an effective policy. And as a generalization, if that happen though, then we have to focus on, okay, we may have disclosed certain kinds of indicators, now what do we have to do in order to tune up our ability to look for other kinds of indicators that will help us. And of course, you don't have to show every kind of whole card you have.

Q: Do you think with the proper intelligence we could have averted tests this time around too?

A: Personal opinion, no. I don't think you were to going to turn them around.

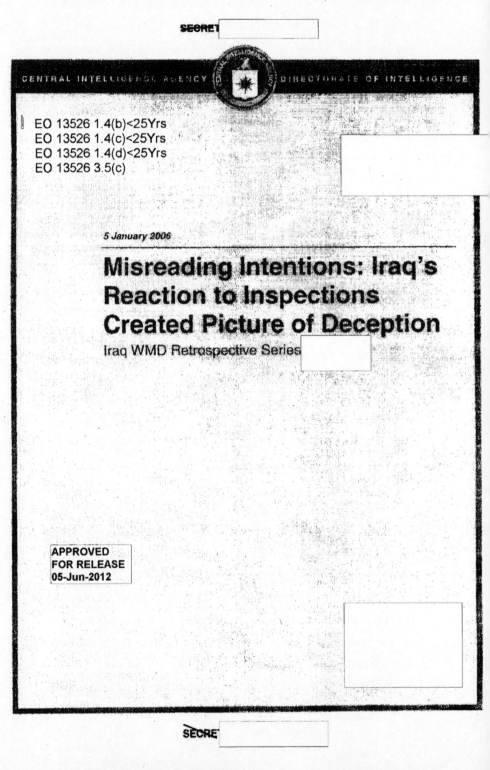

SECRET

CENTRAL INTELLIGENCE AGENCY | DIRECTORATE OF INTELLIGENCE

EO 13526 1.4(b)<25Yrs
EO 13526 1.4(c)<25Yrs
EO 13526 1.4(d)<25Yrs
EO 13526 3.5(c)

5 January 2006

Misreading Intentions: Iraq's Reaction to Inspections Created Picture of Deception

Iraq WMD Retrospective Series

APPROVED
FOR RELEASE
05-Jun-2012

SECRET

**Misreading Intentions: Iraq's Reaction to
Inspections Created Picture of Deception**
Iraq WMD Retrospective Series

Key Findings

Iraq's intransigence and deceptive practices during the periods of UN
inspections between 1991 and 2003 deepened suspicions among many
world governments and intelligence services that Baghdad had ongoing
WMD programs. Ironically, even at key junctures when the regime
attempted to partially or fully comply with UN resolutions, its suspicious
behavior and destruction of authenticating documentation only reinforced
the perception that Iraq was being deceptive.

Key events and Iraqi behaviors that shaped Western perceptions include:

- An early established pattern of "cheat and retreat." Iraq concealed items
  and activities in the early 1990s, and when detected, attempted to rectify
  the shortcomings, usually secretly and without documentation. Those
  coverups were seen to validate analytic assessments that Iraq intended to
  deny, deceive, and maintain forbidden capabilities.

- Shocked by the unexpected aggressiveness of early UN Special
  Commission (UNSCOM) inspections in 1991, Iraq secretly destroyed or
  dismantled most undeclared items and records that could have been used
  to validate the unilateral destruction, leaving Baghdad unable to provide
  convincing proof when it later tried to demonstrate compliance.

- We now judge that the 1995 defection of Saddam's son-in-law Husayn
  Kamil—a critical figure in Iraq's WMD and denial and deception (D&D)
  activities—prompted Iraq to change strategic direction and cease efforts
  to retain WMD programs. Iraqi attempts that year to find face-saving
  means to disclose previously hidden information, however, reinforced the
  idea that Baghdad was deceptive and unreliable. Instead of helping to
  close the books, Iraq's actions reinvigorated the hunt for concealed
  WMD, as analysts perceived that Iraq had both the intent and capability
  to continue WMD efforts during inspections.

- When Iraq's revelations were met by added UN scrutiny and distrust,
  frustrated Iraqi leaders deepened their belief that inspections were
  politically motivated and would not lead to the end of sanctions. As Iraq
  turned its political focus to illicit economic efforts to end its isolation,
  eliminate sanctions, and protect its dual-use infrastructure, these actions
  increased suspicions that Iraq continued to hide WMD.

- Other Iraqi actions that fueled the perception of WMD-related deceptions included Special Security Organization (SSO) and other efforts to hide non-WMD secrets to protect Saddam and the regime   Iraq also continued to provide inaccuracies in UN declarations   for a variety of reasons, not the least of which was an inability to document these statements.

- Iraq did not accurately interpret US and international policy drivers; in 2003, it assessed that the United States would not invade Iraq.

- Several people claimed that Iraqi officials did not believe that all of Iraq's WMD had been destroyed. These officials may in good faith have conveyed the message to others that Iraq retained WMD.

Early 1990s concealment activity combined with unexpected revelations following Husayn Kamil's defection led analysts to view Iraq as a sophisticated D&D practitioner. Faced with inconclusive or uncertain data, analysts made judgments with conviction that Iraq could successfully conceal damaging data.

We recognize that portions of our data were supplied by the same people who were responsible for the deception campaign and provided insight in captivity. Captured documentary evidence exploited to date so far supports the conclusions of this paper.

Contents

Scope Note

This is one in a series of intelligence assessments (IAs) in the CIA's *Iraq WMD Retrospective Series* that addresses our post–Operation Iraqi Freedom (OIF) understanding of Iraq's weapons of mass destruction (WMD), delivery system, and denial and deception (D&D) programs. These IAs reevaluate past assessments and reporting in light of the investigations carried out by the Iraq Survey Group (ISG).

This assessment addresses how the Iraqis perceived and reacted to the international inspection process and the effect these actions had on analyst perceptions. This IA is not intended to be a comprehensive review of all CIA analysis or the analytical process on Iraqi WMD issues. The conclusions of this IA are generally consistent with ISG's findings as reflected in the *Comprehensive Report of the Special Advisor to the DCI on Iraq's WMD* issued on 30 September 2004 and other products. This review of historical reporting and assessments helps to provide additional context on the interplay between Iraqi actions and intelligence judgments.

---

* More comprehensive papers on the individual Iraqi WMD programs, including comparisons of prewar estimates and postwar conclusions, are to be published elsewhere in this *Retrospective Series*.

**Misreading Intentions: Iraq's
Reaction to Inspections Created
Picture of Deception**
Iraq WMD Retrospective Series

Overview

Iraqi leadership reactions to UN resolutions on
weapons inspections between 1991 and 2003 fostered
an atmosphere of distrust with the world community.
Analysts interpreted Iraq's intransigence and ongoing
deceptive practices as indicators of continued WMD
programs or an intent to preserve WMD capabilities,
reinforcing intelligence we were receiving at the time
that Saddam Husayn continued to pursue WMD. A
combination of poorly and hastily considered Iraqi
actions, regime assumptions and beliefs that did not
reflect an accurate understanding of the world outside
Iraq, and the typical paranoia of a security state led to
Baghdad's inability to extricate itself from what it
viewed as oppressive sanctions and outside suspicion.
Instead, Iraq continued to exhibit obstructive and
inconsistent behaviors that perpetuated the belief by
⸻⸻⸻⸻⸻ that Baghdad was
not fully complying with UN resolutions and was
concealing ongoing WMD programs.

1991: Initial Approach to Inspections . . . (U)

Iraq initially tried to end sanctions without fully
revealing WMD programs as required by UN
resolutions, believing that appearing to comply would
be sufficient. Iraqi leaders were optimistic that
inspections and sanctions would end quickly.[1] Their
approach to inspections was to make sure that nothing
was found to contradict their initial false declarations
while they destroyed contradictory evidence:

• Several officials stated after the fall of the regime
that Iraq's original belief was that it would not have
to comply with the inspections, which would be
cursory and only last a few weeks.

⸻⸻⸻⸻⸻ initially believed that it would not have to follow
any UN mandates, because in its view no one had
ever followed a UN mandate ⸻⸻⸻

Iraq planned to gather declared items for presentation,
hide other materials in place, disperse and conceal
nuclear materials, and deny the existence of pre-1991
WMD efforts:

This assessment was prepared by the Office of Iraq Analysis. Comments and queries are welcome and
may be directed to ⸻⸻⸻⸻⸻

Overall Pattern of 'Cheat and Retreat'

The reactions of both sides to the inspection process formed a pattern; Iraq would start to rectify an uncovered shortcoming, usually in secret. The West viewed the discoveries as validation that Iraq had a continued intent to deny, deceive, and maintain forbidden capabilities, especially because Iraqis usually begrudgingly revealed that they had given up those capabilities after being caught with discrepancies.

International weapons inspectors often detected Iraq's concealment activities and discrepancies in WMD-related information, triggering investigations that delayed the lifting of sanctions, thus forming a pattern that deepened mutual suspicion:

- In interviews conducted after the fall of the regime, senior officials indicated that Saddam sought to avoid involvement in a drawn-out process with UNSCOM and the IAEA to investigate every new issue.

- In April 1991, for example, Iraq declared that it had neither a nuclear weapons program nor an enrichment program. Inspections in June and September 1991 proved that Iraq had lied on both counts, had explored multiple enrichment paths, and had a well-developed nuclear weapons program.

Baghdad destroyed rather than revealed items, attempting to make its inaccurate assertions of no programs correct in a legalistic sense.

Decisions to destroy much of the paperwork that could have verified the destruction exacerbated Iraq's inability to later extricate itself from being viewed in the "cheat and retreat" paradigm:

March 1992, Iraq decided to declare the unilateral destruction of certain prohibited items to the Security Council, while continuing to conceal its biological warfare (BW) program and important aspects of the nuclear, chemical, and missile programs

Saddam Husayn ordered Husayn Kamil to hide the weapons in 1991, but gave them up once cornered. He said that Saddam destroyed all WMD in secret after pressure from the UN and inspectors, after initially thinking he could hide weapons also acknowledged the 1991 unilateral destruction.

said that the 1991 order to destroy all documents related to the BW program caused problems later, when Iraq did not have the documentation to support revised declarations in the late 1990s admitting to an offensive program

wondered why he was ordered to destroy the paperwork for the missile destruction in 1991, forcing Iraqis to rely upon personal recollection in later years when trying to prove that destruction had actually taken place

... Leads to Decision on Unilateral Destruction

When the inspections proved more intrusive than expected, the Iraqi leadership appears to have panicked and made a fateful decision to secretly destroy much of the remaining nondeclared items, and eliminate the evidence. According to several officials, Iraq decided to surreptitiously destroy many items and hide others, rather than contradict earlier declarations. Many officials described the regime's shock over inspectors' aggressiveness, citing examples like the June 1991 discovery by IAEA

that Iraqis were moving nuclear electromagnetic isotope separation (EMIS) components away from an inspection:

even after the IAEA inspectors tracked down EMIS components, the regime did not fully understand the implications of its initial false declarations, and Baghdad decided to unilaterally destroy much of the hidden material rather than declare it.

likened this decision to Iraq's fateful 1990 decision to invade Kuwait in terms of having negative consequences for Iraq

July 1991, after consulting with Saddam, to destroy items, although some allegedly were hidden without The bulk of the materials were destroyed in this initial period:

the destruction order for the BW program came in June 1991 recalls getting 48 hours to get rid of everything

time, was their primary BW agent production and storage facility prior to the Gulf war. As with the other programs, orders were given to destroy documentation of the destruction and to retain no copies of other documents. WMD-related organizations received orders to turn over key "know-how" documents to the Special Security Organization (SSO) for safekeeping

said Iraq retained two Scud-type ballistic missiles after the initial unilateral destruction in the summer of 1991 that were destroyed later that year

* Iraq unilaterally destroyed 25 biological al-Husayn warheads and approximately 134 biological R-400 aerial bombs in 1991

noted the destruction of 20 concealed al-Husayn chemical warfare (CW) warheads in the summer of 1991

Weapons Deceptions Maintained After 1992

at the time Iraq still did not admit to having destroyed biological bombs and warheads and represented BW warheads as being CW warheads.

- In November 1993, Iraq accepted UNSCR 715 that allowed for long-term UN monitoring of its weapons programs following two years of Iraqi objections that such monitoring constituted an unacceptable infringement of sovereignty. Baghdad expressed its hope that this step would lead to the immediate lifting of sanctions.

- In October 1994, the regime threatened to end cooperation with the UN and moved forces to the Kuwaiti border after dashed expectations of a positive UNSCOM report in September. Baghdad defused the crisis by agreeing to recognize the Kuwaiti border

By the summer of 1995, international will to sustain sanctions and inspections was dwindling

- Iraqi officials did not admit to weaponized BW agent until after the defection of Husayn Kamil the next month.

and an emboldened Iraq in June had issued an ultimatum to the UN to lift sanctions

Diplomacy 1992-95: Iraq Tries To Break Free (U)

Frustration with continued sanctions led Baghdad to alternate between challenging the UN and taking diplomatic steps during this period that the regime thought would alleviate Iraq's isolation. Saddam's regime also experienced intense economic and security pressure, with the Iraqi dinar falling to its lowest level ever in November 1995 and several notable security threats, including a 1995 coup plot and associated unrest with the Dulaym tribe:

- Baghdad refused to allow a July 1992 inspection of the Ministry of Agriculture, saying it would violate Iraq's sovereignty and was intended for intelligence collection.

Turning Point—August 1995: Iraq 'Scared (Mostly) Straight

Iraq's reaction to the defection of Husayn Kamil—a former Minister of Industry and Military Industrialization, Minister of Defense, and Minister of Oil, among other positions—in August 1995 appears to be the key turning point in Iraq's decision to cooperate more with inspections, but it also strengthened the West's perception of Iraq as a successful and efficient deceiver. Clumsy but genuine Iraqi moves toward transparency—significant alterations in their "cheat and retreat" pattern—not only went undetected but instead seemed to confirm that Iraq could and would conceal evidence of proscribed programs.

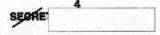

We had previously assessed that Iraq used Kamil's defection as an opportunity to disclose some additional WMD documentation

We now judge that the Iraqis feared that Kamil—a critical figure in Iraq's WMD and D&D activities—would reveal additional undisclosed information. Iraq decided that further widespread deception and attempts to hold onto extensive WMD programs while under UN sanctions was untenable and changed strategic direction by adopting a policy of disclosure and improved cooperation:

states that Iraq tried to conceal everything from the UN prior to 1992, but after Kamil's 1995 defection he was told to release information to the UN without restrictions

- Iraq's attempts to find face-saving means to reveal previously concealed information and extricate itself from sanctions appeared deceptive and reinforced the idea that it was still hiding important elements of its programs.

Confusion at the Top
Several high-ranking detained Iraqi officials described the chain of events surrounding the defection and the resulting panic. Even the highest levels of leadership were unsure what Kamil could reveal, what WMD information was still retained, and what actions to take.

contained elements of an Iraqi damage assessment, laying out what Kamil knew and might not know, and what was still hidden, all of which Iraq later declared.

- Multiple high-level security and government officials affirmed receiving orders to move WMD documents to Kamil's farm, where they were presented to the UN, and Kamil received blame for their concealment.

We now believe the movement of documents to Husayn Kamil's chicken farm and their turnover to the UN represented a genuine attempt to come clean on programs albeit while saving face. Baghdad blamed the previous concealment of aspects of Iraq's WMD programs and the resulting complications with inspectors on an untrustworthy traitor. Captured documentary evidence and interviews support the idea that major concealment operations ended in 1995. Iraqis publicly continued to attribute all WMD and concealment activity to Husayn Kamil—a trend that continued even after the fall of the regime.

Officials Recount Chaotic Document Movements

officials provided first-hand accounts of the confusion and competing orders, and they admitted their roles in the movement, destruction, concealment, and deliberate misrepresentation of the nature of the cache of documents:

Iraq's firmly established "cheat and retreat" pattern made it difficult for UN inspectors and Western analysts to accept new Iraqi assertions at face value, especially when there was evidence at the time that the chicken farm documents were placed there by the regime after the defection.

Proven Deception Underscores Analytic Mindset
Iraqi revelations after Husayn Kamil's flight to
Jordan led to an irrevocable loss of trust by the West.
Iraq was again judged dishonest and deceptive in its
dealings with the UN and determined to retain WMD
capabilities. The new declarations

effectively sidelined previous attempts to
accurately account for material balances of CW agent
production and weaponization:

Some of the information revealed in 1995, such as a
more extensive weaponization effort for BW aerial
bombs, missile warheads, and spray tanks, was not
previously suspected and surprised the UN,
provoking deep suspicion of future Iraqi behaviors
and declarations.

The defection exposed the previously unknown
1991 crash program to develop nuclear weapons,

The 1995 events reinforced the prevailing analytical
paradigm that the Iraqis had been successful in hiding
evidence of significant WMD programs, proved that
they had not intended to cooperate with the UN, and
would only reveal or dismantle programs after being
caught in a lie. Iraq attained the veneer of competence
as a D&D practitioner, and future activities were
viewed through the prism:

The turnover of an incomplete set of documents,
rather than being viewed as a sign of Iraqi
cooperation, opened new issues for UNSCOM and
the IAEA to investigate.

Instead of helping close the books on Iraqi WMD
programs, Iraq's actions reinvigorated the hunt for
concealed WMD

Mutual Suspicion Grows: 1996-98

After the revelations following the defection,
UNSCOM began a series of inspections of Iraq's
security apparatus and concealment mechanisms. Iraq
viewed this new investigation as proof that WMD
was being used as a pretense to bring about regime
change.

passage of the Iraq Liberation
Act by the US Congress enhanced Iraqi suspicions.
Iraq also accepted UNSCR 986 (Oil-For-Food),
which led to growing external trade and decreased
international isolation, as well as an increased Iraqi
willingness to push back against inspections. A series
of standoffs with the UN over inspections culminated
in Operation Desert Fox in December 1998 and the
expulsion of the inspectors.

**Concerns About Never-Ending Inspections and
US, UN Motives**
After 1995, Iraqi leaders solidified their belief that
inspections would not end and sanctions would not be
lifted, especially when Iraq's new disclosures did not
lead to any relief of restrictions. Iraq's focus turned to
protecting its technological infrastructure.

the highest level of Iraqi command
believed that the US   knew that Iraq's
programs were dormant, it could account for some of
Iraq's subsequent behaviors:

• It is possible that Baghdad decided to pursue a more
aggressive strategy toward inspections, convinced
that Washington lacked the proof to convince the
rest of the world.

believed" that the United States thought that Iraq

had nothing ▭ Enough officials recounted this story to suggest that Iraq understood it to be true, and

Many officials expressed the belief that the inspectors wanted to prolong their high UN salaries and did not want to resolve technical issues. Such exchanges support the idea that the Iraqi regime did not understand the West's position on weapons and sanctions, and they sought other reasons to explain continued inspections:

believed that Iraq would never get a clean bill of health from the UN

This was one factor that prompted them to cease cooperation with the UN in August 1998

• After the fall of the regime.

expressed surprise when a former US inspector came into the room to try to resolve old material balance issues, because they felt it had been a ruse for US policy goals and not a legitimate concern.

told debriefers that certain UN inspectors did not want to solve any problems because they were making salaries "100 times higher" than their families back home.

Saddam Resented Inspections, Distrusted Motives. Available reporting suggests that Saddam resented the inspections and thought they infringed upon Iraq's sovereignty and viability. Saddam personally expressed his dissatisfaction with the inspection process on several occasions:

Baghdad's Threat Perception

said that Iraq did not want to come clean about the final destruction of Scuds following the defection of Husayn Kamil, thinking that belief in retained Scuds would deter Iran from invading.

Iraqis viewed Iran and Israel, rather than the United States, as the primary threat to the regime. This could explain why Iraq might have continued to give the impression that it was concealing WMD—to instill fear or at least uncertainty in their neighbors:

emphatically believed in Iran as Iraq's principal enemy—"past, present, and future," asserting the United States was oceans away and did not have long-term designs on Iraq.

Inspections Resume With UNMOVIC 2002-03

By the summer of 2002, it became apparent that Iraq would be willing to accept another round of inspections, this time under the banner of the United Nations Monitoring, Verification and Inspection Commission (UNMOVIC). Iraq again began preparations for active inspections inside its borders.

Leaders Convinced US Would Not Invade

Officials said that the Iraqi leadership in 2002 and 2003 assessed that the United States would not invade Iraq and would at worst institute an air-strike campaign along the lines of Operation Desert Fox:

Saddam still believed that there would be no war, as the United States had achieved its goal of domination in the Gulf and Red Sea area.

and said that the leadership believed the United States did not have the forces to invade Iraq, and press reports said that Washington was not willing to sacrifice US lives.

Iraq's Own Actions Compound Problems

Top regime officials have conceded since Operation Iraqi Freedom (OIF) that past Iraqi deception led to suspicion of Iraq's motives. Iraqi leaders, however, did not understand that they would have had to take specific steps with UNMOVIC to overcome perceptions of dishonesty. Several officials reported that they believed that just presenting the truth would be enough to rectify past problems:

puzzlement at the idea that Iraq needed to do something beyond allowing inspectors access to sites to establish trust with the UN.

felt that if the inspections had only been allowed to continue for seven more months in 2003, all outstanding issues would have been resolved, equating successful inspections with the number of sites visited.

Most senior leaders admitted that the UN and United States could have perceived Iraq's behaviors as suspicious, and offered unprompted examples:

decisions like Iraq's development of missiles with ranges only 20 or 30 km beyond the allowed 150-km range gave the impression that Iraq was defying the UN.

claimed that even though WMD had been destroyed in 1991, not letting inspectors into palaces aroused suspicions.

whether important information had been concealed. He found that people moved "unimportant things," such as furniture, and felt that "what those stupid people did gave the inspectors the right to suspect all kinds of things.

Over-Preparation for Inspections

From many accounts, Iraqis tried hard to make sure the final round of UN inspections went smoothly, conducting their own investigations into potential anomalies.

actions taken by the Iraqi side, however, caused them to continue to give the appearance of deception, especially as Iraq continued to hide some information on lesser points:

official who had hidden missile documents in his house, even though this person had attested to the UN that he had nothing. The investigation concluded that the official had taken the papers to bolster his scientific credentials and to use in a private business. Iraqi leadership worried that these items would affect the content of its 2002 declaration

1994 hid documentation related to the consumption and unilateral destruction of Scud propellant because it would show that Iraq had produced its own oxidizer for its Scud-type ballistic missiles before 1991. This contributed to UNSCOM's and UNMOVIC's inability to account for Iraq's Scud propellant, a gap that suggested Iraq retained a covert Scud-variant SRBM force

Many high-ranking officials did not want to give the appearance of obstructing the UN, and they tried to ensure smooth cooperation. They ordered working-level Iraqi security officers to cooperate with the UN and not cause problems. Steps were taken to make sure that sites and documentation would endure inspectors' scrutiny, but some of the moves were heavyhanded, and seemed more suspicious to the West. The question of intent is still unclear—senior-level officials insist that their motives were benign, but many of their actions are still ambiguous as to whether cooperation or sanitization was intended:

Other Factors Reinforce Deceptive Image

Throughout the 1990s and beyond, other ongoing Iraqi activities, policies, and societal norms reinforced UN and international suspicion that Baghdad continued WMD denial and deception. These internal policies and mindsets—especially the importance of regime security—now appear to be even stronger drivers than earlier assessed, and caused the Iraqi leadership to present an aggressive and unrepentant image

Security State

The Iraqi regime had an extreme distrust of outsiders combined with a fanatical devotion to security that in many cases led to actions that sabotaged efforts to demonstrate that it wanted cooperation. The presence of SSO minders was interpreted as concealment and evasion activity, when their purpose was to warn Saddam of inspections and to handle "sensitive site" inspections as part of their Presidential protection function:

Internal Self-Deception

Fear of retribution and delivering bad news meant that the highest levels of leadership might not have known the true limits of Iraq's technical and military capabilities. Iraqi leaders may have made decisions and projected an image of strength on the basis of inaccurate and inflated capabilities:

Several people claimed that many Iraqi officials did not believe that they had destroyed all of Iraq's WMD. They may have in good faith conveyed the message to others that Iraq retained WMD:

many generals were not necessarily aware that Iraq did not have WMD

Analytic Liabilities (U)

The example of pre-2003 US analysis on Iraq's WMD programs highlights the problem of how to assess ambiguous data in light of past practices. Given Iraq's extensive history of deception and only small changes in outward behavior, analysts did not spend adequate time examining the premise that the Iraqis had undergone a change in their behavior, and that what Iraq was saying by the end of 1995 was, for the most part, accurate. This was combined with the analysts' knowledge that they had underestimated Iraq's programs prior to Operation Desert Storm. A liability of intelligence analysis is that once a party has been proven to be an effective deceiver, that knowledge becomes a heavy factor in the calculations of the analytical observer. In the Iraqi example, this impression was based on a series of undocumented revelations of unilateral destruction combined with unexpected revelations from a high-level, well-placed defector, leading analysts to be more likely predisposed to interpret similar but unrelated behaviors observed after 1996 as proof of continued forbidden activity

The Analysts' Retrospective

The concept for this paper was generated by analysts who had worked Iraq WMD and D&D for several years, including many with experience going back to Operation Desert Storm

Several general themes emerged from our investigation:

• Analysts tended to focus on what was most important to us—the hunt for WMD—and less on what would be most important for a paranoid dictatorship to protect. Viewed through an Iraqi prism, their reputation, their security, their overall technological capabilities, and their status needed to be preserved. Deceptions were perpetrated and detected, but the reasons for those deceptions were misread.

• We were surprised to discover just how broken and ineffective the Iraqi regime was.

• Analysts understood that the Iraqis were working with a different logic system, but did not go far enough in accounting for how greatly Iraqi and Western thought differs.

51918
WB

~~Secret~~

Ficr

(1
(1

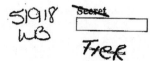

Intelligence Report

Office of Near Eastern, South Asian, and African Analysis · 29 May 1998

India: BJP Flexing Muscles, But How Far Will It Go?

India's recent nuclear tests and sabre-rattling over Kashmir may be a sign that the country's Hindu nationalist Bharatiya Janata Party (BJP)-led government believes it will be able to follow through with its long-range agenda--to remake the country as a powerful Hindu state in accordance with party mythology about India's past. If true, the party's widely popular security posture would help it strengthen its political base and prepare the ground for more controversial domestic reforms down the road.

- *Although the BJP failed to win a majority in the general election, the party is riding a tidal wave of popularity from the tests and is now signaling that resolving Kashmir on India's terms will be next on its agenda.*

- *New Delhi is claiming that its nuclear tests were for national security and to counter China. Nonetheless, last week Home Minister Advani declared publicly that Pakistan must "roll back its anti-India policy immediately" or "it will prove costly" for Islamabad.*

- *Pakistan's decision to conduct nuclear tests is being portrayed by the BJP government as confirmation that its "get tough" policy toward its neighbor was justified.*

The BJP is sending mixed messages on its foreign policy priorities beyond the confines of South Asia, at least in part to keep foreign powers guessing about its intentions. India is calculating that demonstrating its nuclear prowess makes it a state the international community can no longer ignore and will win it a permanent seat on the United Nations Security Council and a place at the table in various regional forums.

It is far from clear how far the BJP will be able to proceed with more controversial aspects of its agenda. The party leads a coalition of diverse political interests and must retain the support of its allies to stay in power. Many BJP partners would oppose party goals to limit special provisions for India's 120 million Muslims on

NESAF IR: 98-40137

(b), (d)
DECL ON: X1, X2, X5
DRV FROM: Multiple Sources

~~Secret~~

CIA\NESAF IR 98-40137

divorce and other religious practices and end the special status of Muslim majority Kashmir, both of which could produce widespread political unrest.

If the party is serious about exploiting its burgeoning popularity to strengthen its hold on national politics, however, one indicator would be the calling of a snap election in the next few months.

- *Some press pundits in India already are predicting such a poll.*

- *BJP insiders estimate that an election held soon could give them a solid majority in a new parliament and possibly enough strength to amend the Constitution.*

Despite the BJP's current popularity, developments could reverse its fortunes, particularly if they occurred before the party is able to reinforce its hold on power through a snap election or other means. The BJP's handling of India's economic slowdown could be its most serious vulnerability.

- *Serious inflation could result if the government expands defense and security spending at the same time it tries to "kickstart" the economy with a broad-based economic stimulus.*

- *Although South East Asian-style meltdown is unlikely, the economy could deteriorate enough to erode the BJP's support as the euphoria from the nuclear tests erodes.*

India: BJP Flexing Muscles, But How Far Will It Go?

India's new Bharatiya Janata Party-led government is riding a tidal wave of public support since its recent nuclear tests. The applause may embolden party leaders to consider pursuing other goals outlined in the coalition government's nationalist agenda, such as ending special provisions for the country's minority Muslims.

- Popular approval of the tests--which were conducted on 11 and 13 May--reached 91 percent in one poll, and shows no sign of diminishing.

- Indian financial markets are shrugging off threatened international sanctions.

- At a press conference with Kashmir Chief Minister Abdullah, Advani said that the nuclear tests ushered in a new era in India-Pakistani relations and warned Islamabad that New Delhi would respond to provocations in Kashmir in a manner "costly for Pakistan." Advani also refused to rule out Indian "hot pursuit" across the Line of Control, cautioned that Indian troops would adopt a more "offensive" posture, and said that the BJP would not hold talks with militant groups.

This memorandum was prepared by [ ] Office of Near Eastern, South Asian, and African Analysis. Comments and queries are welcome and may be directed to [ ]

3

India: Kashmir Policy Turns Proactive

India and Pakistan's mutual claim on Kashmir--the cause of two wars between them--is the primary obstacle to improved ties and remains the most likely flashpoint for war. Several major incidents in the first few months of this year have doused hopes for a significant withdrawal of security forces from Kashmir, as envisioned by the state governor barely a year ago.

- Since January, militants have conducted several high profile attacks on civilians. Entire families of Kashmiri Hindus have been massacred.

- Journalists in Pakistan say that a similar slaughter of 22 villagers in the Pakistani part of Kashmir this month was a retaliatory strike by pro-Indian counter-militants.

The BJP government is adopting an aggressive posture in Kashmir that is certain to raise tensions with Islamabad. In response to increased violence in the state this year, New Delhi announced that senior civilian and military officials would be given "a free hand" to deal with insurgents and terrorists in Kashmir.

- Vajpayee this week gave hardline Home Minister Advani full responsibility for Kashmir policy. He will have carte blanche to approve measures like cross-border raids, "hot pursuit" forays across the line of control, village "sweeps," and crackdowns on infiltration.

The BJP has always endorsed a "get tough" policy in Kashmir, but the issue has taken center stage since India's nuclear tests.

- Last week, Advani announced the tests had "ushered in a new era in Indo-Pak relations," and explicitly linked India's nuclear capability with "finding a lasting solution to the Kashmir problem."

- Vajpayee also hinted at the connection between the tests and New Delhi's Kashmir policy last week when he took Kashmir Chief Minister Farooq Abdullah--who lacks any connection to the scientific, defense, or nuclear establishments--on an official visit to the test site.

Advani's stated goals in Kashmir are to deal with Pakistan's "proxy war"; improve development in the state; and resettle Kashmiri Hindu refugees who had fled the violence in the state. Advani appears to rule out any non-military option, including talks with militant groups and Kashmiri political separatists.

Why Test Now?

The BJP decided to conduct the nuclear tests to enhance its domestic political standing. BJP leaders clearly anticipated that the move would be widely popular and would boost the government's political stock at home, particularly after the Ghauri launch.

- Although the BJP has long called for nuclear testing and inducting nuclear weapons into India's arsenal, Indians of all stripes take pride in standing up to the great powers by demonstrating the country's scientific achievements and military strength.

- Adopting an aggressive posture toward Pakistan also is a sure vote-getter, especially in the northern and western states, which comprise the BJP's main base of support.

- The BJP also knew that it would gain public support by openly defying Western threats of sanctions.

- Prior to the tests, the government had been fending off embarrassing public demands from unruly coalition partners that was fueling press speculation about the coalition's staying power.

Who Knew?

The decision to test was tightly held

The decisionmakers clearly kept the loop small for reasons of secrecy, but the BJP also has a history of ignoring its political allies when considering high-profile policy moves. The BJP has handled its state level alliances in this way, reasoning that partners who depend on BJP strength for their seats at the table should take a back seat on decisionmaking.

Where the BJP Goes from Here

Foreign Policy. India expects its demonstrated nuclear prowess eventually will earn it international respect and a permanent seat on the UN Security Council. Advani's statements indicate that India will be prepared to defend its preeminence with force if necessary, although India would prefer Pakistan make the first move in any conflict.

- Pakistan's nuclear tests will vindicate and embolden those in the BJP government who favor New Delhi's current, harsher stance toward Islamabad.

- New Delhi is unlikely to pick a fight with China, which lies outside India's security orbit, although it clearly regards nuclear weapons as an equalizer and a deterrent against Chinese aggression. Indians--Hindu nationalists in particular--remember bitterly India's humiliating defeat by China in their short 1962 border war, and ill feelings toward its northern neighbor run deep.

- Vajpayee was humiliated by the Chinese during a visit there as Foreign Minister in the late 1970s, however, and Defense Minister Fernandes is an outspoken advocate for the Tibetan cause.

Beyond its immediate neighborhood, New Delhi is likely to send mixed signals on specific aspects of its foreign policy at least in part to keep foreign powers guessing about its intentions. It is already dangling the possibility that it might sign an amended Comprehensive Test Ban Treaty (CTBT) to stifle world criticism in the wake of the tests. Statements by Indian officials, however, vary widely from saying that India "will never sign" to claims that it wants to sign " as soon as possible." In our judgment, India is trying to goad the United States into making an attractive offer on CTBT without tipping its own hand.

- senior BJP officials charged with foreign policymaking support resisting US pressure to sign the CTBT.

The Domestic Agenda. The BJP is a long way from meeting the full range of goals in its manifesto, and it is unclear whether the BJP's burgeoning popularity in the wake of the tests will embolden party leaders to begin implementing the BJP's controversial domestic plans. The BJP may first take steps to consolidate its recent political gains. New Delhi political circles are discussing the probability of a snap election in the next few months, which might enable the BJP to form a majority government in its own right.

- BJP strategists expect they would win over 400 seats in a new parliament, This calculation probably is based on their analysis of 141 constituencies in which it placed second in the most recent election.

- Such a showing would give the BJP a two-thirds majority--enough to amend India's Constitution. It also would allow the party to mount a campaign to change India from a parliamentary to a presidential system, a goal declared in its agenda, which would free the BJP from the threat of no-confidence votes and let it set a fixed time frame for implementing its agenda.

Once the BJP gained sole control in New Delhi, we expect the party's extremist elements--including the party's right-wing parent organization, the Rashtriya Swayamsavak Sangh (RSS)--would become more assertive in driving policy decisions. Vajpayee, Advani, and party President Kushabhau Thakre all hail from the RSS and--with their political power consolidated--would be sympathetic to the organization's wishes.

- RSS assisted the party with policymaking and campaign strategy during the campaign the RSS agreed to drop *Hindutva*-related issues from the coalition's agenda to preserve the political alliance, as its main objective was to have a BJP government installed.

- After the BJP's win, RSS officials kept a low profile in policymaking because they wanted the BJP government to be successful and improve on its position in the next election, a strategy that may pay off much sooner than they expected.

Indicators that the party was implementing its hard-line domestic policy would include:

- Resettling displaced Kashmiri Hindus in their own homes.

- Laying the groundwork for adopting a uniform civil code that would end special provisions for the country's 120 million Muslims.

- Deporting foreign refugees and guest workers.

- Renewing the campaign to erect Hindu temples in place of disputed mosques, such as at Ayodhya.

The BJP's Hindu Blueprint for the Nation

The BJP's election manifesto (*see Annex for excerpts*) calls for revamping Indian politics, society, and economics in accordance with the party's ideology of *Hindutva*, defined as "cultural nationalism" in BJP literature. Party mythology recalls India's "timeless cultural heritage," which the manifesto says is "central to all regions, religions and languages." Key elements of the blueprint include:

A Hawkish Defense Posture. Members of the BJP's defense cell in January established a working plan of action, [   ] include declaring India's nuclear capability, forming a National Security Council; restructuring the Ministry of Defense; restructuring and reorganizing the military; and developing defenses against missile threats.

Cultural Assimilation. The BJP calls for an undivided India that is united by Hindu culture. More immediately, the party's manifesto aims at limiting special provisions for India's 120 million Muslims on divorce and other religious practices and ending special status for the majority Muslim state of Kashmir.

- The party also pledges to rebuild the Hindu temple at Ayodhya, the ascribed birthplace of Hindu God Ram and the site of the bloody destruction by Hindu hard-liners of an historic mosque in 1992. [   ]

Economic Self-Sufficiency. The BJP's *Swadeshi*, or "India first" platform--if implemented fully--would focus the country's economy more inward. The party's manifesto suggests New Delhi will do whatever it takes to protect domestic industry. Specifically, the BJP manifesto calls for "rapid, large-scale internal liberalization, but calibrated globalization so that the Indian industry gets a period of seven to 10 years for substantial integration with the global economy."

Constraints on the BJP

The BJP is not invincible, despite its strong showing in recent days, and a number of developments could cause the party's popular support to erode. These would not include a military conflict with Pakistan, which would generate a national call to arms and probably would strengthen the government further.

The BJP's handling of India's economic slowdown could be its most serious vulnerability. Although an East Asian-style meltdown is unlikely, the economy could deteriorate enough for the BJP's public support to erode as the euphoria from the nuclear tests wears off. Business circles and consumer classes in particular—a critical support base for the BJP—are impatient to return the economy to pre-slowdown growth levels.

The BJP has promised a rosy economic future of healthy growth based on thriving domestic industries protected from foreign competition, expanding agricultural output, beefed up security forces, and a strong and respected currency. These goals may not be compatible, and serious resource constraints complicated by sanctions will force the government to make choices.

- Serious inflation could result soon if the government expands defense and security spending at the same time it tries to "kickstart" the economy with a broad-based fiscal stimulus.

- Sanctions would slow foreign inflows—now averaging about $400 million a month—which the government needs to support the rupee and provide inputs for urgently needed infrastructure projects. Even limited US sanctions imposed narrowly on the Indian government would raise the cost of all foreign investment projects in India by removing the United States Export-Import Bank, the Overseas Private Investment Corporation, and the Trade and Development Association as potential financiers.

Other developments could also produce a sudden fall in the BJP's popularity, in our judgment, including:

- An announcement by China that it will counter India's aggressive posturing by aiding Pakistan in any conflict with India.

- Widespread credible reports of radiation sickness in India from the nuclear tests.

The RSS: The Vanguard of Hindu Nationalism

Founded in 1925, the Rashtriya Swayamsevak Sangh (RSS)--or National Volunteer Corps--is a powerful Hindu revivalist organization that seeks to unite Hindus in an explicitly Hindu state. The organization's strongholds are western India and the Hindi-speaking north Indian heartland, though its members are active in every region and among Indian communities in foreign countries. The RSS publicly shuns politics and prefers to focus on education, charitable work, and partybuilding activities. Behind the scenes, however, it provides the bulk of the BJP's funding, as well as party workers and political direction. RSS members occupy leadership positions at every level of the BJP, though both parties publicly stress their organizational independence. At least one-third of the Indian cabinet--including Prime Minister Vajpayee--are RSS members. New Delhi has banned the RSS three times since independence in 1947. The organization now functions legally and is thriving under the current BJP-led government.

11

ANNEX: The BJP's Optic on the World

Hindu nationalists in the BJP and associated groups that make up the *sangh parivar*, or "family" of like-minded organizations, see the world differently from other Indian political parties. According to party documents, academic studies, ⬚. ⬚ the BJP envisions a world order in which India's unique civilization takes center stage alongside Western, Chinese, and other great civilizations. The vision carries strong allusions to India's "civilizing mission" in the world. ⬚

BJP ideology recalls a pristine--and mythical--Golden Age that predates the arrival of Muslim and European conquerors who they believe sullied India's unique Hindu identity. The BJP, however, does not seek to convert non-Hindus or impose religious uniformity. Its focus is cultural unity. Religious devotions hold little attraction to many BJP stalwarts, including Prime Minister Vajpayee and Home Minister Advani. On the other hand, the concept of *Hindutva*--loosely translated by the BJP as "cultural nationalism"--provides a national identity the BJP believes includes all Indians. The BJP's quarrel is with those Indians—Muslims and Christians, in particular--who reject this transcendent Hindu identity in favor of composite identities that spring from "foreign" civilizations.

- The cultural frontiers of the BJP's world vision extend beyond present-day political boundaries and incorporate all of India's South Asian neighbors--*akhand bharat* ("undivided India") in BJP parlance--and the Indian diaspora spread around the globe. This vision, however, does not encompass non-Indians living outside the Subcontinent. Historically, India has not harbored or pursued expansionist designs beyond its own neighborhood.

- Hindu national theorists reject the pacifist strains of Indian nationalism and champion images of martial prowess and strength. They insist that India's regional primacy be asserted vigorously. Attempts by external powers--the United States and China, in particular--to alter the Delhi-centric balance of power in the Subcontinent by supporting India's neighbors are opposed bitterly.

- The BJP is portraying its decision to test nuclear weapons as a demand for international recognition of Hindu civilization's rightful place in the world and a warning to New Delhi's neighbors to acknowledge India's supremacy. ⬚

ANNEX: Excerpts from the BJP's 1998 election manifesto entitled "Our Vision, Our Will, Our Way."

On Indian civilization: *"The Indian nation evolved not by marching its armies and conquering...but by inner-directed pursuit of universal values by the [Hindu ascetics] living in the forests and mountains of India...It is the ancient Indian mind that formulated the Constitution of India...not the Constitution that shaped the Indian mind."*

On protecting the national interest: *"In the recent past we have seen a tendency [by Indian governments] to bend under pressure. This arises as much out of ignorance of our rightful place and role in world affairs as also from a loss of national self-confidence and resolve. A nation as large and capable as ourselves must make its impact felt on the world arena. A BJP government will demand a premier position for the country in all global fora."*

On WMD policy: *"The BJP rejects the notion of nuclear apartheid...We will not be dictated to by anybody on matters of security requirements and in the exercise of the nuclear option...We expect the United States to be more sensitive to India's security and economic interests... [We will] establish a National Security Council [that will] undertake India's first-ever strategic defense review...[The BJP] will re-evaluate the country's nuclear policy and exercise the option to induct nuclear weapons...[We will] expedite the development of the Agni series of ballistic missiles with a view to increasing their range and accuracy."*

On Kashmir: *[A BJP government will] take active steps to persuade Pakistan to abandon its present policy of hostile interference in our internal affairs by supporting insurgent and terrorist groups. The BJP affirms unequivocally India's sovereignty over the whole of Jammu and Kashmir, including areas under foreign occupations...Our security forces will be given a free hand to deal with armed insurgency and terrorism...Repeated massacres of Hindus in Kashmir show that unless the State Government takes the business of curbing militancy seriously, a durable peace will be hard to achieve...The BJP promises immediate action to help those displaced from the Kashmir Valley and other parts of the state...[We will] place paramilitary forces in sensitive border areas under the full control of the Indian Army."*

On cow protection: *"The BJP will impose a total ban on the slaughter of cows...Cow-protection has remained one of the basics of Indian culture and Indian agriculture."*

13

BIBLIOGRAPHY

The following is a compilation of books that might help you understand how the mind works and how we succeed and fail in decision-making. A lot of these books will help you understand how bias affects thought processes. A few just help simplify the complex world of numbers. This list isn't meant to be exhaustive; it's a compilation of the kinds of materials you might find in a bookstore or on the Internet and a summary of what's on my bookshelf. If you read only a few of these, you'll find that some of the themes, and even some language, grow familiar. Start with Daniel Kahneman's masterpiece and work from there.

Ariely, Dan. *Predictably Irrational: The Hidden Forces That Shape Our Decisions.* New York: Harper Perennial, 2010.
———. *The Upside of Irrationality: The Unexpected Benefits of Defying Logic.* New York: Harper Perennial, 2011.
Brockman, John, ed. *This Will Make You Smarter: New Scientific Concepts to Improve Your Thinking.* New York: Harper Perennial, 2012.
Chabris, Christopher, and Daniel Simons. *The Invisible Gorilla: How Our Intuitions Deceive Us.* New York: Broadway Books, 2009.
Davidson, Richard J., and Sharon Begley. *The Emotional Life of Your Brain: How Its Unique Patterns Affect the Way You Think, Feel, and*

Live—and How You Can Change Them. New York: Hudson Street Press, 2012.

Ellenberg, Jordan. *How Not to Be Wrong: The Power of Mathematical Thinking.* New York: Penguin Press, 2014.

Fingar, Thomas. *Reducing Uncertainty: Intelligence Analysis and National Security.* Stanford, CA: Stanford Security Studies, 2011.

Gardner, Dan. *Future Babble: Why Pundits Are Hedgehogs and Foxes Know Best.* New York: Plume, 2012.

Gigorenzer, Gerd. *Risk Savvy: How to Make Good Decisions.* New York: Viking, 2014.

Gladwell, Malcolm. *Blink: The Power of Thinking Without Thinking.* Boston: Back Bay Books, 2007.

————. *What the Dog Saw and Other Adventures.* New York: Back Bay Books, 2010.

Hand, David J. *The Improbability Principle: Why Coincidences, Miracles, and Rare Events Happen Every Day.* New York: Scientific American/Farrar, Straus and Giroux, 2014.

Harrison, Guy P. *Think: Why You Should Question Everything.* Amherst, NY: Prometheus Books, 2013.

Jervis, Robert. *Why Intelligence Fails: Lessons from the Iranian Revolution and the Iraq War.* Ithaca, NY: Cornell University Press, 2011.

Kahneman, Daniel. *Thinking, Fast and Slow.* New York: Farrar, Straus and Giroux, 2012.

Kandel, Eric R. *In Search of Memory: The Emergence of a New Science of Mind.* New York: W. W. Norton, 2006.

Klein, Gary. *Sources of Power: How People Make Decisions.* Cambridge, MA: MIT Press, 1999.

————. *Streetlights and Shadows: Searching for the Keys to Adaptive Decision Making.* Cambridge, MA: MIT Press, 2011.

Levitt, Steven D., and Stephen J. Dubner. *Freakonomics: A Rogue Economist Explores the Hidden Side of Everything.* New York: William Morrow, 2009.

Mauboussin, Michael J. *Think Twice: Harnessing the Power of Counterintuition.* Boston: Harvard Business Review Press, 2013.

Neill, Humphrey B. *The Art of Contrary Thinking.* Caldwell, ID: Caxton Press, 2010.

Pinker, Steven. *How the Mind Works.* New York: W. W. Norton, 2009.

Schacter, Daniel L. *The Seven Sins of Memory: How the Mind Forgets and Remembers.* Boston: Houghton Mifflin, 2011.

Silver, Nate. *The Signal and the Noise: Why So Many Predictions Fail—But Some Don't.* New York: Penguin Press, 2012.

Surowiecki, James. *The Wisdom of Crowds: Why the Many Are Smarter Than the Few and How Collective Wisdom Shapes Business, Economies, Societies and Nations.* New York: Anchor Books, 2005.

Tavris, Carol, and Elliot Aronson. *Mistakes Were Made (but not by me).* Orlando, FL: Harcourt, 2008.

Tetlock, Philip E. *Expert Political Judgment: How Good Is It? How Can We Know?* Princeton, NJ: Princeton University Press, 2006.

Wheelan, Charles. *Naked Economics: Undressing the Dismal Science.* New York, W. W. Norton, 2010.

——— . *Naked Statistics: Stripping the Dread from the Data.* New York: W. W. Norton, 2013.

ABOUT THE AUTHOR

John Philip Mudd joined the Central Intelligence Agency in 1985 as an analyst specializing in South Asia and then the Middle East. He began work in the CIA's Counterterrorist Center in 1992 and then served on the National Intelligence Council as the deputy national intelligence officer for the Near East and South Asia (1995–98). After a tour as an executive assistant in the front office of the agency's analytic arm, Mudd went on to manage Iraq analysis at the CIA (1999–2001).

Mudd began a policy assignment at the White House in early 2001, detailed from the CIA to serve as the director for Gulf affairs on the White House National Security Council. He left after the September 11 attacks for a short assignment as the CIA member of the small diplomatic team that helped piece together a new government for Afghanistan, and he returned to the CIA in early 2002 to become second-in-charge of counterterrorism analysis in the Counterterrorist Center. He was promoted to the position of deputy director of the center in 2003 and served there until 2005.

At the establishment of the Federal Bureau of Investigation's National Security Branch in 2005, FBI director Robert Mueller appointed Mudd to serve as the branch's first-ever deputy director. He later became the FBI's senior intelligence adviser. Mudd resigned from government service in 2010. Mudd is the recipient of numerous CIA awards and commendations, including the Director's Award; the George H. W. Bush Award for excellence in counterterrorism; the CIA's Distinguished Intelligence Medal and the Distinguished Career Intelligence Medal; the first-ever William Langer Award for excellence in analysis; and numerous Exceptional Performance Awards.

During assignments at the CIA and the FBI, Mudd has commented about terrorism in open and closed congressional testimony. He is a CNN analyst and has also been featured by ABC, NBC, CBS, Fox News, BBC, PBS, MSNBC, CNBC, al-Jazeera, NPR, the *New York Times*, and the *Washington Post*. Mudd has also written in *Newsweek*, the *Wall Street Journal*, *The Atlantic*, *Foreign Policy*, *The Daily Beast*, and *Sentinel*, the journal of the US Military Academy's Combating Terrorism Center. His first book, *Takedown: Inside the Hunt for Al Qaeda*, was published by the University of Pennsylvania Press (2013).

Mudd is the director of enterprise risk at SouthernSun Asset Management in Memphis, Tennessee. He is a senior Fellow at the New America Foundation, and he sits on the advisory boards for the National Counterterrorism Center and the Aspen Institute's Homeland Security Group. He graduated cum laude from Villanova University with a BA in English literature (1983), and he earned an MA in English literature from the University of Virginia (1984).